W9-BTI-827

In 1962 the Supreme Court of the United States ruled that a non-denominational prayer spoken by public school children at the start of each school day was unconstitutional. Was the Court right? What led it to this decision? *Should* the children pray?

Lynda Beck Fenwick began to ask those questions in 1984, when presidential candidates both for and against public school prayer quoted the same historical sources as authorities to back their positions. The more she sought "the truth" behind these claims, the more it became clear that the truth was elusive. Religious history (or history about our country's religious underpinnings) is not routinely taught in our public schools, and even our elected leaders sometimes have little background in the history of their positions. Fenwick began her search by looking at the early history of religious freedom in our nation, and at the writing of the First Amendment, which says that "Congress shall make no law respecting an establishment of religion, or prohibiting the free exercise thereof." She examined the stance taken by the Supreme Court on school prayer cases, and the opinions expressed by our senators in the 1984 debates about a school prayer amendment to the Constitution. Ultimately she was able to answer the questions for herself.

But she does not attempt to answer them for the rest of us. *Should the Children Pray?* seeks only to make available the historical and legal information from which readers can draw their *own* conclusions about this sensitive issue. Whatever those conclusions may be, they "can only benefit from the guidance and wisdom of history."

SHOULD THE CHILDREN PRAY?

SHOULD THE CHILDREN PRAY?

A Historical, Judicial,
and Political Examination
of Public School Prayer

LYNDA BECK FENWICK

Markham Press Fund
Waco, Texas

The following publishers have generously given permission to use extended quotations from copyrighted works: Beehive Press: From *The Most Delightful Country of the Universe, Promotional Literature of the Colony of Georgia, 1717–1734,* introduction by Trevor R. Reese, copyright 1972 by Beehive Press; from *General Oglethorpe's Georgia, Colonial Letters, 1733–1743,* vols. I and II, edited by Mills Lane, copyright 1975 by Beehive Press. Doubleday, a division of Bantam, Doubleday, Dell Publishing Group, Inc.: From *The Indomitable Baptists* by O. K. Armstrong and Marjorie Moore Armstrong, copyright © 1967 by O. K. and Marjorie M. Armstrong; from *The Memoirs of Earl Warren* by Earl Warren, copyright © 1977 by Nina E. Warren. Alfred A. Knopf, Inc.: From *Democracy in America* by Alexis de Tocqueville, copyright © 1960 by Alfred A. Knopf. Macmillan Publishing Company: From *The Establishment Clause* by Leonard W. Levy, copyright © 1986 Macmillan Publishing Company, a Division of Macmillan, Inc. Reprinted with permission of Macmillan Publishing Company.

Library of Congress Cataloging-in-Publication Data

Fenwick, Lynda Beck, 1944–
   Should the children pray? : a historical, judicial, and political
examination of public school prayer / Lynda Beck Fenwick.
     p.   cm.
   Includes bibliographical references (p.).
   ISBN 0–918954–51–7 (alk. paper) : $29.95
   1. Prayer in the public schools—United States—History.
I. Title
LC111.F44   1989
377´.14—dc20   89–62659
                                                 CIP

Cover design by Lynda Beck Fenwick.

This volume is the twenty-second published by the Markham Press Fund of Baylor University Press, established in memory of Dr. L. N. and Princess Finch Markham of Longview, Texas, by their daughters, Mrs. R. Matt Dawson of Waco, Texas, and Mrs. B. Reid Clanton, of Longview, Texas.

Printed in the United States of America on acid-free paper.

To Larry

CONTENTS

INTRODUCTION

Unless we remember we cannot understand.
　　　　　　　　　　　　　　　—Edward M. Forster

The American perception of their ancestors as proponents of religious
freedom recognizes only part of the picture. While it is true that many
colonists sought the freedom to worship as they pleased, the years have
obscured the unattractive fact that these same colonists generally reserved that right for themselves and continued the European practice of
excluding or persecuting all those who wished to worship differently. It
is essential that today's citizens examine the entire picture of religious
history in America, and not just the flattering view.

The founding fathers who met to write the American Constitution
and Bill of Rights knew of the religious persecution in Europe from
which so many had fled, and the intolerance and persecution that had
been continued in America by the early settlers. However, they knew
equally well of those colonial experiments that had proved that religions
could coexist and remain strong.

With that knowledge, the founding fathers wrote the First Amendment, which says in part: "Congress shall make no law respecting an
establishment of religion, or prohibiting the free exercise thereof." To
appreciate their legislative wisdom requires a knowledge of religious history in Europe and early America. Unfortunately, few Americans possess
that historical knowledge. Fearing a violation of the separation of church
and state, educators have generally opted to eliminate references to religion from the public school curriculum, and as a result, Americans lack
the historical knowledge necessary to understand the circumstances leading up to the enactment of the First Amendment.

Equally important is an awareness of the interpretation given those
sixteen words by the courts. The responsibility of interpreting the First
Amendment and applying it to complicated real situations has belonged
ultimately to the United States Supreme Court. For over two hundred
years, the Supreme Court justices have balanced the ideal of religious

1

freedom with the reality of individual Americans exercising that freedom in their daily lives. In one of those cases, *Engel v. Vitale*, decided in 1962, the Court was asked to decide whether a non-denominational prayer, suggested by the New York State Board of Regents, could be used in New York public schools. In finding that the prayer was prohibited by the Constitution, the Court said:

> It is neither sacriligious nor antireligious to say that each separate government in this country should stay out of the business of writing or sanctioning official prayers and leave that purely religious function to the people themselves and to those the people choose to look to for religious guidance.[1]

Although the Court did not include a summary of the decisions preceding the school prayer case within the opinion itself, the legal precedent for the decision should be reviewed in order to understand why the Court ruled as it did.

The Supreme Court in the *Engel v. Vitale* opinion clearly ruled that no prayer could be non-denominational or neutral enough to meet the constitutional test. Those who disagreed with the Court's decision immediately began their campaign for a constitutional amendment; however, the climate of the 1960s was not supportive of their cause. It was not until the social climate shifted back toward more conservative and traditional values that their movement began to pick up momentum.

In March of 1984, the United States Senate debated a resolution proposing an amendment to the Constitution to allow voluntary, spoken school prayer. The amendment had the active support of President Ronald Reagan. Although the senators spoke as legislators in arguing the logical and practical reasons for or against the amendment, they also spoke as individuals, revealing highly personal experiences and beliefs not usually expressed on the Senate floor. Their arguments offer a rare opportunity to examine the wide range of viewpoints held by sincere and intelligent men concerning this issue. Despite a majority of the senators having favored an amendment, the fifty-six senators who voted for the proposal did not constitute the two-thirds majority necessary for passage.

At the time of the Senate debates, the United States Supreme Court had pending before it a case involving an Alabama statute authorizing schools to provide a one-minute period of silence specifically "for meditation or voluntary prayer."[2] Several senators referred to the pending case and expressed the assumption that the Court would uphold the state statute; however, to the surprise of a great many Americans, the Supreme Court found the law to be unconstitutional.

Therefore, the present interpretation given to the First Amendment by the Supreme Court prohibits both spoken and silent group prayer. Many Americans find this prohibition unacceptable and continue to seek ways for public school children to enjoy voluntary, group prayer. Others, equally sincere, fear the threat to religious freedom if school prayer is sanctioned. Both sides agree, however, on the importance of this issue to the spiritual well-being of the nation.

The research for this book was begun during the presidential campaign of 1984. Both candidates referred to certain historical events and quoted the founding fathers as support for their opposite opinions on the school prayer issue. The author undertook to determine the historical context of the events and the quotations in an effort to reconcile the opposite meanings given to them by the candidates.

The purpose of this book is not to conclude which candidate was correct in his interpretation or to advocate any single opinion on the school prayer issue. Rather, it is the intention of the author to make available historical and legal information from which readers can draw their own conclusions.

Since the beginning of this nation its citizens, courts, and politicians have struggled with the balance between religion and government. It is a struggle that by its nature will never end, and " . . . every generation has an obligation to seek anew a healthy relationship between church and state."[3] Our generation faces a particular challenge with respect to the issue of spoken prayer in America's public schools.

The void in the teaching of religious history by public schools has been one of the most unfortunate side effects of court decisions involving the First Amendment. Not only are voters historically ignorant, but also the nation's politicians and judges have suffered from the neglect of religious history in their educations. Yet, nearly a century and a half ago, Philip Schaff warned: "How shall we labour with any effect to build up the Church, if we have no thorough knowledge of her history, or fail to apprehend it from the proper point of observation? History is, and must ever continue to be, next to God's word, the richest foundation of wisdom, and the surest guide to all successful practical activity."[4] Thus the lessons to be learned from history protect both church and state, both God's word and the Constitution.

This book presents historical and contemporary voices and allows them to speak for themselves within the context of their own times. The bibliography offers the curious reader opportunity for wider exploration of the range of opinions presented in the book, but ultimately, the final conclusion on the issue belongs to the reader. Whatever that conclusion may be, it can only benefit from the guidance and wisdom of history.

1
EUROPEAN RELIGIOUS HERITAGE

Among the most inestimable of our blessings is that . . . of liberty to worship our Creator in the way we think most agreeable to His will; a liberty deemed in other countries incompatible with good government and yet proved by our experience to be its best support.
—Thomas Jefferson, 1807

Accustomed to churches of a dozen different denominations in their communities, most Americans find it difficult to imagine a time or place where such religious diversity could not exist. Yet, America's founding settlers would have found today's reality unimaginable. Our earliest colonists came from Europe, particularly from Great Britain, and it was the European religious history with which they were familiar.

That history began with the Catholic church dominating the European continent until 1517 when Martin Luther posted his 95 theses on the church door in Wittenburg in protest of certain abuses he saw in the Catholic church. With his act, Protestantism was born. Less visible but certainly a part of Europe's religious population were the Jews, who, having lost their homeland centuries before, had wandered among the other countries of the world, including countries in Europe. They faced such hostility from Christians that they largely insulated themselves from persecution as best they could by living in Jewish ghettos away from the rest of the population. The Jews were not alone, however, in facing the persecution of Christians. Once Luther had shown the way, other protestors arose, that is, other Protestant sects, and now Christians not only were opposing infidels, pagans and Jews, but also other Christians. Thus, only a few years after America was discovered in 1492, Protestantism had emerged to challenge the Catholic church.

The very name Protestant came from the fact that these sects broke away from the Catholic church in protest. In fact, some of their protests and demands for reform led to the desired changes, and initially the Catholic church hoped the protestors would be satisfied with the reforms that were made and return to the church. However, it became apparent that not all of the demands for reform could be met. Efforts to compromise were abandoned by the Catholic church during the Counter Reformation, and instead of compromise the church determined to strengthen itself and fight for the souls of those being tempted astray by the Protestant sects. These were bloody and cruel years of wars, Inquisitions, massacres, population shifts, and executions. Sins were not left for the punishment of God but were defined in law and punished as crimes against the state. Often heads of state, such as Philip II of Spain, defended the church and punished dissenters more vigorously and cruelly than the church itself.

In many localities it was complicated or even impossible to separate the church from the state. When there had been only one dominant religion, the Roman Catholic church, it was natural that the ruler and all the people shared that common religion and its moral and spiritual code. When dissenting sects arose, the acceptance of a common code was shattered as well, and since matters of faith and religious practice had been codified as law, the opponents of the church were law breakers as well as dissenters. The state, therefore, treated these lawbreakers just as they would treat any criminals. If the dissenters refused to stop breaking the law, they faced the punishment of the state, including the severe fate of exile or execution. Such extreme measures were seen as necessary for the good of both church and state.

Examples of religious persecution and wars fought for religious reasons can be cited throughout Europe during this historical period. The more the head of state identified himself with the church, the harsher the punishments. Probably no head of state felt more strongly the duty to serve the church than the Spanish king.

When the Reformation began, the Netherlands were linked politically to Spain, and the Protestants trying to worship there felt the strict restraint of the Roman Catholic Spanish king, Charles V. Meetings were forbidden, books were banned, and an estimated thirty thousand people were put to death for matters of faith. Conditions did not improve for Protestants when the king was followed in power by his son, Philip II, who initiated the Spanish Inquisition at home and sanctioned the killing of ten thousand more martyrs in the low countries. Ironically, Protestantism endured in the Netherlands despite all the bloodshed, and the Dutch people became a very tolerant nation, providing a refuge for sects seeking a place to settle when their own homelands became intolerable.

The religious history of England must be of particular interest to Americans. All of the original thirteen colonies were English (although New York's beginnings were Dutch), and the colonists were overwhelmingly British. English was the language of the colonies, and to a large extent, the colonial religions were English as well.

The birth of Protestantism in Europe had resulted from conflicts of theology, and the political ramifications followed. In England, the reverse was true. Henry VIII was more concerned with the political consequences of having to answer to the Pope in Rome than with any real theological differences when, in 1534, he declared himself head of the Church of England. Thereafter, out of his largely political act, theological ramifications followed.

Henry VIII, although he is well remembered for his quarrel with the Roman Catholic church, did not initially oppose the Pope. In fact, in 1521 he printed a book called *In Defence of the Seven Sacraments* which he dedicated to Pope Leo X. In the king's book, he pointed out the heresies of the Protestant, Martin Luther. In response, the Pope gave him the title, Defender of the Faith. Henry's disagreement with the Catholic church grew out of his personal, not his spiritual life, and in the case of this king, his personal life was also his political life.

Henry's personal and political problem was that his wife could not give him a male heir. As troubling as this alone was to the king, it was complicated by the fact that his wife, Catherine, was Spanish and the aunt of Charles V. Henry complicated it even further by falling in love with Anne Boleyn. By 1527 Henry had decided that he had offended God by marrying Catherine, who was his deceased brother's widow, and on that basis, he asked the Pope, now Pope Clement, for an annulment. Unfortunately for English Catholics, Pope Clement was strongly influenced by Charles V, and Henry's petition was denied. It is impossible to understand the events of this royal love triangle without appreciating the entanglements of the Catholic church in European politics at that time. Since the Pope would not grant the annulment and recognize his marriage to Anne, Henry broke with the Catholic church and set himself up as Supreme Head of the Church in England. Thus, England became Protestant.

The evolution of how this new Church of England was to be different from the old, Catholic church actually followed its creation, in a sequence obviously reversed from the evolution of Protestant sects on the European continent. Eventually, an important part in defining the new church was played by Thomas Cranmer, the Archbishop of Canterbury, in his creation of the Book of Common Prayer and the Forty-two Articles. Later, during the reign of the Catholic Mary Tudor, Cranmer would sacrifice his life for the role he had played in defining English Protestantism. The important thing to remember in all of this transition is, however, that Protestantism was not added to the English religious tradition; rather, it was substituted for the old religion, and the English people were still left with *one* established church. The unity of church and state was absolute with the king as the head of both.

For the common people there was probably little initial feeling of change. They were accustomed to loyalty to the king and now could feel a unified loyalty of both soul and body to the King of England. Where in the past they had been forced to divide their spiritual and secular loyalties between the foreign Pope in Rome and the English king at home, they could now look to the King of England as head of both church and state. There were, of course, those, such as Sir Thomas More, for whom this realignment of faith was impossible, but for most Englishmen the transition was easier. The changes to church ritual were gradual, and so the day-to-day religious observances were altered little in the beginning.

For those who could not abandon their Roman Catholic faith, challenges remained ahead for many years. They would struggle to return England to Catholicism, as they did briefly under Mary Tudor, and the consequences of their religiously motivated political intrigues were often fatal. The idea of there being only one acceptable church was common to both adherents to the Roman Catholic church and to the Church of England, and whoever was in power persecuted the nonbelievers. The desirability of a single, established church may have been the one thing about which they could agree!

Not all of the challenges to the Church of England were external. In terms of the significance to the American colonization movement, the more important challenges came from within the church itself.

When Henry VIII declared himself head of the Church of England, the allegiance to the Pope ended. Otherwise, however, the Church of England retained the rituals and creeds of its past, and one group within the church, the Anglicans, were in favor of continuing without change the old traditions. This group consisted largely of the upper classes and the landed gentry, and they were loyal to the king. They were in control and content to stay at home in England during the early years of America's colonization. Only when they lost control, along with the king during England's Civil War, did they migrate to America in significant numbers.

Within the Church of England there was a second group who wanted not only to break with the Pope but also to change the rituals and traditions of the church itself. They believed the changes they sought would purify the church, and from their desire to purify came their name, Puritans. They saw their mission as working for change from within, and although they disagreed with the Anglicans about the direction the church should take, they believed as did the Anglicans in a single, established state church.

The fact that they remained within the church did not protect them from persecution. The religious climate of the times, as it was enforced by the state, demanded not only membership in the established church but also beliefs consistent with the majority of that church. Since 1559, when Queen Elizabeth I had caused the Act of Uniformity to be passed, ministers had been forbidden from using any liturgy or service other than what was established by Parliament. While Elizabeth was still on the throne, the Puritans had expressed their objection to mandatory use of the Book of Common Prayer and other church traditions and had been persecuted as a result. (It is ironic that many of the Puritans who vexed the Protestant Anglicans and the crown had been exposed to the teachings of John Calvin during the time they had fled England while the Catholic Mary ruled. That is, the Catholics drove these Protestants out of England and into Switzerland for refuge where they were exposed to the ideas for reform that later caused their fellow Protestants so much annoyance when they returned to England upon the death of Queen Mary.)

In 1603 the Puritans presented to King James I a list of changes they felt were necessary to purify the church, such as omitting a ring in the marriage ceremony, ending the wearing of the cap and surplice by the priest, enforcing better observance of the Sabbath day, and modifying the music of the church. James not only did not implement their proposed reforms, he declared that they would either conform or be forced out of England—or worse! The king saw these challenges to the church as attacks upon himself, and in a certain sense, he was right. Many of the changes the Puritans desired were more in the nature of improving the social morality of England, such as better observance of the Sabbath, than strictly matters of church doctrine. As they intruded into social matters, they affected political matters as well, and threatened, perhaps unintentionally, the position of the king.

Eventually, even the members of the Puritan movement itself were divided. While one branch remained steadfast in their mission to stay within the established church, working for its reform, another branch decided that the purity they sought could never be achieved within the established church. Only by separating from the established church, they believed, could they accomplish the desired purification of faith, and from their decision to separate came their name, Separatists. The harshest persecutions were applied to this group.

There were among both the Puritans and Separatists few members of the highest class. Among the Puritans were more merchants and artisans, but both the Puritans and Separatists attracted many of the common people. The upper class of Englishmen adhered to their Anglican creed, and therefore, the Anglicans held not only religious control but also economic and political control in England.

The division among Puritans had its counterpart among Protestants on the European continent. One branch had retained the traditional structure of an organized church for their new Protestant faith, but another branch had emphasized the importance of individual thinking in matters of faith and rejected any formal, organized church. Most of the members of this nontraditional branch of Protestantism had come from the common people, and they were called Anabaptists or Rebaptizers.[1] Since the emphasis was upon individual thought without the support of an organized church, the Anabaptists had no single creed. However, many important ideas grew out of the thinking of these early Anabaptists, and one of the most important ideas of all was the commitment to complete separation of church and state. Perhaps this commitment arose from the fact that most of their number were not powerful or wealthy and thus not influential in matters of state. Perhaps because of their political and economic impotence they had felt the special persecution reserved for the powerless. For whatever reasons, they believed that churches could only achieve spiritual purity if they were absolutely separate from the state, and they argued for the establishment of a dualism of church and state, with each having absolute authority within its own realm but without intrusion into the other's territory. Only with the assurance that the state could not intrude could these common people believe that they could worship as they chose.

Having no structure, the Anabaptist movement itself did not survive for very long, but it gave birth to other Protestant movements, such as the Baptists, Mennonites, Dunkers, and Moravians, and many of the Anabaptist ideas survived in them.

When the English Puritans felt they could no longer exist within the established Church of England, they were drawn to some of the ideas of these Protestants on the continent. Others actually fled to Europe to avoid religious persecution in England, particularly to the Netherlands. One of these Separatist congregations established itself for a time in Leyden in the Netherlands, and from this group came the Pilgrims who founded Plymouth Colony.

Among the Puritans who remained in England, the idea developed that as long as they remained in England they were a minority facing the entrenched Anglican majority, but if they could go to America and establish a reformed Puritan church, it could serve as an example of what they were trying to accomplish in the established English church. By going to the colonies, they reasoned, they could become the majority and obtain the control they were denied in England, and by their example, they could still accomplish the reform of the Church of England. From this motivation came the impetus for the Massachusetts Bay Colony.

Ironically, by 1642 the Puritans had gained control of the English church. During the English Civil War the Anglicans had largely allied themselves with the king, and when he lost his throne, and eventually his head, the Anglicans lost both their political power and their control of the church. Under Oliver Cromwell they became the ones subjected to religious persecution, which motivated their migration to America just as religious persecution had prompted the Puritans to settle New England. The Anglicans, however, headed for the southern colonies of Virginia, Maryland, and the Carolinas.

This, then, was the tradition the English colonists, and in fact the tradition almost all of the European colonists, brought to America with them—a single established church with the king at its head, and persecution of religious minorities. When we say the colonists came to America for religious freedom, we must understand that they regarded that freedom as something personal to them and not as something to be extended to others who worshipped differently. Religious tolerance was not part of the tradition brought by the colonists to America.

2
COLONIZATION

. . . haveing undertaken, for the glorie of God, and advancemente of the
Christian faith, and honour of our king and countrie, a voyage to plant
the first colonie in the Northerne parts of Virginia, doe by these presents
solemnly and mutualy in the presence of God, and one of another, covenant and combine our selves together into a civill body politick . . .
                                    —from the Mayflower Compact, 1620

The personalities differed and the means they chose to accomplish
their goals differed as well, but the leaders of the earliest American colonies expressed the common ideal of claiming this new land for the
glory of God and country. Up and down the eastern coast of colonial
America, the English flag and the Christian cross were planted together.
Despite the common national heritage and religious motivation, the colonial leaders created unique communities whose differences were
largely a result of the religious character of the leading citizens. The
development of these religious communities defined the earliest development of America, and to understand the birth of the American nation
we must examine these colonial communities and their leaders.

This examination should not ignore the fact that there were many
immigrants who were not possessed of any strong religious faith. Many
of these people—whether adventurer or poor laborer—came to America
for economic rather than spiritual reasons, and their industry provided
the sweat that allowed colonial America to succeed. But without the
framework of the religious colonies, the America we know could never
have been born.[1]

It was a common belief among the Protestant clergy that the timing
of the birth of Protestantism following so closely the discovery of the
American continent was not merely coincidence but rather Divine Providence. They truly believed that God had kept the existence of America
a secret, saving this new land for the Protestant Christians to pioneer
and build a Christian nation. Whether their belief was true or not, they

believed it to be true, and that belief controlled many of the decisions they made in the colonization of America.

Spanish

Although the English were most successful in establishing permanent colonies in North America, they were neither the first nor the only Europeans to attempt colonization. The oldest permanently inhabited city in the United States is St. Augustine, Florida, founded in 1565 by the Spanish. During the height of Spanish power in the New World, the area they called La Florida extended north as far as Chesapeake Bay.

During the sixteenth century it was the French and not the English who challenged the Spanish colonial venture in the New World. As with the later colonists, both nations saw their colonial mission as serving both king and church, and the battles between the French and Spanish in America were therefore both political and religious. In 1563 the French attempted to establish a Protestant colony in La Florida which they called Fort Caroline. The colony failed, and starvation and hostility from the Indians had nearly defeated the French colonists, even before Catholic Spain sent military forces to drive out the intruding French Huguenots. The Spanish killed nearly the entire male population of Frenchmen, and it is reported that in doing so their leader said, "I do this not as to Frenchmen but as to Lutherans."[2]

In 1566 the Spanish established a community on what is now Parris Island in South Carolina, which they called Santa Elena. Until 1587 it served as Spain's colonial capital and included families, as well as soldiers and priests, among its population.[3]

While the Spanish soldiers pushed inland in search of wealth, the priests built more than fifty missions in La Florida, where they brought Roman Catholicism to the native Indians. Many priests gave their lives to that effort. After the killing of one Spanish priest in 1597, the son of the Indian chief described the reasons for the priest's death and the anticipated revenge upon his tribe by the Spanish.

> Although the friar is dead he would not have been if he had not prevented us from living as before we were Christians: let us return to our ancient customs, and let us prepare to defend ourselves against the punishment which the governor of Florida will attempt to inflict upon us, . . . let us restore the liberty of which these friars have robbed us, with promises of benefits which we have not seen, in hopes of which they wish that those of us who call ourselves Christians experience at once the losses and discomforts: they take from us women, leaving us only one and that in perpetuity, prohibiting us from changing her; they obstruct our dances, banquets, feasts, celebrations, fires and wars, so that by failing to use them we lose the ancient valor and dexterity inherited from our ancestors; they persecute our old people, calling them witches; even our

labor disturbs them, since they want to command us to avoid it on some days, and be prepared to execute all that they say, although they are not satisfied; they always reprimand us, injure us, oppress us, preach to us, call us bad Christians, and deprive us of all happiness, which our ancestors enjoyed, with the hope that they will give us heaven. These are deceptions in order to subject us, in holding us disposed after their manner; already what can we expect, except to be slaves?[4]

Despite the failure of the Spanish to have left any permanent colony among the original thirteen colonies from which this nation was formed, the lasting success of the Spanish priests in converting the native Americans has contributed to the nation's religious diversity, and their influence throughout the American continent may still be seen, particularly in Central America and the American Southwest.

French

As for the French, they were more successful in settling the northern parts of the Atlantic coast. Their earliest settlement in what is now the United States was on Ste. Croix Island in the Scoodic River in Maine, but their primary settlements were in what became Canada. A wealthy French Calvinist was given a trade monopoly in the North American territory between the 40th and 46th parallels, which also mandated that he establish agricultural settlements. Although the Huguenots he recruited were allowed to bring their own ministers, Roman Catholic priests were required to minister to the Indians.[5] Among the missionaries to the Indians, perhaps none were more diligent than the French Jesuits who brought Christianity to the Hurons.[6] French influence upon the American colonies resulted, however, not from government sanctioned settlements or church sponsored missions but rather from individual French families who were scattered among the colonies. Between twenty and forty thousand French Protestants immigrated after the revocation of the Edit of Nantes in 1685. Perhaps another five thousand Acadian French were deported in 1755.[7] These French were assimilated into their colonies, wherever they settled, and the French surnames among prominent families in many early communities reflect how successful they were.

German

The immigration of many groups can be identified as resulting from a particular historical event that made practice of their religion difficult or impossible. This is perhaps especially true of the German immigrants. The Thirty Years' War had been devastating for the German people. Then, in 1648, the Treaty of Westphalia which ended that war gave the leader of each territorial area the right to decide the religion of all his subjects. Thereafter, each leader was free to establish his own faith and exclude or persecute all others. Under this scheme, smaller sects, such as the Mennonites, Dunkers, and German Quakers, suffered particularly. This persecution, coupled with hard economic times, prompted large numbers of Germans to emigrate.[8] Most of these immigrants were farmers, and they continued that livelihood in America.

Scotch-Irish

Another wave of immigrants came from Ireland during the first half of the eighteenth century. A century before, a group of Lowland Scotch Protestants had been given land in Ireland. Although they were often referred to as Scotch-Irish when they came to America, their heritage was almost purely Scottish. They did not intermarry with the native Irish, who were Catholic and who resented the Scots having been given Irish lands, so the relocated Scots retained their own religion and customs with little modification. English laws were not supportive of their Presbyterian faith, and when England enacted restrictive laws against colonial commercial enterprises in America, the impact was equally restrictive in Ireland. Finally, several crop failures were the inducement to bring these Scotch-Irish people to America.[9] More than two centuries after the first English colony was established in Virginia, these later British immigrants played a significant role in the fight for religious liberty in that colony.

Dutch

The Dutch deserve particular mention among the early colonists, for their influence was strongly felt in the middle colonies. Unfortunately for the Dutch, they were always surrounded and outnumbered by the English, who eventually overwhelmed them. Nevertheless, next to the English, the Dutch played the most important part in colonial America.

Because of wars at home, the Dutch had few people to spare for colonization. Therefore, most of the Dutch settlements were trading centers rather than true colonies. Even before surrender to the English in 1664, the few Dutch settlers were nearly absorbed by the sea of Englishmen around them. After the explorers and traders, the first permanent Dutch settlers in New Netherlands were, in fact, French speaking, having come from the southern region of the Netherlands. They were thirty families of Protestant Walloons.

However, their settlement was not to come until fourteen years after the Dutch ship, *Half Moon,* anchored in New York harbor. During the early years, the Dutch were devoted to an active trade between Old and New Netherlands, when beaver skins were such a valued commodity that they were used as currency. The focus of Dutch trade is revealed through one ship's manifest which included the skins of 7,246 beavers, 675 otters, 48 minks, and 36 wildcats, cargo obtainable without permanent settlers.[10]

Permanent settlement was required by the 1621 charter granted to the Dutch West India Company, and in 1623 they sent the thirty families of Walloons, descendants of Protestant refugees. In order to populate a greater area, the Walloons were scattered through the region rather than being formed into a single community. "Most of them could neither read nor write. They were a wild, uncouth, rough, and most of the time a drunken crowd. They lived in small log huts, thatched with straw. They wore rough clothes, and in the winter were dressed in skins. They subsisted on a little corn, game, and fish. They were afraid of neither man, God, nor the Devil."[11]

Encouragement of agricultural development also gave rise to the patroon system, under which the Dutch West India Company gave a patroon four years to settle a colony of fifty persons above the age of fifteen in an area of sixteen miles along a navigable river. The Dutch settlers brought over by the patroons resented this medieval system of agriculture, especially when they could see English neighbors who settled their own farms. By 1664, when the English took possession of New Netherlands, there were patroonships in existence, which the English recognized as manorial grants, and the Dutch colonial heritage of patroons may still be seen in land holdings along the banks of the Hudson River.

The greatest Dutch colonial influence was not in its farms but rather in the bustling port city of New Amsterdam, and this was the part of the colony so coveted by the English. The last Dutch governor of New Amsterdam was Peter Stuyvesant, and in 1654 his city was such a mix of peoples that his minister complained to the Dutch West India Company. "For as we have here Papists, Mennonites and Lutherans among the Dutch; also many Puritans or Independents, and many Atheists and various other servants of Baal among the English under this Government, who conceal themselves under the name of Christians; it would create a still greater confusion, if the obstinate and immovable Jews came to settle here."[12] Despite his complaints, the Dutch West India Company permitted the Jews to come, primarily because they were able to provide investment capital to the financially troubled company.

The resultant conglomeration of religious sects was too much for Governor Stuyvesant, and with the support of the ministers of the Dutch church, he passed an ordinance forbidding preaching by unqualified persons. The best known persecution under this law was of a Quaker named John Browne, who then complained to the Dutch West India Company about the treatment he had received. The company rebuked the governor for his policy and reminded him of the Dutch traditions of moderation and asylum. " . . . the consciences of men, at least ought to remain free and unshackled. Let every one be unmolested as long as he is modest, moderate, his political conduct irreproachable, and as long as he does not offend others or oppose the government. The maxim of moderation has always been the guide of our magistrates in this city, and the consequence has been that people have flocked from every land to this asylum. Tread thus in their steps, and we doubt not you will be blessed."[13] With so few Dutch available to the company as colonists, not only the traditions of moderation and asylum may have prompted their rebuke to Governor Stuyvesant but also their desperate need to attract colonists.

The English resentment of the Dutch wedge driven in the midst of their colonies was at last resolved in 1664 when they finally seized control. The series of English laws that followed represent the first example in America of an establishment of religion different from the classic European establishment of a single preferred church over all others.[14] The instructions that the English gave to the governor allowed any church of the Protestant religion to become an established church. Every township was obligated to support some Protestant church and minister, but the denomination of the church was not mandated. Therefore, whatever Protestant denomination predominated in a particular locality could become the established church. The New York Assembly confirmed the system of multiple establishments in 1683 with the Charter of Liberties, which provided: " . . . the Churches already in New York do appear to be privileged Churches . . . Provided also that all other Christian Churches, that shall hereafter come and settle in the province, shall have the same privileges."[15]

Later there were attempts to establish the Anglican church, but the difficulty in accomplishing such an establishment is revealed by the Catholic governor's description of the population of the colony in 1687. "Here bee not many of the Church of England; few Roman Catholicks; abundance of Quakers preachers men and women especially; singing Quakers; Ranting Quakers; Sabbatarians; Antisabbatarians; some Anabaptists some Independents; some Jews; in short of all sorts of opinion there are some, and the most part, of none at all."[16]

In 1693 an act was passed that the royal governors and the Anglicans in the colony claimed had established the Anglican church, although the act never named that church. However, the dissenters and the legislature that had passed the act disagreed. Disputes arose, and in 1731 the New York provincial court heard a dispute between Anglicans and dissenting Presbyterians to determine the ownership of a church that had been built with funds from the town tax. The court ruled in favor of the Presbyterians. That holding is extremely important, for it shows that in colonial America there was such a thing as a multiple establishment of religion in which public support was mandated on an impartial, nonpreferential basis.[17] Therefore, when the founding fathers spoke of an establishment, their meaning was not necessarily limited to a single preferred church, since multiple religious establishments were a part of their colonial experience.

Jamestown

There were other nationalities represented among the early settlers; however, the English were definitely most successful in establishing permanent colonies in the New World, and it is the English influence that predominates in the birth of this nation. The English colonies succeeded because of the proper economic, political, and religious mix. Economically, there were Englishmen with money to invest in colonial business ventures, and there were common people who were hungry for land and a chance to get ahead with a fresh start in America. Politically, English kings were eager to establish colonies in America and manipulate people both at home in England and abroad in the colonies by the granting, denying, and withdrawing of charters for these colonies. Religiously, there were enough devout colonists to be willing to take the risks involved in settling this unknown and frightening land for the glory of God, and their presence formed a structure for many others, without any particular religious motivation, to join in establishing a colony.

The first enduring English colony was established in Jamestown, Virginia in 1607. This initial effort was not a colony in the true sense of individuals relocating with their families to establish a new home. Many of the so-called colonists were actually servants and laborers under contract to the company which had obtained the patent for establishing a colony. An examination of this colony is more beneficial to understanding how the King of England controlled development of the new land than in studying the colony itself, for in the early years the experiment in Virginia was largely unsuccessful.

By the time England began colonizing America, it controlled the seas, having defeated the Spanish Armada in 1588. England developed a practice of encouraging private companies to establish colonies overseas as investments. These companies obtained a patent or charter from the king which defined the area of colonization and the rights and privileges the company would enjoy with respect to that colony.

On April 10, 1606, a patent was granted to the Virginia Company to colonize America's Atlantic coast, from Cape Fear to Halifax. Within the company there were to be two subordinate companies, the London Company, which controlled the southern portion of the grant, and the Plymouth Company, which controlled the northern portion. The division included an overlapping area which was to be shared. With respect to the colony, the king acted through a royal council, which he appointed. The company consisted of separate councils in England for each subordinate company, as well as resident councils in each colony. The patentees were obligated to provide ships, supplies, and colonists, and the resident councils were to supervise the colonial government, building, and work.

When the terms of the original patent were not met to the king's satisfaction, a new charter was granted in 1609, modified in 1612, which covered a lesser area consisting of only 400 miles along the Atlantic coast. The reorganization met with little more success than had the original colony, and during this period a succession of men served as governors of the colony. Certainly a contributing factor in the failure of the colony was the lack of any sense of community among the colonists. The colonies that were organized around a strong religious community were much more successful.

In 1611 this absence of community identity and goals was seen as a lack of discipline, and the new governor decided to enforce the necessary discipline through a series of strict laws. These laws included the first English law concerning religion that was passed in America: " . . . I do strictly and commaund and charge all Captains and Officers . . . to have a care that the Almighty God bee duly and daily served, and that they call upon their people to heare Sermons, as that also they diligently frequent Morning and Evening prayer themselves by their owne exemplar and daily life, and duty herein, encouraging others thereunto, and that such, who shall often and wilfully absent themselves, be duly punished according to the martial law in that case provided."[18]

The punishments prescribed for failing to observe proper attendance at worship and other crimes, such as blasphemy and failing to keep the Sabbath, were often harsh, but in fact, such punishments were rarely enforced. By 1618, the laws had been modified, but it remains interesting to recognize that the first law in America to deal with religion included a direction to remember morning and evening prayers.[19] It is also significant to recognize that the laws were enacted at that time in an effort to impose discipline upon the colonists, and that the government employed religion as an instrument of such disciplinary control.

Despite such efforts, the Virginia Company eventually failed. Its downfall resulted from factional disputes within the company itself, Spanish intrigues to sabotage any success by the English in establishing colonies, unfriendly Indians, (whose unfriendliness may have been the result of earlier exposure to the Spanish),[20] sickness, disputes with the king, and the significant fact that certain company leaders opposed the king in Parliament. In 1623 the king caused the Virginia Company to be investigated, which led to the revocation of its charter in 1624. As a result, Virginia became a royal colony.

Although Virginia was not a religious community of colonists like the other colonies that will be considered in the following pages, an analysis of the failures of the Virginia Company to deal with the hardships and political realities of colonizing America focuses our respect upon the successes of the religious communities. It also introduces us to the English system of obtaining patents or charters from the king, a system with which the religious colonies had to comply as well. Within twenty years, the influx of Anglicans after the English Civil War was underway, and their influence upon the religious character of Virginia will demand a reexamination later in this book. But, for now our attention should be shifted northward to New England.

This brief summary of the earliest colonial efforts is not intended to ignore the rich traditions other nationalities have brought to America; however, it does recognize that during the colonial and revolutionary years of this nation's history, the predominant influence was English. Although present-day Americans rightly regard their nation as a melting pot, the early ingredients in the pot were mainly British. Even as late as 1790, nearly ninety-two percent of the white population had come from England, Scotland, or Ireland. The Germans constituted 5.6 percent of that population and the Dutch 2 percent. All the others combined made up only 0.6 percent.[21] Although there was also a large African population during this period, they were essentially powerless in any political sense. The rich addition of ingredients from all over the world to America's melting pot occurred after the American Revolution.[22]

It is therefore obvious why the English religious traditions played such an important part in the religious life of the colonies. And the American colonies with the strongest identities and greatest unity gained their strength and unity primarily from the personality of their leaders and the religious commitment of their colonists. To best understand the original thirteen colonies, six of them will be considered separately. The experiences of the other seven colonies were similar, and by isolating these six for study—Massachusetts, Rhode Island, Pennsylvania, Maryland, Virginia, and Georgia—the details of the colonial experience can be better understood.

Such separate consideration of the six colonies is somewhat artificial, since events were happening beyond their borders, both in the other colonies and in the rest of the world. However, a separate examination of each colony is not so illogical as it might be today with communication and transportation linking all regions of this nation almost immediately. In those early years there was very little interaction among the colonies. Physical barriers of distance, forest, and swamp isolated the colonies, and philosophical barriers of their respective colonial leaders isolated them as well. Although they shared many common problems of survival in the new land and they shared the common impact of political influences from England, they existed on a day to day basis with very little effect upon each other. This study isolates them much as circumstances isolated them at that time, so that we can better examine the gradual coming together of common roots and goals that led to the birth of a new nation. It also allows a more detailed consideration of the colonial experiences that were known to the founding fathers and that influenced their decisions in the creation of the Constitution and Bill of Rights.

3
NEW ENGLAND

The Pilgrims

If he have but the taste of virtue and magninimity, what to such a mind can bee more pleasant, than planting and building a foundation for his Posteritie, gotte from the rude earth, by Gods blessing and his owne industry without prejudice to any.

—Captain John Smith, 1616

After having visited New England, John Smith returned to England, eager to describe the wonders to be had in America, "wherein the most curious may finde pleasure, profit, and content."[1] In writing *A Description of New England,* Captain Smith intended not only to describe the new land but also to encourage settlement. "If hee have any graine of faith or zeale in Religion, what can hee doe lesse hurtfull to any: or more agreeable to God, then to seeke to convert those poore Salvages to know Christ, and humanitie," he implored.[2] One group of Englishmen who heeded his advice to colonize New England were the small group of Separatists who had left England for Holland in 1609.

Although the earliest English colonists were in Jamestown, Virginia, the Pilgrims have come to symbolize America's first settlers. In fact, the Pilgrims obtained their patent to settle in Virginia, but when winds and weather drove their ship north to New England, they chose to land in Massachusetts and stay there.

Massachusetts was not the first move the Pilgrims had made. Originally their religious group had been among the Puritans in England trying to purify the Church of England from within. By 1609 they had left church and country behind them, having come to believe that the purity of faith they sought could not be achieved with the Church of England, and having felt too harshly the religious persecution shown to Separatists to even remain in their homeland. They established themselves first in the Netherlands, using up most of their funds in making that move. Holland, with its different language and culture, proved to be a disappointment to them, even though they were not harrassed by

22

the Dutch. They determined that they would establish an English-speaking colony in America, far away from the distractions which threatened to contaminate their children. Outside investors had to be found to finance their trip, and, as a result, colonists from outside their group had to be included.

One of the group's leaders, William Bradford, tells in his *History of Plymouth Plantation* that when the ship was about to land in New England, rather than Virginia for which the patent had been obtained, some of the outsiders began to express their belief that "when they came a shore they would use their owne libertie; for none had power to command them, the patente they had being for Virginia, and not for Newengland."[3] In order to obtain control over the mutinous outsiders, the colonists decided to enter into an agreement, fashioned after the covenant of their religious congregation, which would bind the signers by contract to form a political body empowered to enact laws for the common good, to which everyone would submit and obey. Out of the immediate need to meet the threatened mutiny, these non-lawyers drafted a legal document which served the Plymouth Colony for seventy-one years, the Mayflower Compact.

> In the name of God, Amen. We whose names are underwriten, the loyall subjects of our dread soveraigne Lord King James, by the grace of God, of Great Britaine, Franc, and Ireland king, defender of the faith, etc., haveing undertaken, for the glorie of God, and advancemente of the Christian faith, and honour of our king and countrie, a voyage to plant the first colonie in the Northerne parts of Virginia, doe by these presents solemnly and mutualy in the presence of God, and one of another, covenant and combine our selves together into a civill body politick, for our better ordering and preservation and furtherance of the ends aforesaid; and by vertue hearof to enacte, constitute, and frame such just and equall lawes, ordinances, acts, constitutions, and offices, from time to time, as shall be thought most meete and convenient for the generall good of the Colonie, unto which we promise all due submission and obedience. In witnes wherof we have hereunder subscribed our names at Cap-Codd the 11. of November, in the year of the raigne of our soveraigne lord, King James, of England, France and Ireland the eighteenth, and of Scotland the fiftie fourth. Ano: Dom. 1620.[4]

Although their legal claim to Plymouth Colony was not established until 1691, when they were incorporated within the Massachusetts Bay Colony, the Pilgrims endured and eventually prevailed. They are remembered for their hard work and determination to survive. While other English investors had seen their colonial ventures fail, the London merchants who had financed the Pilgrims were paid back their investment in full. The original agreement had been that the joint venture would run for seven years, at the end of which time the company would be dissolved and the stock divided. True to their word, the Pilgrims

dissolved the venture in 1627 and agreed to pay the investors install-
ments upon their investment over a period of nine years. Despite the
sacrifice involved, they met their obligation, and they are remembered
today for that integrity, and for the Mayflower Compact.

The Mayflower Compact which they created was the result of their
religious practices. One of the differences the Separatists had with the
Church of England was their manner of forming a congregation. They
believed a group of people could come together and write a covenant,
that is, a contract of their faith. Each member of the group bound himself to follow that covenant, and thereby a church was created. Each
church formed in this way was independent and self-governing, an idea
totally opposite to the established Church of England. Yet, it was only
natural that when the Pilgrims arrived in America and determined to
settle in an area to which their patent did not apply, they employed the
practice of their church to establish a form of government in their new
land. Thus, democracy came to America out of necessity when the ocean
winds carried the Pilgrims away from the lands to which their royal
charter applied, and they drafted a document for civil government patterned after their church covenent.

The Puritans

I dare take upon me, to be the Herauld of New-England so farre, as to
proclaime to the world, in the name of our Colony, that all Familists,
Antinomians, Anabaptists, and other Enthusiasts, shall have free Liberty
to keep away from us, and such as will come to be gone as fast as they
can, the sooner the better.
—The Reverend Nathaniel Ward (1578–1652)

The leaders of the Massachusetts Bay Colony accomplished a unique
structuring of their colony by convincing the company to legally transfer
the charter to those who actually lived in the colony. By removing the
supervision of stockholders in England, the colony became as nearly independent as it could be under the English king. The Puritan leadership
of Massachusetts Bay was not reluctant to exercise that independence.
They envisioned a religious colony in which the citizens acted according
to God's will. It was for the leaders to interpret God's will from the
Bible, and disobedience naturally had both civil and religious consequences. Since the motivation for establishing the colony had been to
create an example of Puritan living for all to see, any challenge to the
leadership was seen as a direct threat to the Colony. There simply was no
separation between religion and government insofar as the Puritans were
concerned.

The principal purpose of the colony, according to their charter, went
beyond the formation of a Puritan settlement. Their charter closed with

the direction to the people that they " . . . may be soe religiously, peaceablie, and civilly governed, as their good Life and orderlie Conversacon, maie wynn and incite the Natives of Country, to the Knowledg and Obedience of the onlie true God and Savior of Mankinde, and the Christian Fayth, which in our Royall Intencon, and the Adventurers free Profession, is the principall Ende of this Plantacion."[5] Except by the example of their own lives, the Puritans, in fact, made few efforts to convert the Indians. With the exception of a few people, of whom Roger Williams was one, the Puritans did not go out of their way to satisfy the king's intention to acquaint the native Americans with God.

Rather, they occupied themselves with the unique opportunity their charter presented them to conduct this experiment in creating a Bible commonwealth. The nature of the land they settled contributed to it as well. Unlike the agricultural-based society of Virginia in which towns were few and residences were far apart, New England was smaller in overall area, and society developed naturally into towns, not unlike the towns and villages in England from which the Puritans had come, wherein the people were employed in many of the same industries they had pursued in England.

Occupying a central location in each village was the meeting house or church. Its interior was simple, even harsh, and the hard pews lacked even the slight comfort of backs. Not until the middle of the seventeenth century did seating arrangements change to allow the church committee to assign pews or boxes according to social position, with each family paying for its own. No stoves appeared in churches until the nineteenth century, and both minister and congregation wore coats and gloves during services to withstand the winter cold. Prayers lasting an hour were not uncommon, and sermons were longer. Sundays were filled with religious obligations, for there were two services each Sunday, separated by a break for lunch. The meal had to be eaten cold since there could be no cooking fires on the Sabbath, and the mealtime break was also used for catechism, after which the people returned for the afternoon service.[6]

The presence of the church dominated not only the village landscape but also the daily lives of the villagers. Clustered in near proximity to the church and to each other, their homes served as vantage points for the villagers to keep a close eye on their neighbors. The acts which they regarded as criminal reflect just how watchful of one another they must have been. The ten crimes that were punishable by death under the first code enacted in Massachusetts, the Body of Liberties of 1641, were not only murder and poisoning but also heresy or idolatry, witchcraft, blasphemy, bestiality, sodomy, adultery, manstealing, and treason. Physical mutilation by branding, cutting off ears, slitting the nose or boring through the tongue was also employed to deter criminals from such activities as profanity, Sabbath breaking, speaking evil of preachers or officers, and drunkenness.[7]

The community also employed public humiliation to punish wrongdoers of lesser crimes. Hawthorne's *The Scarlet Letter* has acquainted many readers with the Puritan practice of forcing an adulteress to wear the letter "A" as a constant reminder to all she met of her crime of adultery. Other offenders might have been forced to wear a "D" for their drunkenness or a "T" for committing a theft. Punishments also intended to shame the offenders were the stocks and the ducking stool, and these were used to greatest effect in the public square or in front of the meeting house on days when the largest number of people would be in those places.

Although the colony was self-governing and the governor and his assistants were elected, until 1691 the right to vote was dependent upon membership in the church. To gain membership in the church, the applicant had to convince the members that he also was one of God's chosen, and only about one-fifth of the free males in the colony met the criteria. Once again, the linkage of church and state by the Puritans was absolute.

This examination of the Massachusetts Bay Colony, which focuses upon the role of religion in the community, particularly with regard to civil affairs, reveals the most severe side of life in the colony. To balance that picture, it should be mentioned that most of the leaders were intelligent, well-educated men. Plans for the colony had been well thought out, and thereby the suffering and hardships were greatly reduced. The church provided not only a governmental and religious framework but a social unity as well. Since large numbers had come to the colony, there was not the isolation settlers in rural communities endured. Economically, the colony's industries were successful enough to be in direct competition with England's own. And, the early colonists were filled with the exciting sense of creating the religious and social community they had envisioned.

As severe as the Puritan life style sounds today, the leaders of the colony were willing to take extreme steps in protecting it from the influence of outside religious sects. The Reverend Ward expressed the common sentiment of his day when he said that the only religious freedom the Puritans were willing to extend to other religious sects was the freedom to stay away from the Massachusetts Bay Colony. The restrictions against religious outsiders entering the colony went beyond empty threats from the pulpit.

The primary sources of danger to the spiritual safety of the colony, in the eyes of the Puritans, came from Roman Catholics, Quakers, and Baptists. One of the witches hanged in Boston Common in 1688 told the magistrates, "I die a Catholic," which certainly would not have helped her cause.[8] As late as 1732, when the governor of the colony· learned that a handful of Catholics might be living in Boston, he directed the following order to the sheriff:

> These are therefore to will and require you and each of you respectively in His Majesty's Name forthwith to make diligent Enquiry after and search for the said Popish Priest and other Papists of his Faith and Perswasion and (if need be) in order to apprehend them or any of them you are Directed and Impowered to break open any Dwelling houses shops or other Places or appartments where you shall suspect they or any of them are kept concealed and them or any of them having found you are to Convent before lawful Authority in order to their being secured and proceeded against as to Law and Justice appertains. Hereof fail not at your Peril . . . [9]

The Quakers were especially threatening to the Puritans, for while the Puritans believed that the Bible, as interpreted by learned religious leaders, was the source of all spiritual information, the Quakers believed in the "inner light," a process of personal revelation whereby the least educated person might receive as worthy a message from God as the most learned. This belief challenged the very foundations of the Puritan colony. It is only fair to add that certain Quakers felt the call to appear in shocking stages of dress and undress at Puritan gatherings, and we should not imagine all of the offending Quakers as looking and acting like the genteel, pacifist stereotype often portrayed in the movies. Laws were passed which ordered all Quakers to leave the colony. If they returned once after banishment, they lost one ear; again, they lost the other ear; and for a third time, a hole was thrust through the tongue. If they were foolhardy enough to return after all of this, they faced the death penalty. In addition, any ship's captain who knowingly brought a Quaker to the colony faced a fine of one hundred pounds.[10]

Executions of Quakers were, in fact, carried out. The most famous of these was of a woman, Mary Dyer. The Quakers were actively and openly challenging the laws against them, and Mary was among twenty others the day she was arrested. Three of them, two young men and Mary, were selected for hanging, and although both of the men were hanged, Mary was released at the last possible moment. She was sent back to jail, where she wrote the governor that she preferred· death to being shown mercy by the people who had killed her two companions. Unwilling to grant her demand for martyrdom, the governor had her taken by force from the jail and led fifteen miles outside of Boston. Mary awaited her chance and later returned. Although she was again put in jail, she was told that if she would leave Massachusetts, she was free to go. She replied, "I came here before to warn you to repeal your wicked law. I am upon the same mission now." This time, there was no reprieve for Mary, and on June 1, 1660, she was again taken to Boston

Common for hanging. She was urged to recant but she refused and actually signaled the hangman to proceed with her own hanging. A year later on September 1, 1661, King Charles II ordered the Puritans to relent in their persecution of the Quakers, and thus, Mary's mission was won.[11]

The most famous Baptist to face banishment by the Puritans was the founder of the first Baptist church in America, Roger Williams. His particular experience with the Puritans will be discussed later in connection with the establishment of Rhode Island.

A consideration of the Puritans could not ignore the period in their history during which the colony became obsessed with punishing witches. Witch hunts were not peculiar to the Massachusetts Bay Colony. They had occurred in England and Europe for centuries, and in other American colonies, but for such a small geographic area and population, the Puritans seem to have found and punished more than their share of witches. During the early 1690s when the trials were at their peak, at least twenty persons were executed as witches.

The second and third generation Puritans were not as severe in their faith as were their fathers and grandfathers, and many great men and ideas grew from New England's soil. One leader in the mid-seventeenth century cited a proverb: " . . . they that will find must as well seek where a thing is not, as where it is. . . . And this liberty of free disquisition is as great a means to keep the truth as to find it. The running water keeps pure and clear, when the standing pool corrupts."[12] Although such a proverb seems inconsistent with the rigid control of society practiced by the New England Puritans, they nevertheless appreciated well-reasoned discussions based upon thorough Bible study, and the sermons of their ministers were logical and scholarly. It is not surprising that during the Revolution and the founding of this nation, America found many of its leaders in New England.

From the early settlements along the Atlantic coast, colonists moved inland. The early settlers of Connecticut were primarily former Massachusetts colonists, although the Dutch had been there before them but had abandoned Fort Good Hope near Hartford as the English population increased. Originally Connecticut and New Haven were separate colonies, although they later merged. In most respects they were patterned after the Puritan system of Massachusetts. New Hampshire also reflected the character of Massachusetts. Only Rhode Island, among its New England neighbors, truly had a character of its own.

In 1642 delegates from Plymouth, Connecticut, New Haven, and the Massachusetts Bay Colony met together to form a confederation of the New England colonies, but specifically excluding Rhode Island. On May 19, 1643, the New England Confederation agreed in part:

Whereas we all came into these parts of America with one and the same end and aim, namely, to advance the Kingdom of our Lord Jesus Christ and to enjoy the liberties of the Gospel in purity and peace; and whereas in our settling (by a wise providence of God) we are further dispersed upon the sea coasts and rivers than was at first intended, so that we can not according to our desire with convenience communicate in one government and jursidiction; . . . The said United Colonies for themselves and their posterities do jointly and severally hereby enter into a firm and perpetual league of friendship and amity for offence and defence, mutual advice and succor upon all just occasions both for preserving and propagating the truth and liberties of the Gospel and for their own mutual safety and welfare. [13]

The intentional exclusion of neighboring Rhode Island from their confederation serves to emphasize the distaste the Puritans felt for that colony, and for its leader, Roger Williams. The friendship and common purposes expressed in the statement of confederation were not shared with the little colony of exiles and outcasts. As much as they felt disgust toward the colony, the Puritans also felt fear, frightened by the unorthodox ideas of Roger Williams.

4
RHODE ISLAND

God requireth not an uniformity of Religion to be inacted and inforced in any civill state; which inforced uniformity (sooner or later) is the greatest occasion of civill Warre, ravishing of conscience, persecution of Jesus Christ in his servants, and of the hypocrisie and destruction of millions of souls.

—Roger Williams, *The Bloody Tenent of Persecution*

More than is true of any other colony, the history of Rhode Island is the history of its leader and founder. Roger Williams did not, however, make his way directly from England to Rhode Island. Rather, he arrived in the Massachusetts Bay Colony where he was warmly received, to the extent even of having been asked to serve as a pastor-teacher in Boston. His refusal of that position was only the first shock of many the Puritan leaders would receive from him.

Before leaving England, Williams had aligned himself with the Separatists, and he was disappointed upon coming to New England to find that the Puritans bound church and state together as tightly as had the Anglicans in England. "According to Divine Law, officers of the Crown cannot rightfully interfere with the right of a person to worship as he pleases!" he preached.[1] Further, he stated, "I affirm that there was never civil state in the world that ever did or ever shall make good work of it, with a civil sword in spiritual matters."[2] Trying to find a community more suited to his views, Williams left Boston for Salem, then moved on to Plymouth, and finally returned to Salem. Wherever he went, his opinions disturbed the religious leaders, but the warnings of the Puritan leadership did not silence him, and within four and a half years of his arrival, he was brought to trial for his opinions which, in the eyes of the Puritan leadership, constituted sedition against the Commonwealth.

The opinions that the Puritans found dangerous to the state were the following: "First, That we have not our land by patent from the king, but that the natives are the true owners of it, and that we ought to repent of such a receiving it by patent. Secondly, that it is not lawful to

30

call a wicked person to swear, to pray, as being actions of God's worship. Thirdly, that it is not lawful to hear any of the ministers of the parish assemblies in England. Fourthly, That the civil magistrate's power extends only to the bodies, and goods, and outward state of men."[3] Obviously, the offending opinions were both religious and political. As might be expected, the Puritans convicted him. The pronouncement of guilt and punishment was made with these words: "Whereas Mr. Roger Williams, one of the elders of the church of Salem, hath broached & dyvulged dyvers newe & dangerous opinions, against the aucthoritie of magistrates . . . & yet maintaineth the same without retraccon, it is therefore ordered, that the said Mr. Williams shall departe out of this jurisidiction within sixe weekes noew nexte ensueing . . . "[4]

Because of his wife's pregnancy and his own poor health, Williams was granted six weeks to make the necessary preparations for his exile, but he was enjoined from expressing the opinions that had been found "newe and dangerous" during this period. Ignoring the injunction, he angered the Puritans by continuing to express his views, and they made plans to seize him and put him aboard a ship bound for England. Williams learned of their intentions and escaped into the night during a snow storm. He would probably not have survived the winter without the Indians. Their friendship had existed long before his exile, and his respect for the Indians and their rights to their native land had constituted the first of the charges for which he was convicted. During that winter, he decided to establish his own colony wherein all would be welcome to live and practice their faith. Practicing what he preached, he acquired the land for his colony not from the king but rather from the Indians, by gift and by purchase. Only later would he deal with the problems of gaining legal recognition from England. More importantly, he had been true to his own conscience in first honoring the rights of the Indians.[5]

He sent word to his followers of his colony and invited them to join him. The citizens of the colony were required to sign the following compact:

> We whose names are hereunder written, being desirous to inhabit the town of Providence, do promise to submit ourselves in active or passive obedience to all such orders or agreements as shall be made for the public consent of the present inhabitants, masters of families incorporated together in a township, and such others when they shall admit into the same, only in civil things.[6]

The startling and significant language for its time which was contained in the compact was the last limitation, "only in civil things." With those four words Williams and his followers made it clear that the government in Providence had no power to intrude in matters of religion. Nearly ten years after founding the colony, Williams was given a patent for The Rhode Island and Providence Plantations on March 14, 1644. It was yet another twenty years before a royal charter was issued by the king.

The unique experiment in religious freedom that was begun by the compact of the citizens of Providence was preserved in the petition they addressed to the king for the purpose of requesting a charter. The petition asked, "to hold forth a lively experiment, that a flourishing civill state may stand, yea, and best be maintained, and that among English spirits, with a full liberty in religious concernments."[7] The king honored the request, providing in the charter his royal endorsement of the religious experiment: "Our royall will and pleasure is, that noe person within the sayd colonye, at any time hereafter, shall be any wise molested, punished, disquieted, or called in question, for any differences in opinione in matters of religion, and doe not actually disturb the civill peace of our sayd colony; but that all and everye person and persons may, from tyme to tyme, and at all tymes hereafter, freelye and fullye have and enjoye his and theire own judgments and consciences, in matters of religious concernments . . . "[8] Despite the hostility and political intrigues of the neighboring Puritans, Rhode Island had secured the royal approval needed to continue Williams' dream.

Not only were Williams' ideas regarding religious liberty innovative; for the times in which he lived, his ideas regarding the source of civil authority, as expressed in the charter, were perhaps even more novel.

> The Civill Power is originally and fundamentally in the People . . . a People may erect and establish what forme of Government seemes to them most meete for their civill condition: It is evident that such Governments as are by them erected and established, have no more power, nor for a longer time, than the civill power of people consenting and agreeing shall betrust them with.[9]

By the time the founding fathers met in Philidelphia to declare a new nation, the idea of authority coming from the people themselves had gained general acceptance, but in the seventeenth century, when the world was controlled by kings and princes of the church, the idea was radical.

Upon coming to Rhode Island, Williams had been baptized by immersion in a stream near his home, and he established the first Baptist church in America. He was determined, however, that people of all faiths were welcome in Rhode Island, even going so far as to extend freedom of conscience to the Catholics,[10] a privilege denied them by law in most of the colonies. About the Catholics Williams said: "I have impartially pleaded for the freedom of the consciences of the Papists themselves, the greatest enemies and persecutors (in Europe) of the saints and truths of Jesus: yet I have pleaded for no more than is their due and right."[11]

Williams was also offended by many of the views held by the Quakers, but he protected their rights to hold such views. In 1657 the United New England colonies asked Rhode Island to join them in excluding Quakers. Rhode Island refused to exclude the Quakers and explained to its New England neighbors: "We have no law among us, whereby to punish any for only declaring by words, etc., theire minds and understanding concerning the things and ways of God, as to salvation and an eternal condition."[12] Freedom of conscience was the rule in Rhode Island, and there was no church establishment.

Williams himself had passed through the various groups within the Church of England on his way to becoming a Baptist, and he continued on his journey of conscience, eventually moving beyond a leadership role within the Baptist church to an independent search outside any organized church during the last years of his life. He did not see this constant seeking as a loss of faith, however. As he said, "None shall see the Truth but the Soul that loves it, and digs for it as for treasures of gold and silver, and is impartial, patient, and pitiful to the opposers."[13]

Certainly the Puritans were irritated by the odd ideas of Roger Williams and had little respect for the mixed assortment of people who settled in his colony. However, even the tolerant Dutch were perplexed by his willingness to not only accept practitioners of any religion but also his insistence upon their right to such freedom of conscience. Upon turning away a ship of Quakers from the dock at New Amsterdam, the Dutch master of the port recorded the following: "We suppose they went to Rhode Island, for that is the receptacle of all sorts of riffraff people, and is nothing else than the sewer of New England."[14]

It was not tolerance that was extended to these newcomers in Rhode Island, for tolerance implies a rightness of one's own religion and a willingness to endure other faiths less right. Williams advocated not tolerance but equality of all faiths. Later in his life, he recognized that the price of such freedom was a certain amount of abuse, for he wrote in 1654 that "a sweet cup hath rendered many of us wanton and too active, for we have long drunk of the cup of as great liberties as any people that we can hear of under the whole heaven."[15] Nonetheless, he maintained throughout his life in both word and deed his commitment to the freedom and equality of treatment toward all faiths.

Rhode Island and her people were a small minority in the colonial world, but the impact they made upon the emerging nation was enormous. Regarded in its own time as the "sewer of New England," Rhode Island was nevertheless the only place in the Christian world during the mid-seventeenth century where any religious sect could practice its faith freely. By their example, the citizens of Rhode Island showed that religious liberty could be made to work, and they made it work in a colony founded upon the radical idea that the people themselves hold the authority to grant the power to be governed.

5
PENNSYLVANIA

Every person that does or shall reside therein shall have and enjoy the free possession of his or her faith and exercise of worship towards God, in such way and manner as every person shall in conscience believe is most acceptable to God.

—William Penn

It was not until the latter quarter of the seventeenth century that William Penn was successful in persuading the king to grant him a colony for Penn's own religious experiment. By that time, there were already settlers residing in the area covered by the grant. These settlers, joined by the variety of nationalities recruited by Penn, gave the colony a greater mixture of non-British colonists than was found in most of the other colonies. That ethnic diversity it shared with New York. Like Rhode Island, Pennsylvania was the dream of a single man, whose motivation in establishing the colony was religious. Unwilling to extend religious freedom without reserve as Roger Williams had insisted upon doing, William Penn nevertheless established greater religious freedom in his colony than its citizens had known in their prior homelands. Although it was Penn's intention to extend religious freedom to all persons who believed in one God, his primary purpose in founding the colony was to provide a haven for members of his own faith, the Quakers. As a result, Pennsylvania shared in common with New England the influence of a single, founding religion upon the character of the colony. Therefore, Pennsylvania had certain characteristics in common with the other colonies already discussed, but the application of those characteristics was uniquely Pennsylvania's own.

In order to understand the unique development of Pennsylvania, one must examine the equally unique, even contradictory characteristics of the founder of the colony, William Penn. The son of a naval hero and a member of the wealthy class, Penn was drawn to the Quaker faith while he was still in school, and as a result of the opinions he expressed at Oxford, he was expelled. His fellow Quakers were, according to one of their own, "a plain lowly-minded people,"[1] yet Penn was a personal friend of King Charles II. His father had commanded victorious English forces against the Spanish and the Dutch, but Penn led a pacifist sect. What was it about the Quakers that had attracted this privileged young man?

The earliest Christians had believed that it was necessary for a priest to intercede between God and His followers. It was a revolutionary change of faith when people came to believe they could read and interpret the word of God for themselves, with the help of learned church leaders. Eventually, some people moved even further away from the traditional view and came to believe they could read and interpret the Bible without the guidance of any church leadership. However, the Quakers shocked even those who accepted the right of individuals to read and interpret the Bible for themselves by going so far as to believe that a person could experience a direct revelation from God. This personal revelation was the Inner Light which the Quakers possessed and which distinguished them from all other sects. They were often poor, common people, but since they believed anyone could experience this inner light, matters of education, wealth, and social position were unimportant within their society. They called themselves the Society of Friends, but they were more generally known by the name first applied to them as an insult, Quakers.

The Quakers regarded all the members within their Society of Friends as equals. This had several important effects. First, there was no elevated clergy in their church. Second, wealth and social class had no special privileges. In fact, at that time in England, the terms "thee" and "thou" were reserved for children and servants, and so the Quakers adopted that form of address for everyone to show the removal of class distinctions. Third, men and women were of equal importance in their church, and women were among the most active of their missionaries. The first two Quakers jailed in Boston were women, and it was the hanging of Mary Dyer that offended public opinion to such an extent that the king ordered an end to harassment of the Quakers in Massachusetts. Ultimately, this insistence upon equality led Quakers to the forefront in the fight against slavery, but in colonial times even some of the Quakers owned slaves.[2]

Upperclass Englishmen and figures of authority found the refusal of the Quakers to address them by their titles most offensive. Another means of showing this equality was for the men to refuse to remove their hats indoors, except when they were in the presence of God within their church. This sign of disrespect, particularly when practiced in a courtroom, sent more than one Quaker to jail. However, the story was told that when William Penn failed to remove his hat in the presence of the king, Charles made a joke of it by saying that since it was customary that only one man in the room when the king was present should wear a hat, he would remove his own and allow Penn to retain his. Penn's friendship with the king did not always keep him out of jail, but he did not spend as much time there as did many of the Quakers.

By the time Penn approached the king with his request for a colony, the time of severest persecution of the Quakers, both in England and in the colonies, had passed, and some degree of religious tolerance was being practiced. Even so, the Quakers were not welcomed anywhere. In granting Penn's request in 1681, Charles II settled a sixteen thousand pound debt he owed Penn and rid England of a great number of the troublesome Quakers. Thus, both friends were satisfied with the bargain.

Penn referred to the colony as his "holy experiment." He expressed his intentions in forming the colony in this way: "My God that has given it me through many difficulties, will, I believe, bless and make it the seed of a nation. . . . which may answer His kind providence and serve His Truth and people; that an example may be set up to the nations.. There may be room there, though not here, for such an experiment."[3] Thus, like the Puritans, Penn wanted to build a religious community that would be an example to the world. Like Roger Williams he wanted to welcome people of differing faiths. And, like the Dutch West India Company, he actively recruited colonists from outside England to come to his colony.

Since his colony was founded rather late in the colonial adventure, earlier settlers preceded him. In 1698, a friend of Penn's wrote to him, including in his communication a short history of the colony and describing the early inhabitants: "The Natives, or first Inhabitants of this Country in their Original, are suppos'd by most People to have been of the Ten Scattered Tribes. . . . The next that came there, were the Dutch, (who call'd the Country New Neitherland) between Fifty and Sixty Years ago, and were the first Planters in those Parts; but they made little or no Improvement, (applying themselves wholly to Trafique in Skins and Furs), . . . Soon after them came the Swedes and Fins, who apply'd themselves to Husbandry, and were the first Christian People that made any considerable Improvement there."[4]

Of the settlers recruited by Penn, many were Quakers from England and Wales, but he was also especially successful in recruiting Germans to Pennsylvania. Those who came reported back to Germany that in Pennsylvania were both the religious toleration that had been promised and farms similar to those in Germany to which they were accustomed. As a result of their favorable reports, other Germans came to join them. In fact about seventy percent of the Germans who came to America within the century after Pennsylvania was founded came to the middle colonies, and half of the total came to Pennsylvania itself.[5] The smaller German religious sects, like the Mennonites, arrived earliest, and, on the whole, were most like the Quakers. Later arrivals belonged to the Reformed and Lutheran churches.

All of the arrivals found that the colony, especially the beautifully designed city of Philadelphia, had been well planned for settlement. Upon their arrival they set to work to make the colony and the city even better. Penn's correspondent of 1698 described the city in these words: " . . . the Industrious (nay Indefatigable) Inhabitants have built a Noble and Beautiful City, and called it Philadelphia"; and of the rest of the colony he said: "What is Inhabited of this Country, is divided into Six Counties, though there is not the Twentieth Part of it yet Peopled by the Christians"; and of both city and country: "Now the true Reason why this Fruitful Countrey and Flourishing City advance so considerably . . . is their great and extended Traffique and Commerce both by Sea and Land." Upon the subject of religion he added: "[T]here is no Persecution for Religion, nor ever like to be; 'tis this that knocks all Commerce on the Head, together with high Imposts, strict Laws, and cramping Orders."[6]

Penn had been in England during the period of which his friend wrote. Early in the 1690s the king had taken Penn's colony from him, and although he regained it after two years, he did not return until 1699. Thereafter, the Great Charter and Frame of Government of 1683, which had replaced the original Frame of Government of 1682, was replaced itself by the Pennsylvania Charter of Privileges of October 18, 1701. This document was drafted not by Penn himself but rather by committees from the council. Nevertheless, they showed their commitment to carry forward his dream of religious freedom by placing the provision for religion foremost in the charter. It provided:

> BECAUSE no People can be truly happy under the greatest Enjoyment of Civil Liberties, if abridged of the Freedom of their Consciences, as to their Religious Profession and Worship: And Almighty God being the only Lord of Conscience, Father of Lights and Spirits; and the Author as well as Object of all divine Knowledge, Faith and Worship, who only doth enlighten the Mind and persuade and convince the Understandings of People, I do hereby grant and declare, That no Person or Persons, inhabiting in this province or Territories, who shall confess and acknowledge One almighty God, the Creator, Upholder and Ruler of the World; and profess him or themselves obliged to live quietly under the Civil Government, shall be in any Case molested or prejudiced, in his or their Person or Estate, because of his or their conscientious Persuasion or Practice, nor be compelled to frequent or maintain any religious Worship, Place or Ministry, contrary to his or their Mind, or to do or suffer any other Act or Thing, contrary to their religious Persuasion.[7]

With this charter, freedom of religion was extended to all who accepted one God. The right to serve in any governmental post, however, was limited by the following language: " . . . all Persons who also profess to believe in Jesus Christ, the Saviour of the World, shall be capable (notwithstanding their other Persuasions and Practices in Point of Conscience and Religion) to serve this Government in any Capacity, both legislatively and executively, he or they solemnly promising, when lawfully required, alligiance to the King as Sovereign, and Fidelity to the Proprietary and Governor, and taking the attests now established by the Law . . . "[8] If Catholics could, in good conscience swear allegiance to the King of England and pass the other tests established by law, they could serve the government. But, in 1757 greater restrictions were imposed upon any "papist or one reputed to be such" by requiring him to surrender all arms and ammunition and exempting him from military service while at the same time fining him for his failure to serve in the army.[9] While making great strides toward religious liberty, Pennsylvania could not extend the absolute equality of religions found in Rhode Island.

William Penn shared with Roger Williams not only the desire to create a place where people could freely enjoy their religion, but also his respect for the native Indians, and, like Williams, Penn evidenced this respect by learning the language of the natives. Penn entered into a treaty with the Indians, and although its terms are not known to us today, it was unbroken for seventy years. The Quaker Penn was put to an awkward test upon its signing, for the Indians chose to celebrate not with the formality of seals and oaths but rather with dancing. Although the Quakers disapproved of dancing, on this occasion Penn joined in the ceremony. [10]

The colony was so successful in attracting people of differing nationalities and religions that soon the Quakers were outnumbered by non-Quakers many times over. Until 1756, however, the Quakers held all of the important elective and appointive posts. These positions had been denied them elsewhere because of their religious refusal to take oaths.

Since most of the non-English colonists came from the more humble classes of Europe, they had little experience in matters of government. This, coupled with the fact that the language of government and commerce was primarily English, led to a dominance by the majority English in matters of colonial government. However, the enrichment contributed by the other nationalities could easily be seen in farming practices, architecture, and social customs.

Philadelphia quickly became the largest colonial city, and because of its diverse population it was a cultural center for the colonies. It was not just its geographic location that led to its selection by the founding fathers for their early meetings. Philadelphia had become, as Penn had envisioned, "an example to the nations" of the success of his "holy experiment" in establishing a colony where men of many faiths were welcome. In his own lifetime, Penn had become disheartened by the enthusiasm with which his citizens had grasped his dream and begun to carry it beyond the dimensions he had planned, with demands that he found rather ungrateful. But, the contrast of ideas and customs that Penn himself had brought together created a colony, centered in Philadelphia, astir with intellectual and commercial activity. When the American colonies reached the historical moment when they were ready to embark upon the American Revolution, Philadelphia led the way. William Penn had planted the seed of a new nation in which things that had been impossible in the Old World could be achieved.

6
MARYLAND

No person or persons whatsoever, within this province . . . professing to believe in Jesus Christ, shall from henceforth be in any ways troubled, molested, or discountenanced, for in respect of his or her Religion, nor in the free exercise thereof . . .

—Maryland Toleration Act, 1649

Like other colonies, Maryland was founded for the purpose of providing a colony of refuge for a religious minority to worship without persecution. Tragically, the minority Catholics of Maryland did not find refuge in America, only further years of religious conflict, and eventual reduction to the status of second class citizens in the very colony that they had founded.

When Henry VIII established the Church of England, there remained Englishmen who could not abandon their Roman Catholic faith. Ironically, the same character trait that made them adhere to the old traditions in matters of religion also discouraged them from leaving their traditional home in England; therefore, there were few Catholics willing to emigrate, despite the persecution of members of their faith. Nevertheless, by 1632, a Catholic member of the upper class had convinced King Charles I to give the Catholics a colony in America.

Between the Anglicans in Virginia to the south and the Puritans in New England to the north, the Catholic Lord Baltimore, George Calvert, was granted a colony. When he died, his son Leonard, the second Lord Baltimore, carried on the project. The charter, granted by Charles I in April of 1632, described the Calvert family project: "Whereas our well beloved and right trusty Subject Caecilius Calvert, Baron of Baltimore, in our Kingdom of Ireland, . . . being animated with a laudable, and pious Zeal for extending the Christian Religion, and also the Territories of our Empire, hath humbly besought Leave of Us, that he may transport, by his own Industry, and Expence, a numerous Colony of the English Nation, to a certain Region, herein after described, in a Country hitherto uncultivated, in the Parts of America, and partly occupied

41

by Savages, having no Knowledge of the Divine Being . . . "[1] Unfortunately, despite his "pious Zeal," Leonard was not successful in recruiting large numbers of Catholics willing to face the risks of colonization. In fact, neither Leonard nor his father before him chose to settle in or even visit his colony. Most of the Catholics who settled in Maryland arrived in the first two ships, and subsequent immigrants were almost entirely Protestant. Within fifty years, they outnumbered the Catholics about twenty to one. From the beginning, they resented the powerful positions held by the Catholics in the colony.[2]

Leonard Calvert had not been insensitive to the difficulty of managing a colony where the controlling Catholic minority had to work with and attract a non-Catholic population if the colony were to succeed. In 1636 he drafted an oath for Maryland governors to take which made clear his position that non-Catholics were not to be harassed.

> I will not myself or any other, directly or indirectly, trouble, molest, or discountenance any person professing to believe in Jesus Christ, for or in respect to religion: I will make no difference of persons in conferring offices, favors, or rewards, for or in respect of religion: but merely as they shall be found faithful and well deserving, and endued with moral virtues and abilities: my aim shall be public unity, and if any person or officer shall molest any person professing to believe in Jesus Christ, on account of his religion, I will protect the person molested, and punish the offender.[3]

Going even further, Calvert instructed the Catholic colonists to "be very careful to preserve unity and peace amongst all the passengers on Shipp-board, and . . . suffer no scandal or offense to be given to any of the Protestants, whereby any just complaint may hereafter be made by them, in Virginea or in England, and . . . for that end . . . cause all Acts of Romane Catholique Religion to be done as privately as may be, and . . . instruct all Romane Catholoques to be silent upon all occasions of discourse concerning matters of Religion; and . . . treat the Protestants with as much mildness and favor as Justice will permit."[4]

Despite his careful precautions, Calvert was unable to avert the friction between Catholics and Protestants in his colony. Religious resentments were compounded by the fact that most of the colonial leadership was Catholic, while the working classes were Protestants, resulting in class-based as well as religious differences.

In addition, the Virginia colonists, who had earlier claimed the land granted to Lord Baltimore under their forfeited charter, were not happy with their Catholic neighbor. In 1630 the Virginia Council had learned of Lord Baltimore's plan to establish a colony for Catholic settlement in America, and with great concern the council had petitioned King Charles I that of all the blessings they enjoyed in their new land, "there is none whereby it hath beene made more happy then in the freedome of our Religion, which wee have enjoyed, and that noe papists have bene suffered to settle their aboad amongst us."[5] When the king ignored their petition and granted Baltimore his Catholic colony, the Virginians continued their animosity indirectly by doing whatever they could to help the Protestants in Maryland. Obviously, when they spoke in their petition to the king of enjoying religious freedom, they did not mean freedom for all faiths—and certainly not for Catholics!

Not only did Catholics face the religious intolerance of all English religious minorities. They faced the additional distrust born of the fact that Spain, the long-time enemy of England, was a Catholic country, and it was easy for the English in America to assume that a Catholic colony might be in league with Spain.

The early years of the Maryland colony were unsettled years in England as well. The English Civil War began in 1642 and King Charles, who had approved the colony, was executed in 1649. Under Lord Protector Cromwell, permission was given to settlers to occupy land in Maryland without swearing allegiance to the Catholic proprietor, thereby weakening the Catholics' position further.

Some measure of the religious mixture of the population in Maryland in 1649 may be found by reviewing the list of groups which the Act of Toleration forbid its citizens to berate. It included the prohibition against calling anyone in a derogative way a "Heretic, Schismatic, Idolater, Independent, Presbyterian, Popish Priest, Jesuit, Jesuited Papist, Lutheran, Calvinist, Anabaptist, Brownist, Antinomian, Barrowist, Roundhead, Separatist, or any other Name or term, in a reproachful manner."[6]

To accommodate all of these people, Lord Baltimore urged the Maryland Assembly to pass the Act of Toleration. It contained the following provision:

> And whereas the enforcing of the conscience in matter of religion, hath frequently fallen out to be of dangerous consequence in those common wealths where it has been practiced, and for the more quiet and peaceable government of this Province, and the better to preserve mutual love and unity among the inhabitants, etc. No person or persons whatsoever, within this Province . . . professing to believe in Jesus Christ, shall from henceforth be in any ways troubled, molested, or discountenanced, for in respect of his or her Religion, nor in the free exercise thereof . . . nor any way compelled to the belief or exercise of any other religion, against his or her consent, so as they be not unfaithful to the Lord Proprietor, or molest or conspire against the civil government established, or to be established, in this Province, under him or his heirs.[7]

Unfortunately, the act did not resolve the religious jealousies and friction. At the time of its passage, Lord Baltimore had appointed a Protestant governor, but the governor was away from the colony when

Charles I was executed and his deputy, a Catholic, declared allegiance to the exiled Charles II. Lord Baltimore repudiated this foolhardy act, but a commission was sent, nevertheless, to determine the loyalty of the colony to Parliament. As a result of political maneuvering, the Maryland Puritans gained control. Five years after its enactment the Act of Toleration was repealed by the Maryland General Assembly, which passed a new act unfavorable to the Catholics. Although the proprietor regained control in 1657 and reestablished the Act of Toleration, matters were not settled. When William and Mary assumed the throne in 1688 following the English Revolution, the Protestants acquired the royal encouragement they had been awaiting and overthrew the Catholic proprietor, the third Lord Baltimore. Maryland became a royal province in 1692, although the proprietorship was restored in 1715. With the overthrow of the proprietorship, however, the Church of England was made the established church of Maryland and taxes were imposed upon the population to build Anglican churches and support the Anglican clergy. This was done even though about one-twelfth of the population remained Catholic.

Only sixty years after its founding as a Catholic colony where people of all Christian faiths could enjoy religious freedom, Maryland had thrust aside the Act of Religious Tolerance and established the Church of England. Catholics were denied suffrage, the right to hold office, and were taxed twice as much as were Protestants.[8]

The motives of the Lord Baltimore proprietors in founding a colony open to all Christians may have been economic, knowing that there were not enough Catholics willing to emigrate. Nevertheless, they did open their colony to other Christians. Whatever their motives, they struggled for three generations to maintain a colony based upon religious tolerance. Perhaps their experiment failed because it was not until the third Lord Baltimore that the proprietor actually came to his colony to live. Perhaps it failed because of political events in England. Or perhaps the prejudices against the Catholics made its success impossible. Although the experiment failed insofar as religious tolerance is concerned, the Maryland Act of Religious Tolerance is often cited as one of the earliest examples of religious liberty in America.

7
VIRGINIA

. . . Which said Counsellors and Council we earnestly pray and desire . . . they bend their Care and Endeavors to assist the said Governor; first and principally in the Advancement of the Honour and Service of God, and the Enlargement of his Kingdom amongst the Heathen People; and next, in erecting of the said Colony in due obedience to his Majesty . . .

—from the document authorizing the Virginia Assembly, 1621

As the earliest English colonists, the Jamestown adventurers had the fewest assurances of safety and success in their venture, and only those with very little to lose by leaving England would take such risks. Of course, the investors and colonial leaders came from positions of some wealth and social standing, but most of the original colonists were of the lowest economic and social class. The harsh punishments of poverty, and often of the criminal courts, were what they were abandoning in England to face the risks of Virginia. About his fellow colonists, John Rolfe said: "I speake on my owne experience for these 11 years, I never amongst so few, have seene so many falsehearted, envious and malicious people (yea amongst some who march in the better rank)."[1] The high mortality rate during the early years resulted not only from conditions in the colony but also from the fact that many of the colonists were malnourished when they left England, or suffering from jail fever or other diseases. Shipboard conditions further weakened them. Almost all of the early colonists were too poor to pay for their own passage, and so they arrived as indentured servants. In the beginning, the colonists were almost entirely men, and even later when the women also came, there were not enough of them to provide wives for all of the men. During the early years, it was not a colony of families, and in 1611 the governor had to admit that sometimes "everie man allmost laments himself of being here, and murmers at his present state, though haply he would not better it in England."[2] In addition, their life was unsettled by the quick passage through Jamestown on their way to some plantation where they would serve out their indenture. As can be imagined, religious freedom was not a high priority among these people.

As grim as the Jamestown colony may have been, it nevertheless endured and served as the port of entry to Virginia. Colonial Virginia spread itself along its waterways, rather than carving roads through the wilderness, and it was at Jamestown that incoming ships first docked. The treasures these ships carried back to England were not what the king and the investors had anticipated.

The English, like the Spanish before them, had come to the new world with expectations of gold and other treasures to be found. In fact, the fortunes to be made in Virginia came from another discovery brought back to Europe by the Spanish—tobacco. Between the time when Columbus had brought the plant back from the West Indies and the settlement of Virginia, the use of tobacco had spread throughout Europe. Despite the warnings of King James I that tobacco was "loathesome to the eye, hateful to the nose, harmful to the brain, and dangerous to the lungs,"[3] and his imposition in 1604 of a fine upon users, its popularity continued. The tobacco plant, not religion, defined the development of early Virginia.

Plantations for raising tobacco were stretched in narrow bands along the rivers, and because the soil was quickly exhausted by the crop, each planter's farm had to be large. Therefore, an agricultural economy developed, with plantation homes spaced far apart. Throughout the colonial period, no really large cities developed, and the plantations, rather than villages or towns, formed the social structure. Without close neighbors, it was difficult to select a church site convenient for very many colonists to attend. Additionally, the absence of close neighbors to monitor their activities led many Virginians to do as they pleased, and attending church every Sunday was not always what they pleased to do. With no one living nearby, who knew whether they attended or not? Even those who wanted to attend church services were often unable to attend regularly because of the great distances between their homes and the nearest church. As a result, a different attitude about church attendance developed in Virginia. In 1661, one writer excused the poor church attendance by explaining that "many of them were very remote from the House of God, though placed in the middest of them . . . and divers of the more remote Families being discouraged by the length or tediousness of the way, through extremities of heat in Summer, frost and snow in Winter, and temptestuous weather in both, do very seldome repair thither."[4] While it was possible for the Puritans in New England to establish towns and villages centered around their church in much the same way they had done in England, the Virginians could not duplicate English village life in their vast new land. Without the guidance of the clergy and the fellowship of townspeople sharing the weekly ritual of church attendance, even the more pious of the Virginia colonists gradually drifted away from traditional church observances.

That is not to say that religion was forgotten in Virginia. From the laws they enacted, it is obvious that the influential men regarded religious beliefs, specifically belief in accordance with the Church of England, as important. However, the Anglican planters saw their church as much a necessary social institution as a controlling force in their personal lives. In truth, the church structure had been utilized as a political or social subdivision. Citizens of a parish elected vestrymen, and once elected the vestries filled their own vacancies. The vestries were responsible for fixing the minister's salary, for church expenses, for assessment to support their expenditures, and for caring for the poor. By filling their own vacancies as they occurred over the years, the vestrymen were able to select other like-minded gentlemen and to run the vestry business with little interference.[5]

Just as the isolation and distances were impediments to religion for laymen, they also impeded the clergy. It was difficult to convince an Anglican minister to give up his position in England to face the hardships of Virginia. Of those who were convinced, many did not remain in the colony for very long. Too often the only ones willing to come were those unacceptable, for some reason, to churches in England. Writing to the Bishop of London, one Virginia rector complained about the poor quality of some of his fellow clergymen. He reported: "Several ministers have caused such high scandals of late and have raised such prejudices amongst the people against the clergy, that hardly can they be persuaded to take a clergyman into their parish."[6]

Those clergymen who stayed and strived to minister to all for whom they were responsible faced a nearly impossible task. In 1661, only about one-fifth of the Anglican parishes actually had clergy. As late as 1738, one Anglican minister wrote to the Bishop of London, describing his work load in this way: "I have three churches, 23 and 25 miles from the Glebe, in which I officiate every Sunday; and besides these three I have seven places of service up in the mountains, where the clerks read prayers, four clerks in the seven places. I go twice a year to preach at twelve places which I reckon better than 400 miles backwards and forwards, and ford 19 times the North and South Rivers."[7]

It was permissible, because of the circumstances, to use laymen, approved and hired by the vestries of the parishes, to fill in for the absent ministers. A clergyman who had spent some time in Virginia wrote to Sir William Berkeley in 1681 that the system led to abuses by vestries who hired layreaders instead of ministers because it was cheaper to do so, and not because ministers were unavailable. The minister complained: "Two-thirds of the Preachers are made up of leaden Lay-Priests of the Vestries Ordination: and are both the shame and grief of the rightly ordained Clergie there."[8]

To attempt to remedy the unsatisfactory religious conditions in Virginia, in 1689 the Bishop of London sent a commissary to the colony, the Reverend James Blair. Blair perceived that the answer to the shortage of Anglican ministers willing to come to Virginia and the unsuitable nature of many who came was to establish a college in Virginia where native sons could be educated as ministers. When the Virginians sent him to England to ask for a charter for their college, Blair explained the importance of his mission by stating that creating the college would save colonial souls. The English attorney general replied: "Souls! Damn your souls. Make tobacco."[9] Nevertheless, King William and Queen Mary were supportive of the request and a charter for the college bearing their names was granted in 1693. The purpose for William and Mary College was defined as being "that the church in Virginia may be furnished with a seminary of ministers of the Gospel, and that the youth may be piously educated in good manners and that the Christian faith may be propagated amongst the western Indians to the glory of almighty God."[10]

Educating the Indians had been an expressed priority from the time of the first charter in 1606. It provided: "We, greatly commending, and graciously accepting of, their Desires for the Furtherance of so noble a Work, which may, by the Providence of Almighty God, hereafter tend to the Glory of his divine Majesty, in propagating of Christian Religion to such People, as yet live in Darkness and miserable Ignorance of the true Knowledge and Worship of God, and may in time bring the Infidels and Savages, living in those Parts, to human Civility, and to a settled and quiet Government; Do, by these our Letters Patents, graciously accept of, and agree to, their humble and well-intended desires . . . "[11] Since there were not even enough ministers to serve the English colonists, however, converting the Indians had been given very little attention.

The initial influx of members of the poorest class was relieved as the colony prospered. Especially during the English Civil Wars beginning in 1642, families who had followed the king in his unsuccessful defense of the throne came to Virginia when the king was defeated. During the years of the Commonwealth, from 1649 to 1660, the Puritans gained control of the Church of England, and the Anglicans were prompted to emigrate by many of the same reasons that had prompted the Puritans to leave England twenty years before.

Not only were the immigrants of a higher class, but also the indentured servants who lasted out the terms of their indentures often acquired plantations of their own and joined the propertied class of Virginia. This was possible because most agreements of indenture required the master to provide the servant with a certain number of acres at the completion of his term. In the early years of the colony, anyone willing to work hard in the tobacco fields of his farm could eventually earn enough to purchase indentured servants of his own, and more land for raising tobacco, and thereby rise to the highest levels of society. The introduction of slave labor closed this route of social mobility. No longer could the small farmer compete against the plantations using cheap slave labor. Nevertheless, in the beginning many successful Virginia planters had originally come to America as indentured servants.

While social class distinctions in England had become fixed over many generations, in Virginia anyone could achieve social prominence through prosperous farming. The Virginia aristocrats were the planters. The introduction of slaves into the social equation practically eliminated the middle class in Virginia. There were left only the aristocratic plant-ers with their slaves and the poor white farmers or tenant farmers who could not compete. Many of those who were not willing to be trapped at the lowest social level of the white population left Virginia and headed west.

In seventeenth-century Virginia the Church of England was not only the established church, it was also the socially acceptable church of the planter class. The faith of the Anglican planter aristocrats did not pro-hibit them from enjoying worldly pleasures, and their religious emphasis was upon praise of the Creator and confidence in His power to redeem them from their sins. The music and liturgy of their church served as a tie to the traditions of the civilized England from which they had come, although many of them would not have been a part of the English soci-ety they were emulating. The formal prayers and responses employed in the Anglican service required instruction and signified that members ca-pable of participating in the service were learned and initiates of a spe-cial group. In contrast, most of the common people lacked the teaching and sophistication necessary to participate in the service or understand the sermons. The Church of England was almost a private club for the Anglican planter society, and even the seating in the church was accord-ing to social rank.

When it is remembered that the vestries, composed of the leading gentlemen of the community, determined the minister's salary and con-ducted church business, it is easy to understand how the common people became more and more estranged from the church. By under-standing the neglect of the religious training of the common people in Virginia, and the emphasis, even in church, upon their lowly social position, it will be easier to appreciate the enormous appeal of the preachers who reached out to them during the Great Awakening of the eighteenth century. But, throughout the seventeenth century, the Church of England prevailed in Virginia.

During the civil wars and the period of the Commonwealth of England, the Anglicans were displaced by the Puritans within the Church of England. Realignment of existing sects was not the only consequence of these events. This was also a particularly fertile period for the birth of new Protestant sects. These new sects disagreed not only with the traditional Anglican rituals and creeds but also with the strict Puritans.

Among the new sects that arose during this time were the Quakers, and early in their history they sent missionaries to Virginia, just as they had to New England. Like the Puritans in New England, the Anglicans in the Virginia Assembly enacted laws to exclude the Quakers from the colony. The Act for Suppressing the Quakers was passed in 1660 and stated in part: "Whereas there is an unreasonable and turbulent sort of people commonly called Quakers, who contrary to the law do daily gather together unto them unlawfull assemblies and congregation of people, teaching and publishing lies, miracles, false visions, prophecies and doctrines . . . It is enacted . . . that all such Quakers as have been questioned, or shall hereafter arrive shall be apprehended, wheresoever they shall be found, and they be imprisoned without bail or mainprize till they do adjure this country . . . And that no person do presume on their peril to dispose or publish their books, pamphlets, or libels, bearing the title of their tenets and opinions."[12] Also like the Puritans, the Virginians provided for a fine of one hundred pounds to be assessed against any ship's captain who transported Quakers to the colony. To assure diligence in searching out these unwelcome Quakers, Governor Berkeley spent one-half of the money collected in fines from the Quakers in paying rewards to informers.

The Quakers were not the only sect the Virginians had attempted to exclude. Even earlier, a few Puritans had come to Virginia, as the Pilgrims had originally planned to do, and they had obtained clergymen from Massachusetts to join their communities. However, in 1642 the Virginia General Assembly had passed a law requiring all ministers to conform to the tenets of the Church of England or immediately leave the colony. Thereafter, the Puritans who remained in Virginia had practiced their faith discreetly.

Roman Catholics had been excluded from Virginia from the beginning. The second charter of 1609 had provided, " . . . we should be loath, that any Person should be permitted to pass, that we suspected to affect the Superstitions of the Church of *Rome,* we do hereby *Declare* that it is our Will and Pleasure, that none be permitted to pass in any Voyage, from time to time to be made into the said Country, but such, as first shall have taken the Oath of Supremacy; . . . "[13] This hostility continued and was even directed beyond the boundaries of Virginia, especially with reference to the Catholic population in Maryland.

During the seventeenth century in England, along with the Quakers, numerous other Protestant sects had arisen. In response to the changed religious climate, the English Parliament enacted a law called by the long but descriptive name, An Act for Exempting Their Majesties' Protestant Subjects Dissenting from the Church of England from the Penalties of Certain Laws. This act for Protestant religious tolerance was passed in England in 1689, but the Virginia General Assembly did not extend it to the colony until 1699. Thereafter, although Virginian Protestant groups, such as the Quakers and Puritans just mentioned, benefitted from it, the terms of the act did not apply to Catholics or Unitarians.

Nevertheless, the Toleration Act encouraged non-English settlers to come to Virginia. In 1685, the loss of religious freedom of the Protestant Huguenots by order of King Louis of France had encouraged large numbers of their faith to leave France for Virginia. There are many French names among the leading citizens of early Virginia, and in general they were absorbed within the established communities rather than forming separate settlements.

The conditions at home that had encouraged many Germans to come to Pennsylvania also worked toward their migration to Virginia. In fact, a great many came down from Pennsylvania. As with the later immigrants to Penn's colony, most of the eighteenth-century arrivals were Lutherans or United Brethren, but some of them were Mennonites. They brought with them their knowledge of crop rotation. Instead of exhausting the soil with a single crop as the English tobacco planters had done, they employed soil conservation on farms of fewer acres and were therefore able to settle in farming communities centered around their churches.[14]

The so-called Scotch-Irish, who were actually Protestant Scots who had lived for a time in Ireland, also arrived in Virginia in great numbers during the first half of the eighteenth century. They also farmed or became merchants in the port towns that were developing. With them they brought their Presbyterian faith.

As a result of this influx of non-English small farmers and merchants, Virginia began to acquire a middle class. The religious diversity divided along class lines. The planter class remained Anglican, with the other religious groups spread among the remaining white population. There was also a very large percentage of the population that had no particular interest in religion. Also included in the population by this time were the African slaves who had been brought to Virginia, but in the early years the slaves were not actively converted to Christianity.

Among the last Protestant sects to arrive in Virginia before the American Revolution were the Methodists. At first they remained within the established Church of England, and thus attracted no special attention. Only later did they acquire a separate identity and play their part in bringing religious liberty to Virgina.[15]

Virginia was the setting for the earliest English colonial venture, and throughout the colonial period it remained important. Originally the southernmost colony, by the end of the seventeenth century both North and South Carolina lay to Virginia's south. Spain continued to threaten from Florida, and between the Carolinas and Florida there remained an area still peopled primarily by Indians. Claimed by England, France, and Spain, the area was called the Debatable Lands because of the un-resolved claims. From this disputed southern frontier England created the last of the original thirteen colonies, the only English colony named after a Hanoverian monarch, King George II.

8
GEORGIA

It will be then an Act of Charity to these, and of Merit to the Publick, for any one to propose, forward, and perfect a better Expedient for making them useful; if he cannot, it is surely just to acquiesce, 'till a better is found, in the present Design of settling them in Georgia.
—Benjamin Martyn, 1733

The motives of the Georgia founders were unique among the colonies, for whatever benefits they foresaw were intended for others and not themselves. The Georgia Charter of 1732 expressly prohibited the founding trustees of the colony from receiving any personal benefit from its creation, specifically providing that no trustee "shall have take or receive directly or Indirectly any Salary Fee perquisite benefit or profit whatsoever for or by reason of his or their serving the said Corporation of Common Council."[1] Only one of the seventy-one trustees who served during the two decades of the trust ever went to the colony, and his purpose was not to make a home for himself. Unlike the other colonial founders who sought profit or a safe haven for religious practices, the original twenty-one trustees named in the charter lacked financial or religious motives.

Although there had been talk for many years of colonizing the Debatable Lands claimed not only by England but also by France and Spain, the talk had come to nothing until two Englishmen, known for their humanitarian deeds, came together. Dr. Thomas Bray, an Anglican clergyman, was known for having worked toward educating Negroes and sending missionaries to the colonies. James Edward Oglethorpe, a privileged member of Parliament, had gained his reputation fighting for reform of debtors' prisons. They and their acquaintances conceived the idea of a colony for the debtors and the unemployed of England, open as well to European Protestants who were suffering persecution for their beliefs. However, the trustees were deprived of the benefit of Dr. Bray's assistance in the administration of the colony by his death in 1730.

The Earl of Egmont described the plan presented to him by Oglethorpe on February 13, 1730: "[T]o settle a hundred miserable
wretches, lately relieved out of jayl, on the Continent of America, and
for that end to petition his Majesty for a grant of a suitable quantity of
acres, whereon to place these persons, who now they are at liberty starve
about the streets, or lye an incumbrance on their friends."[2] John Vis-
count Percival, who became the Earl of Egmont in 1733, proved to be
an excellent man for Oglethorpe to have made aware of the scheme, for
he became the corporation's first president and one of its most diligent
trustees.

On July 30, 1730, Oglethorpe, Percival, and nineteen other men petitioned George II for the colony. Among the original twenty-one petitioners, who became its trustees, five were Anglican clergymen, some
were members of the Parliamentary committee chaired by Oglethorpe
that had investigated the condition of the debtors' prisons, and some
had served on hospital boards. None was particularly prominent but all
were known for their religious or humanitarian works. Until Georgia
became a royal colony twenty-two years later, a total of seventy-one men
served as trustees, but the bulk of the responsibility was borne by only
seven.[3] Among those seven, the only clergyman was Reverend Stephen
Hales. The trustees were described in the promotional material for the
colony as having, "for the Benefit of Mankind, given up that Ease and
Indolence to which they were entitled by their Fortunes and the too
prevalent Custom of their Native Country. They, in some Degree, imi-
tate their Redeemer in Sympathizing with the Miserable, and in Labour-
ing to Relieve them."[4] Thus, the trustees may have served the colony
out of a sense of Christian duty, if the saintly motives ascribed to them
by the promotional literature are correct, but their goals for the colony
were not specifically religious.

The charter provided for "liberty of conscience" and "that all such
persons Except Papists shall have a Free Exercise of their Religion."[5] No
detailed instructions were issued by the trustees for the implementation
of this provision, or regarding any other provision contained in the charter, until April 27, 1737, when they sent to Georgia as their representative a secretary. His instructions regarding religion were in the nature
of reports and recommendations, and were summarized by Dr. McCain
as follows: "1. To tell how the people, and especially the magistrates,
attend services; 2. To write how the lands set aside for religious uses
were cultivated; 3. To recommend to magistrates the punishing of vice
and immorality and the encouragement of reverence; and also to encourage the ministers; 4. To encourage magistrates to place the children of
the colony in school; to inspect the schools; and also to exhort parents to
send their children to school; and 5. To recommend to the magistrates
that they do the same for the Indian children."[6]

Early in the planning for the colony, the trustees did seek the assistance of certain well-known religious and philanthropic groups. These
included the Society for Promoting Christian Knowledge, organized in
1698 by Dr. Bray, and devoted to instructing the poor and distributing
Bibles and religious literature; the Society for the Propagation of the
Gospel in Foreign Parts, also called the Venerable Society or the S.P.G.,
which evolved from Dr. Bray's original Society and assumed the responsibility of coordinating missionaries; The Associates of the Late Rev. Dr.
Bray, formed in 1733 to carry on his work providing libraries for ministers and ministering to Negroes; and later, the Society in Scotland for
Promoting Christian Knowledge, which was affiliated with the Presbyterian Church and engaged in the religious objectives shared among the
three English organizations. These four groups all contributed to the
religious needs of the colony, particularly by paying the ministers who
served there.[7]

The trustees' own financial resources originally came from two different charity legacies of £15,000 and £900 respectively. To these legacies
was added an initial grant from Parliament of £10,000. Further, the
charter authorized the trustees "to take Subscriptions and to gather and
Collect such moneys as shall be by any person or persons Contributed. . . ,"[8] and as a result, the Georgia Trust was perhaps the most
popular charity of the decade.[9] Sermons praising the humanitarian goals
of the Georgia Trust were preached to encourage contributions. "No
beneficence can be more lasting in its nature, or more serviceable to the
poor themselves, and therefore none can be more agreeable to a generous
mind. Relieving present hunger indeed is necessary, but in a few hours
the want returns and the duty is to be repeated. Employing the poor in
some industry which cannot but be successful, is securing them happiness, and enabling them to hand it down to their posterity; . . . No
settlement was ever before established on so humane a plan."[10]

Without belittling the humanitarian motivation for establishing the
colony, other motives were equally influential. The need for soldier settlers to defend the southern border of South Carolina from Indians and
the Spanish in Florida constituted a significant political inducement
which was specifically recognized in the charter.

The third motive was economic. Not only would the poor themselves
benefit from their labors in Georgia, it was argued, but also England
would benefit from the raw materials produced by the colonists. The
two products upon whose manufacture the planners placed great hopes
were wine and silk.

The colonists originally envisioned by Oglethorpe were the debtors
released as a result of Parliament's prison reforms. He communicated
this intention to the Earl of Egmont in 1730, and even at Oglethorpe's
death in 1785, his widow caused to be inscribed on his tombstone the

following: " . . . Of these, about seven hundred, rendered, by long confinement for debt, strangers and helpless in the country of their birth, and desirous of seeking an asylum in the wilds of America, were by him conducted thither in 1732."[11] Efforts by historians to identify which of the colonists may have been debtors have been fruitless, and it is now believed that their numbers were few.[12]

The trustees shifted their emphasis from a colony for debtors to one for the "worthy poor." Such colonists included not only the "miserable wretches" starving in London's streets but also, according to promotional literature attributed to Oglethorpe, worthy poor from reputable families. "Let us in the mean Time cast our Eyes on the Multitude of unfortunate People in the Kingdom of reputable Families, and of liberal, or at least, easy Education: Some undone by Guardians, some by Law-Suits, some by Accidents in Commerce, some by Stocks and Bubbles, and some by Suretyship."[13]

A third group of charity colonists were encouraged to go to Georgia; these were European Protestants. There was apparently some criticism of the trustees for expending English trust funds on foreigners, for one author of promotional literature stated: "Since I have mention'd the foreign Protestants, it may not be improper to consider their present Situation, and to show how prudent it is to establish such a Colony as Georgia, if only on their Account. As Men, as fellow Christians, and as persecuted Christians, they have, as well as our own Poor a Claim on our Humanity, notwithstanding the narrow Opinions, and mistaken Politicks of some, who think their Charity should begin, continue, and end at home."[14]

The would-be English colonists were scrutinized by the trustees to eliminate those who were unworthy or whose services were needed at home in England. According to the promotional literature, the trustees "use the utmost Care, by a strict Examination of those who desire to go over, and by their Enquiries otherwise, to send none, who are in any Respect useful at home. . . . They suffer none to go, who would leave their Wives and Families without a Support; none, who have the Character of lazy and immoral Men; and none, who are in Debt, and would go without the Consent of their Creditors."[15]

At the trustees' meeting on November 9, 1732, James Oglethorpe offered "to go in person and conduct the people."[16] The Governor of South Carolina wrote to warn Oglethorpe, "Send none but People used to Labour and of Sober Life and Conversation, for others will never be govern'd nor make good Settlers, for much hardship, sickness and Labour will attend their first Settling, which will not be born by People used to Idleness or Luxury, and So far from being thankfull for the Bounty bestowed upon them, will be discontended and mutinous."[17] Unfortunately, Oglethorpe did not benefit from Governor Johnson's advice since the first colonists aboard the *Anne* had already sailed by the time the letter was received in England. Among the colonists on board were a potash-maker, two merchants, five carpenters, two wig-makers, two tailors, a miller and baker, a writer, a surgeon, one gardener, five farmers, an upholsterer, a basket-maker, two sawyers, an apothecary, a vintner, a wheelwright, one stocking-maker, and a reduced military officer.[18] Clearly there would appear to be little need in the wilderness for some of those occupations, but the limitation on removing productive occupations from England must have hindered the selection of appropriate colonists. As for the colonists' skills as settler-soldiers, *The Gentlemen's Magazine* reported that as the *Anne* readied to sail, "[t]he men were learning military discipline of the guards, as must all that go thither, and to carry muskets, bayonets and swords, to defend the colony."[19] Donations for the first shipload of charity colonists included not only the monetary grants to the Georgia Trust but also more beer, wine, Egyptian kale, bamboo plants, Lippora raisins, mulberry seeds, olive plants, cotton seeds, Burgundy vines, bayonets, swords, drums, cartridge boxes, tools, clothes, and religious books than the *Anne* could carry.[20]

The settlers of the earlier British colonies would have been amazed at such generosity. The Georgia colonists certainly departed under different circumstances, and they left behind an England whose religious attitudes had altered in obvious ways from the narrow intolerance from which earlier colonists had fled. Contributions paid the passage of over eighteen hundred charity colonists between 1732 and 1741, and over eight hundred of those were foreign Protestants from dissenting sects.[21] Not all of the Georgia colonists went at Trust expense, however. The lure of the promotional literature attracted adventurers as well.

Who were the colonists who had been attracted by the trustees? They were a widely varied group, from different national, religious, and cultural backgrounds, further separated by the different languages they spoke. The colony started strongly but very quickly floundered, due primarily to the well-intentioned but paternalistic policies of the trustees in distant London. The two most successful communities were those whose inhabitants shared a common religion and which enjoyed the guidance of a strong religious leader—the Salzburgers and the Highland Scots.

The Salzburgers were German Lutherans. They were among those who had taken the Covenant of Salt, by which they swore to remain loyal to their faith. In response, Archbishop Leopold issued a decree in October of 1731, ordering them to leave the province within eight days. Although the time limit was extended, they were forced to leave their homes. The Society for the Promotion of Christian Knowledge published *An Account of the Sufferings of the Persecuted Protestants in the Arch-*

bishoprick of Saltzburg to raise money for their aid. One of the trustees, James Vernon, took a special interest in encouraging their settlement in Georgia. On July 26, 1732, the Earl of Egmont recorded the following action taken by the trustees: "Agreed that a proposal be made to the Collectors of charity for the persecuted Saltzburgers, that we would Settle a number of them in Georgia, with promise of lands in Freehold, & maintenance for one year, pay their passage from Frankfort to Rotterdam, & from thence to Georgia."[22] There were four different transports of Salzburgers, and they settled in their own community of Ebenezer. They were led by the Reverend John Martin Bolzius until his death in 1765, and he described his community in this way. "Every year God gives them what they need. And since they have been able to earn something apart from agriculture, through the mills which have been built and in many other ways, they have managed rather well with God's blessing, and have led a calm and quiet life of blessedness and honesty. They love the calmness, the church, and the school, do not begrudge others the glory of good and extensive plantations. . . . I do not wish to live and to die anywhere except among and with them at Ebenezer."[23]

The other successful early community, called Darien, was founded by Highland Scots, recruited by the trustees as fighters. The trustees paid the passage for one hundred forty-six persons, who arrived in January of 1736 and were then located on the southern frontier as protection against the Spanish. Their Presbyterian minister was John MacLeod, sent to them by the Society in Scotland for Promoting Christian Knowledge. When Oglethorpe led the colonists into battle against the Spanish, many of the Highland Scots were killed, and this, together with his dissatisfaction with the trustees' policies, led MacLeod to leave the colony. From his new church in South Carolina he wrote to the Society in Scotland, and the criticisms contained in his letters resulted in the Society declining to provide further religious support for Georgia.

Although their numbers were small, there were many other groups present in Georgia during the period of the Trust. Other Germans came, settling around Ebenezer. One German sect, the Moravians, was particularly noteworthy. They came at their own expense and were only about forty in number, consisting primarily of young men. They started a school for the Indians at Irene and were successful, productive members of the colony until a disagreement over military service arose. When the Spanish threatened the colony, all able-bodied men were expected to join the militia. The Moravians not only refused to join but also refused to pay for a substitute soldier, a common way then to avoid service. Their faith prohibited bearing arms, a belief other Georgians did not understand in light of the real danger to the colony from the Spanish. The disagreement led the Moravians to leave Georgia for North Carolina and Pennsylvania. John Wesley, the Anglican minister who founded Methodism, encountered the Moravians while he served in Georgia, and he later said his religious thought was greatly influenced by them.

On January 10, 1733, the trustees "[r]esolv'd to admit no Jews to go over to Settle in the Colony, and to recall the Deputation made to Some principal Jews in London to collect mony."[24] Neither resolution was performed.

Three members of the Sephardic Congregation in London had secured a commission to take subscriptions and collect money for the Georgia Trust. When the trustees learned that the money was being collected to transport Jews to the colony, they demanded forfeiture of the commission, but the three men, who were among the wealthiest men in England, refused. In the meantime a shipload of Jews arrived in Savannah harbor at a time when the colony was ravaged with fever. The first among the Georgia colonists to die was the doctor, and so they were left without a physician to tend the sick when the fevers came. Oglethorpe attributed the cause of the fever to rum, although it is more likely to have come from the drinking of polluted river water.[25] In a letter to the trustees Oglethorpe described the situation as the ship of Jews arrived: " . . . the illness being once frequent became contagious. It appeared chiefly in burning fevers or else in bloody fluxes attended by convulsions and other terrible symptoms. . . . So that we had neither doctor, surgeon nor nurse, and about the 15th of July we had above sixty people sick, many of whose lives we despaired of. At which time Captain Horton arrived here with some Jews and amongst them a doctor of physick, who immediately undertook our people and refused to take any pay for it. He proceeded by cold baths, cooling drinks and other cooling applications. Since which the sick have wonderfully recovered, and we have not lost one who would follow his prescriptions. Next to the blessing of God and this new regimen I believe one of the greatest occasions of the people's recovery has been that by my constant watching of them I have restrained the drinking of rum."[26]

In his journal, the Earl of Egmont described why the trustees had decided to exclude Jews. "There was Some disposition to allow the Jews to Settle in Georgia, but the Majority were not for it, because they generally are not cultivators of land, but Small hedge Shopkeepers, and might keep private correspondence with the Spaniards. However a considerable number went over, without the Trustees knowledge, to whom Mr. Oglethorpe gave Lots. A few of them proved industrious, but the greater number not. They were in all 43. Mr. Oglethorpe was much displeas'd at their arrival, and took advice of Lawyers in Carolina whether he could not send them away, but they gave him their opinion he could not. Besides eating Capt. Hansons provisions who carry'd them over, they cheated him of their passage money, So that he lost by them about

3 or 400£. Many ran away from their Christian Creditors."[27] Later, however, Egmont remembered it differently, for he wrote, "They had a good Physitian with them and behaved so well as to their morals, peacableness and charity, that they were a reproach to the Christian Inhabitants."[28] At the end of the colony's first year, one-sixth of the population of Savannah was Jewish, some of whom were German (Ashkenazim) and some of whom were Spanish or Portuguese (Sephardim).

Other groups that came to Georgia deserve mention. A ship of forty starving Irish indentured servants came into the harbor, and as Oglethorpe reported to the trustees, "I thought it an act of charity to buy them, which I did giving £5 a head."[29] There were also French settlers, who tended to assimilate more quickly than the Germans.

In considering the groups present in Georgia during the trustees' administration of the colony, the Indians should not be ignored, for Oglethorpe immediately established friendly relations with them. In a letter to the trustees only one week after the colonists' arrival, he wrote, "A little Indian Nation, the only one within Fifty Miles, is not only at Amity, but desirous to be Subjects to his Majesty King George, to have lands given them among us, and to breed their Children at our Schools. Their Chief and his beloved Man, who is the Second Man in the Nation, desire to be instructed in the Christian Religion."[30] Letters from Oglethorpe concerning the desire of the Indians to be instructed in Christianity continued throughout the spring of 1733. On March 12 he wrote, "The king comes constantly to church . . . " and on May 14, " . . . there is great hopes of one town's being converted."[31] However, difficulties arose in providing missionaries for the Indians. In December of 1735, John and Charles Wesley came to Georgia specifically as missionaries to the Indians, but ministers for the colonists were needed, and so, they were diverted from their mission.

The trustees' greatest problems came not from troublesome Indians but from a group of Lowland Scots who came to be called the Malcontents. In truth, some of the Scots' criticisms of trustee policies were probably valid, since unlike the trustees, they were more interested in making the colony profitable than in creating a model community. The trustees withheld title to protect the colonists against losing their land to mortgages or unscrupulous buyers, and limited ownership to fifty acres and to males to encourage small farms worked by their owners, but the Malcontents resented such paternalistic restrictions. The trustees refused to allow slaves, but the Malcontents saw the plantations in the other southern colonies and demanded the slave labor required for such farming. The trustees made the rules and selected the officers for the colony, but the Malcontents wanted certain rights of self-government, particularly the right to choose their own magistrates. When their demands were refused by the trustees the Malcontents, along with many other colonists, left Georgia. Between 1737 and 1741, the population may have dropped from five thousand to five hundred people.[32]

Parliament refused for the first time to vote funds for the Georgia colony in 1742. The trustees were losing interest in the project. The Earl of Egmont complained, "It is a melancholoy thing to see how zeal for a good thing abates when the novelty is over and when there is no pecuniary reward."[33] Oglethorpe confided to another trustee, "I am daily teared with impertinencies, insults and abuses from the people of the colony, in such a manner that I really do not know what measures to take. Did I not love them as my children, I should let them perish in their follies."[34]

In the midst of all this disappointment, one venture was flourishing. Although Georgia had provided for its orphans from the beginning, George Whitefield resolved to build an orphanage. Previously, the trustees had relied primarily upon placement in foster homes. Whitefield objected to this practice as neglecting spiritual training and as allowing the children's work to benefit private individuals, saying, "they are provided for as to their bodies, yet they are destitute of means to improve their souls. And if they can work, I think the Orphan House has a better claim to it than any private person."[35] On June 2, 1739, the trustees' minutes show, "Sealed a grant of five hundred acres of land to the Rev. George Whitefield, in trust for the use of the house to be erected and maintained for the receiving such children as now are, and shall hereafter be, left orphans in the colony of Georgia."[36]

According to a letter received by the trustees, "Certain it is that this town [Savannah] for near these twelve months past has been almost wholly supported by the money expended in building the Orphan House, Mr. Whitefield having daily employed at a medium for the above-mentioned space of time, 60 persons . . . "[37]

Life for the orphans at Bethesda was described in a report to the trustees:

> They rise about five o'clock, and each is seen to kneel down by himself for a quarter of an hour, . . .
> At six all the family goes to church, . . .
> At our return home about 7, we sing Bishop Ken's Morning Hymn; and whoever is president of the house uses family prayer as the spirit gives him utterance, . . .
> From eight to ten the children go to their respective employs, as carding, spinning, picking cotton or wool, sewing, knitting. . . .
> At ten they go to school, . . .
> At noon we go to dinner all in the same room, and between that and two o'clock every one is employed in something useful, but no time is allowed for idleness or play, which are Satan's darling hours to tempt children to all manner of wickedness, as lying, cursing, swearing, uncleanness &c., . . .

From 2 'till 4 they go again to school, as in the morning, and from 4 to 6 to work in their respective stations as before mentioned. At six the children go to supper, . . .

At seven the family all goes to church, . . . At nine o'clock we go to supper, and the children up to their bedroom, where some person commonly sings and prays again with them. Before they go to bed, each boy, as in the morning, is seen to kneel by his bedside, and is ordered to pray from his own heart for a quarter of an hour, some person instructing them how to pray as in the morning. And at ten o'clock all the family goes to rest, unless any one or more chooses to sit up an hour or two for their private devotion, or meditation, or conference.

. . . And thus is our time all laid out in the service of God, the variety of which is a sufficient relaxation to a well-disposed mind and obviates idle pretenses for what is called innocent (though in reality damnable) recreations.[38]

The trustees were not happy with the harshness of the orphans' lives. Egmont objected, "Not a moment of innocent recreation tho necessary to the health and strengthening of growing children is allow'd in the whole day."[39] The trustees ordered the magistrates to inspect the orphanage frequently and sent Bethesda's superintendent a stinging rebuke. "Religion should be shewn and recommended to them in an amiable Light, nor should they be fill'd with ill grounded Terrours, which must probably give their Minds an Enthusaistick Turn, or by bending them too much one way, make them hereafter fly back another with greater Force, and may give them a Distaste even to Religion it Self."[40]

During the last decade of the trustees' administration of Georgia, it limped along with little success. No public contributions were received during the last eleven years of the Trust, and only the regular societies and the few loyal trustees paid much attention to Georgia. Financially, the trustees had not failed to carry out the donors' purposes, and from their records every contribution can be accounted for as having been spent as designated: "(1) For building churches about £702; (2) For Indian missions about £679; and (3) for general religious purposes a little more than £522."[41] In addition to the public funds, it is estimated that various societies spent between £3,500 and £4,000 for ministers' salaries, supplemented by the trustees' own expenditures for religious purposes, together with the granting of 1,400 acres for religious uses.[42]

The trustees built three Anglican churches in Georgia, the most elaborate being in Savannah, but more humble structures having been built in Frederica and Augusta. The Salzburgers also built three churches, which they called Jerusalem, Aion, and Bethany. Most of the other religious groups either used public buildings or rented rooms for their services.

While religion may not have fared particularly well in Georgia under the trustees, it seems to have fared at least as well as their other efforts. In 1752 the trustees surrendered the charter and Georgia became a royal colony. While the accomplishments may have been a disappointment, the trustees remained true to their humanitarian purposes and the core of a colonial society was created.

Under the royal governors Georgia moved forward, but at the cost of certain ideals the trustees had preserved. One of the most obvious regarded slavery. During the Trust, slavery was prohibited for reasons of defense. The law provided that "Experience hath Shewn that the manner of Settling Colonys and Plantations with Black Slaves or Negroes hath Obstructed the Increase of English and Christian Inhabitants therein who alone can in case of a War be relyed on for the Defence and Security of the same, . . . "[43] As further inducement for the prohibition against slavery, the trustees wished to encourage small farms rather than the plantations maintained by slave labor in the other southern colonies. The Salzburgers also opposed slavery, but even their motives were not humanitarian: " . . . we humbly beseech the Honourable Trustees not to allow it that any Negro might be brought to our place or in our neighbourhood, knowing by experience that houses and gardens will be robbed always by them and white people are in danger of life because of them, besides other great inconveniencies."[44]

However, those nonhumanitarian motives do not exclude equally strong moral reasons felt by others as the basis for the prohibition of slavery in Georgia. In a sermon preached to recommend contributions for the colony, a London minister stated, "Slavery is absolutely proscribed from this Colony; the misfortune, if not the dishonour of other plantations. Let avarice defend it as it will, there is an honest reluctance in humanity against buying and selling and regarding those of our own species as our wealth and possessions."[45] From the beginning Oglethorpe opposed slavery in the colony for moral reasons. "[I]f we allow slaves we act against the very principles by which we associated together, which was to relieve the distressed. Whereas, now we should occasion the misery of thousands in Africa, by setting men upon using arts to buy and bring into perpetual slavery the poor people who now live free there."[46]

There were definitely Blacks in trustee-administered Georgia, for The Associates of Dr. Bray allowed a catechist £25 a year for instructing Negroes, and the trustees paid his passage. At that time, which was near the end of the Trust period, there were said to be three hundred Blacks in Georgia.[47]

The royal governors lifted the prohibition and the new legislators passed laws that barred the teaching of writing to Blacks, and later, reading. The school supported by The Associates of Dr. Bray was discontinued in 1760.[48] By 1770 there were 11,000 Blacks in Georgia, chiefly slaves, among only 13,000 Whites.[49]

Another attack upon the ideals of the trustees was brought about by the first session of the new legislature in February of 1755, when they attempted to provide for an establishment of the Church of England, even though a large part of the population (if not the majority) were dissenters. Opposition came primarily from two groups—the Salzburgers, who had practiced their Lutheran faith throughout nearly the entire Trust period, and the Puritans, who had come to the Midway district south of Savannah late in the Trust period. The absence of strong opposition from other large groups of dissenters is probably explained by the lack of ministers present in Georgia to speak for them.

The Salzburgers, speaking through their minister, Martin Bolzius, reminded the legislators "that the Province of Georgia was intended by His Majesty for an Asylum for all sorts of Protestants to enjoy full Liberty of Conscience Preferrable to any other American Colonies in order to Invite Numbers of Oppressed or persecuted People to Strengthen this Barrier Colony by their coming over."[50] Despite the opposition, a bill establishing the Church of England was passed in 1757.

However, the effect, at least for the Salzburgers, was very much like the multiple establishment in New York discussed in Chapter 2. Under the Georgia establishment, churchwardens and vestrymen were elected by all freeholders and householders, including dissenters. Since the Salzburger Lutherans were a substantial majority in their parish, they were free to elect their own deacons as churchwardens and vestrymen. That the legislators had intended this result is indicated from the fact that the German community discussed with the legislative floor manager certain "favors in the bill which might give them Ease."[51] By being assured that dissenters could vote for the churchwardens and vestrymen, the Lutheran majority knew they could control the outcome and elect Lutheran deacons, thereby complying with the letter of the establishment law without accomplishing its true intent of establishing the Anglican church in their parish. From 1758 until 1766, so long as they had a unified majority, that is exactly what they did.

The Georgia establishment provided, even as to parishes in which the Anglican church was established, that dissenting churches were free to function without interference. In 1768, the Anglican priest of Savannah decided that as the rector of the established church in the parish, he was the official clergyman for the entire parish and was therefore entitled to all fees for religious services, whether or not he officiated. To test his theory he shrewdly urged it, not on his own behalf, but on behalf of his sexton. Specifically, he demanded that the fees for ringing the funeral bell be paid to the Anglican sexton, even though the sexton of the Presbyterian church had rung the Presbyterian funeral bell and the Anglican church bell was never rung.

Prior to the trial for the fees, the judge had revealed his bias by commenting on the merits of the case (in favor of the Anglican clergyman). The three-man jury consisted of an Anglican vestryman of the parish and the church clerk, both of whom predictably voted in favor of the Anglican clergyman, with the third member of the jury, a taverner, alone in his dissent. The judge not only ruled for the clergyman but also added that dissenters had no right to a bell of their own and that the Anglican clergyman should pull the Presbyterians' bell to the ground.[52]

The newspaper account of the trial editorialized by saying, "If a parish sexton is entitled to a fee for every burial, it will be a double hardship upon such parishes as are chiefly inhabited by Dissenters, such as St. Matthew's, St. John's, and St. Andrew's parishes. And if any Justice should have a right to pick a jury of choice, he is more than morally sure that they concurred with him in prejudging the matter before it comes to a hearing; a trial in that case will be worse than a mere formality."[53]

The religious diversity of Georgia's citizens was far different from the earliest colonies, and during the intervening years many dissenting sects had grown in both membership and acceptability. The settling of Georgia, late in the colonial period, nearly coincided with the Great Awakening, in which Whitefield and the frontier circuit riders played such significant roles. Frontier settlers in remote areas of all thirteen colonies, lacking pastors of their own, were especially affected by the evangelistic preachers of the Great Awakening.

9
THE GREAT AWAKENING

My brethren, I would now warn you against this wretched, mischievous spirit of party. . . . A Christian! a christian! let that be your highest distinction; let that be the name which you labor to deserve.
—Samuel Davies (1723–1761)

The wilderness of the New World had taken its toll on religious fervor. As Jonathan Edwards, the minister of Northampton, Massachusetts, saw it in 1727, it was a time of "extraordinary dullness in religion" and "[l]icentiousness for some years [had] greatly prevailed among the youth of the town."[1] In fact, the religious stupor he observed had crept into not only New England but all of the colonies, and into England and Europe as well.

Such "extraordinary dullness" merely served to emphasize the brilliance of the spiritual oratory of several men who stepped forward to preach. In both the Old World and the New, a resurgence of religion occurred, carried forward by the oratorical gifts of these preachers. Although this period came to be known as the Great Awakening, it had no such name in its own lifetime, and there was no central organization controlling and coordinating events. In retrospect, however, the Great Awakening must be viewed as one of the most important events in the making of the new nation of America. The effects of this movement were as much social and political as they were religious, and although only about ten percent of the colonial population participated in the religious events, the ideas of all colonists were affected.

Until the mid-eighteenth century, most colonies had established a specific church which was supported by taxes. Even those colonies without an established church generally had a majority denomination which exerted influence over all the citizens, or at least all the citizens of a particular locality, as in the case of the multiple establishments. Increased religious tolerance had permitted minority sects to exist, but they did so in a powerless way, without the benefit of taxes to support their ministers, teachers, and churches and with church membership composed primarily of common people lacking in economic and political influence. In addition, as had always been the case in America, there remained those colonists with no particular interest in religion. A missionary described preaching to a group in South Carolina that had never, before his sermon, heard a minister preach. Writing in his journal, the minister regretted the ineffectiveness of his message, for as soon as he had finished the service, he wrote, "they went out to Revelling, Drinking, Singing, Dancing and Whoring, and most of the Company was drunk before I quitted the Spott."[2] Many of these colonists relied upon the occult to fill the spiritual needs of their lives, practicing astrology and divination, as well as witchcraft. Although New England became known for the trials of witches, witchcraft was practiced throughout the colonies, and most villages had certain men and women wise in the ways of herbs and potions, or reputed to possess supernatural powers, whom the other villagers either avoided or consulted, depending on their own fears and beliefs. Belief in the occult was prevalent among all classes.

Gradually, however, the religious complexion of the colonies began to change. Church members themselves had lost the religious fervor of the earliest colonists. Perhaps more significantly, the population of the colonies was becoming more diverse in terms of national origins and religious sects. In 1660 the Congregationalists and the Anglicans together comprised approximately seventy-five percent of the colonial churches, and although both their numbers continued to grow during the next one hundred years, they did not keep pace with the growth of other colonial churches. By 1740, the Congregationalists and Anglicans comprised only fifty-seven percent of the colonial churches.[3] To a large extent, this was the result of immigrants bringing their own sects with them to America. From Scotland and Ireland had come large numbers of Presbyterians, together with Mennonites from Switzerland and Lutherans, German Reformed, Moravians, Bretherans and other Protestant sects from Germany. Nevertheless, in almost, if not all of the colonies, there could still be found either an established church or a denomination that maintained its powerful influence over the colony. Such religious dominance was the status quo that the Great Awakening changed forever.

It is inaccurate to identify any single man or event as beginning the Great Awakening, for unrelated surges giving the movement momentum were occurring throughout the Protestant world. However, one of the leaders of this period was certainly Jonathan Edwards. He deserves his reputation in this regard, although his style differed greatly from the other preachers associated with the Great Awakening. Jonathan Edwards came to Northampton, Massachusetts in 1727. Unlike the other accessible preachers of the Great Awakening, Edwards withdrew from society to devote hours to the preparation of his sermons, which he delivered in a serious, stiff style. He structured his sermons in the traditional way, stating first the scripture, then the doctrine or proposition from that scripture, and finally the uses or applications for his congregation. Yet, somehow his intellectual style reached into the hearts of his listeners, and in 1734 what he described as "a glorious alteration" occurred. Nearly the entire town became involved in religious concerns, and as Edwards described it, "all other talk but about spiritual and eternal things was soon thrown by; all the conversation in all companies, and upon all occasions, was upon these things only, unless so much as was necessary for people carrying on their ordinary secular business. Other discourse than of the things of religion would scarcely be tolerated in any company."[4]

Although his sermons were presented in a logical and formal way, Edwards did not fail to address the emotional terrors of Hell. In describing the torture of souls in Hell, he likened the suffering of the unsaved to "a spider or some loathesome insect [held] over the fire." In fact, the chief emotion to which Edwards appealed in his sermons was terror.

He had in common with the other preachers of the Great Awakening his success in stirring the emotions of the people, although his style in doing so was very different. He also contributed to the social and political implications of the Great Awakening by referring to colonial America as a source of the resurgence of religious faith. Relying on the biblical prophesy that this religious revival would come from a remote part of the world, Edwards interpreted the Bible to mean that colonial America was to be the source of the new religion. His interpretation evoked a new sense of nationalism in colonial Americans which went beyond matters of religion.

Eventually the excitement Edwards had caused waned, and by 1750 the male members of his church voted overwhelmingly to eject him as their minister. But seeds of religious revival had sprouted throughout New England, especially in the Connecticut Valley. Intertwined with the growth of religion was the new spirit of nationalism, and by the time of the American Revolution, some of the strongest calls for colonial patriotism came from New England pulpits.

In the middle colonies a Dutch Reformed clergyman, Theodore Jacob Frelinghuysen, was one of the earliest preachers to stir the emotions of his listeners. Ironically, he was greatly influenced by having read Puritan literature, and he, in turn, had a great influence on a minister outside the Dutch Reformed church.

Frelinghuysen's neighbor was a Presbyterian minister named William Tennent. Although belonging to different denominations, the two men became friends, and Frelinghuysen served as a ministerial model to Tennent. Later, this religious fervor was passed to a new generation of ministers by Tennent. Near his home, he built a log cabin wherein he could train his young sons for the ministry. This cabin came to be known as the "Log College," and in it he trained not only three of his sons but also fifteen other young men. His training included language, logic, theology, and most importantly, his own evangelical passion. By 1741, this core of young ministers had split the Presbyterian church into Old Side believers, who adhered to the strict, traditional ways, and New Side believers, who followed the emotional appeal of the Log College preachers. Rather than having an overall negative effect upon the church, however, the furor invigorated it and helped spread Presbyterianism into other regions. In 1758 the two sides reunited, but dominance was held thereafter by the former New Siders.[5]

One of these New Side preachers was Samuel Davies. He was preaching in Virginia, in the heart of the established Church of England. At that time colonial governments were recruiting soldiers to fight the Indians and the French, and Davies incorporated into his sermons two themes: "to save my country, and, which is of more consequence, to save souls." After one of his sermons in 1758, so many men volunteered that the military had to refuse some of them. Because of his patriotic usefulness, Davies was not bothered by the Anglican government. He is an excellent example of the joinder of religion and patriotism that the Great Awakening represented. In fact, one regular listener at his sermons was Patrick Henry, who came to learn from Davies the oratorical skills Henry would later employ as a politician.[6]

Perhaps the most significant figure among the preachers of the Great Awakening was an Englishman. From his first visit to America in 1740 until his death in 1770, George Whitefield traveled between England and America thirteen times and converted souls on both sides of the Atlantic. Unlike Jonathan Edwards in Northampton, who preached only two sermons a week in the pulpit of his own church, Whitefield preached whenever and wherever people gathered to hear him. Without a church of his own, and often facing opposition from the established ministers, Whitefield preached many of his sermons out of doors, and huge crowds of people came to hear. In Philadelphia he preached from the courthouse steps, and Benjamin Franklin, who had been skeptical of the estimates of crowd size at other gatherings for Whitefield, stepped off the boundaries of the crowd himself and calculated its number at thirty thousand.[7] A like number were said to have attended his sermon on Boston Commons. The significant fact about such numbers of people crowding to hear him as he spoke throughout the colonies was that finally the common people were able to participate in a religious event on an equal footing with the upperclass. Taken out of the elitist churches and into the open air, these revivals were entirely democratic. Further,

Whitefield and most of the other revivalists appealed to the emotions of the people rather than to their reason. The message of these sermons could be felt, and it did not take special education or training by the minister to understand them, for the preachers spoke in the language of the people. The crowds responded in ways totally alien to the formal responses given in established churches; they shouted, jumped about, fainted, groaned, sang, or did whatever they personally felt in response to the message they heard. One minister described the preachers and congregations at these revival meetings in this way: "Their manner of preaching was, if possible, much more novel than their doctrines . . . [they] had acquired a very warm and pathetic address, accompanied by strong gestures and a singular tone of voice. Being often deeply affected themselves while preaching, correspondent affections were felt by their pious hearers, which were frequently expressed by tears, trembling, screams, shouts, and acclamations."[8]

In a climate where established or majority churches controlled entire regions or colonies, Whitefield and the other itinerant preachers belittled the importance of denominational labels. Preaching from the courthouse balcony in Philadelphia in 1740, Whitefield staged a mock conversation with God, asking: " 'Father Abraham, whom have you in Heaven? Any Episcopalians?' 'No.' 'Any Presbyterians?' 'No.' 'Have you any Independents or Seceders?' 'No.' 'Have you any Methodists?' 'No, no, no!!' 'Whom have you there?' 'We don't know those names here. All who are here are Christians . . . Oh, is this the case? Then God help us to forget party names and to become Christians in deed and truth.' "[9] It is understandable that such preaching angered established ministers. It is also predictable that a strong opposition was mounted against these revivalists.

Whitefield escaped some of this criticism by justifying his preaching journeys as charitable endeavors on behalf of his orphanage in Georgia, Bethesda. Thus, while Whitefield devotedly served Bethesda throughout his life, the orphanage also served him by providing an excuse for his preaching throughout the colonies. On his journeys, he collected not only contributions but also orphans beyond the borders of Georgia.

The pastor of one of the largest congregations in the colonies, Reverend Increase Mather, objected to the intrusion of itinerant preachers into territory in which a minister was already established. Mather challenged the right of these traveling revivalists to call themselves ministers. "To say that a Wandering Levite who has no flock is a Pastor, is as good sense as to say, that he that has no Children is a Father," argued Mather.[10]

Opposition went beyond mere words from the leading clergy, however. At the request of the ministry, the Connecticut Assembly passed a law in 1743 requiring itinerant preachers to obtain the consent of both the pastor and the people before coming to their region to preach, and constables were empowered to escort vagrant ministers out of the colony.[11] In Virginia in 1745 the governor charged the grand jury with the responsibility of searching out and indicting "false teachers that are lately crept into this government professing themselves ministers under the pretended influence of new light, extraordinary impulse and such like fanatical enthusiastical knowledge [who] lead the innocent and ignorant people into all kinds of delusion."[12]

Not all of the itinerant preachers intruded into the territory already served by a minister. This was also the era of the circuit riders who sought out isolated communities not served by a regular church. The two denominations particularly known for their circuit riders and frontier preachers were the Baptists and the Methodists. About them, one writer has said, "They spent a good part of their lives hungry, wet, cold, verminous and saddlesore, and if they did not die young of consumption, they could expect an old age of rheumatism and dyspepsia."[13]

Nevertheless, despite hostility and hardship, the Great Awakening could not be stopped. The social and political changes the religious movement had stimulated altered the American consciousness forever. First of all, the idea that a new religious movement was to be born in America and spread to the rest of the world gave the colonists a sense of national destiny. Second, the itinerant preachers gave the common people new role models for leadership and a new voice. The preachers' style of speaking was adopted by many of the young men who would play such major political roles in the birth of America. Third, the common people learned of their own power to challenge the establishment when they challenged the established churches. By discovering freedom of choice in matters of faith, they had also discovered the right to choose in political matters as well. Fourth, the itinerant preachers traveled throughout the colonies, and the religious interchange of ideas gave churches a national character that they had not previously possessed. This character spread into social and political matters, and at just the same time that many denominations were trying to build a national church organization, the founding fathers were also meeting to build a national political organization. Fifth, the revivalists shattered the elitist image of the clergy. Many of the preachers came from the common class of people, and by preaching out of doors without elevated pulpits, they removed the trappings of superiority employed by other church leaders. They gained their followers through their powers of persuasion, using the common words of the people. The destruction of the elitist image of church leaders extended over to the image that the people found appropriate for political leaders. Sixth, the Great Awakening included whole segments of the population that had previously been ignored or excluded, particularly the poor and the Negro slaves, many of whom were converted to Christianity. Although true equality had many years to wait, the concept was certainly stimulated by the Great Awakening. Finally, the use of emotionalism as well as logic won not only many souls to God but later many patriots to the revolutionary cause.

Many churches were altered by the movement, as in the case of the Presbyterians. Many denominations gained strength in regions in which they had previously held little influence. This was particularly true of the Baptists, Presbyterians, and Quakers in Virginia, and later the Methodists benefitted from the groundwork laid by those three groups when they came to Virginia. Of all the churches that suffered from the effects of the Great Awakening, never to recover their former power, the Church of England lost the most. Its adherence to conservatism left it out of step with the times, but more damaging still was the unavoidable connection with England at a time when colonial America was ready to sever that connection.

The Great Awakening was not only a religious movement, which in its oddly disorganized way unified colonial America. It was a dress rehearsal for the rallies, shifts in allegiance, and changes in the colonial consciousness that were necessary for the American Revolution.

10
THE AMERICAN REVOLUTION

> If the Americans shall be taught to believe Resistance to be lawful and consistent with their duty to God, it will not be long before they sound the Trumpet of War, and publicly appear in Arms.
> —St. James's Chronicle, September 29, 1774

The effects of the Great Awakening had gone far beyond religious rebirth, giving the colonies a sense of national destiny and the colonists a democratic recognition of the importance of the individual. Another religious movement during the middle of the eighteenth century contributed toward the colonies' desire for independence from Great Britain. This movement was instigated by the Society for Propagating the Gospel in Foreign Parts, and its goal was to place a bishop of the Church of England in America.

Ironically, the colonial support for the American bishop did not come from the southern colonies, where the established church was Anglican. During the disestablishment proceedings in Virginia, which will be explored in detail in the next chapter, payment of the Anglican clergy had been suspended for several years. The Anglican clergy had appealed to the king to intercede on their behalf with the Virginia legislature. The timing of such a request, at the historical moment when America was breaking away from England, was a tactical mistake, regardless of the merits of their claim for compensation or the genuineness of their financial need. That mistake had weakened their confidence, and besides, they were busy defending the southern colonies against the encroachment of the dissenters. The Anglicans in the south, both clergy and laity, were more interested in restoring the control and stability of the local Anglican establishment than in agitating for an American bishop.

It was in the northern colonies, where the Anglicans had been far outnumbered, that the movement for a colonial bishop found supporters. This had come about because the Royal Governors had tended to be members of the Church of England, or as they were also called, Churchmen. To the extent that association with the Royal Governor and his practices was fashionable, gradually socially prominent, wealthy colonists had been drawn to the Anglican church. Just as the Church of England was the church of the southern aristocracy, so it had become for many of the northern aristocrats. It was among this group that advocates of an American bishop were found.

Naturally the opponents saw the class distinctions involved and couched much of their opposition in terms of a struggle between the wealthy aristocrats versus the common people. The mood of the times gave the definite propaganda advantage to the common people in such a contest. More importantly, however, the American bishop became a symbol of British intrusion in colonial matters. It was argued that the presence of an American bishop would allow Anglicans, and those sympathetic to the Crown, to dominate colonial governments, that it would result in dissenters being driven from politics by a Test Act, and that the Church of England would be established in all of the colonies, with all dissenters taxed for its support. The reason an American bishop was perceived as having so much potential power was not only a result of his connection with the king, who was, of course, the head of the Church of England. It also resulted from the awareness that no denomination had a member of the church hierarchy present in America, and therefore an Anglican bishop would hold a unique status in the colonies.

The fear that an Anglican bishop would bring about the loss of rights for non-Anglicans led denominations that had formerly distrusted one another to unite against this common foe. In the 1760s the Presbyterians joined with the Congregationalists, under the leadership of the Reverend Ezra Stiles. A letter written in 1766 to Stiles from a fellow opponent of the episcopacy expressed their fear: "What we dread is their political power, and their courts, of which Americans can have no notion adequate to the mischiefs that they introduce."[1]

The movement for an American bishop was unsuccessful. What it accomplished instead was to intensify colonial dislike for English meddling and to unify different denominations in the fight against a common foe, the English.

The propaganda during the campaign for an American bishop had stirred religious hatred against the Anglicans, associating them with the king and accusing all of them of being Tories. In fact, not all Anglicans were Tories and not all non-Anglicans were Whigs. Particularly in the South, the loyalty of the members to the Church of England did not mean loyalty to England, and many Anglicans fought for the American cause. In the North, there was more likelihood that a Churchman was also a Tory. While a generalization can be made that colonists clinging to England in religious matters were more likely to want to preserve English political control as well, there were, in fact, patriots to be found in all churches.

The colonial churches were very much a part of the American Revolution. The desire for religious liberty naturally merged with the political quest, and calls for patriotism had been coming from pulpits for several years before the Revolution actually began. Those sympathetic to the English complained: "As to their Pulpits, many of them were converted into Gutters of Sedition, . . . the Clergy had quite unlearned the Gospel, and had substituted Politicks in its Stead."[2] After the Revolution began, the clergy continued to urge patriotism. A Presbyterian minister preaching in Massachusetts in 1777 unified the causes of God and Country when he preached that the American Revolution was " . . . the cause of truth, against error and falsehood, . . . the cause of pure and undefiled religion, against bigotry, superstition, and human inventions. . . . In short, it is the cause of heaven against hell—of the kind Parent of the universe against the prince of darkness, and the destroyer of the human race."[3] Another Presbyterian minister, preaching in Pennsylvania, stated: "The cause of America is the cause of Christ."[4]

Colonial ministers served the Revolution beyond their pulpits as well. A Lutheran minister serving a church in Virginia just after the Battle of Bunker Hill in 1775, the Reverend John Peter Gabriel Muhlenberg, left his church with these words: "The Bible tells us 'there is a time for all things,' and there is a time to preach, and a time to pray, but the time for me to preach has passed away; and there is a time to fight, and that time has now come." He stepped from his pulpit into the vestryroom, and when he returned he was wearing the uniform of an American colonel. Most of the men in his congregation enlisted, and Reverend Muhlenberg became a general and served in several crucial revolutionary battles.[5]

The clergy from dissenting as well as established colonial churches also served as chaplains. In 1775 the Baptists asked the convention in Virginia, which at that time still had the established Anglican church, to approve Baptist ministers to preach to the colonial troops. The convention agreed, passing a resolution that directed commanding officers to allow dissenting clergymen to celebrate divine worship and to preach to the soldiers who chose not to attend the services celebrated by the Anglican chaplains.[6]

The story is told of one Presbyterian chaplain who contributed more than his prayers to the troops. When the American troops began to run out of wadding paper to ram powder and ball into their muskets during a battle near his home church, the chaplain dashed to the church and gathered up the hymnals of Isaac Watts, which he distributed to the soldiers with the cry, "Now put Watts into them, boys!"[7]

The response of the youngest colony to the call for revolution was especially wrenching since many Georgians had only recently come to America and some of them owed the generosity of the British people and their king for their passage, expenses, and land. Georgia sent no delegates to the Continental Congress, although a letter was sent which admitted " . . . the sense and disposition of the people in general seemed to fluctuate between liberty and convenience."[8] The dilemma was particularly poignant for the Salzburgers, nearly all of whom had come as charity colonists, and for a while many tried to remain neutral. It was foolish for the British to convert the Salzburgers' beloved Jerusalem church into first a hospital and then a stable, and to destroy the records kept there. That was enough to turn many neutral Salzburgers into Patriots. The Jews were always strongly patriotic, and when the British temporarily regained control of Georgia during the course of the Revolution, the British governor objected to any Jews being allowed to return to the colony because he had found "These people . . . to a Man to have been violent Rebels and Persecutors of the King's Loyal Subjects."[9]

The Revolution did a great deal to eliminate the old religious prejudices and distrust. The national cause was more important than any denominational differences, and after having fought together, patriots found new respect and trust for the beliefs of their fellow soldiers. Even the Roman Catholics, who had been so disliked throughout the colonies, benefitted from the effects of fighting shoulder to shoulder with other patriots. In addition, the Roman Catholic French government had been America's ally. The religious communities had played their part in the Revolution, but the Revolution had also played its part in changing forever the way that Americans looked at people of differing religious faiths.

Unfortunately, patriotic fervor had displaced religious fervor for many people, and there appeared to be a decline in religion immediately after the Revolution. Many of the church buildings had suffered damage or destruction during the war, for there were few public buildings in America at that time, and it was only natural that many churches were utilized as hospitals, barracks, and storehouses. One of the petitions presented to the Virginia legislature in 1784 urged the need for state support for religion by saying, "Petitioners have with much concern observed a general Declension of Religion for a number of Years past, occasioned in Part, we conceive by the late War, . . . "[10] George Mason wrote to Patrick Henry in 1783 that "among us a depravity of manners and morals prevails, to the destruction of all confidence between man and man." Despite such contemporary observations, religious concerns continued to involve both the founding fathers of America and the common citizens as the new nation emerged. No doubt religious practices and prejudices were changing, but the goal of religious liberty and freedom of conscience remained an important priority of the American people.

11
RELIGIOUS FREEDOM IN VIRGINIA

We are teaching the world the great truth that Governments do better without Kings & Nobles than with them. The merit will be doubled by the other lesson that Religion flourishes in greater purity, without than with the aid of Government.

—James Madison

Entering the revolutionary period, nine of the thirteen colonies had a religious establishment. The extent of the establishment varied from one colony to another, but it generally meant tithes or taxes were imposed upon all the citizens to build churches and pay the salaries of clergymen of the established churches. Sometimes establishment meant compulsory church attendance, submission to tests or oaths, privileges of citizenship, and rights to vote or hold political office as well. Obviously, the effects of an establishment were social, economic, and political as well as religious. The persons in control of the governments of the various colonies were generally members of the established church, and disestablishment was a direct threat to their powers.

In three of the New England colonies, the Congregational church was established, but in the five southern colonies the established church was Anglican, as it was in a portion of New York. (See Chapter 2 for a discussion of the multiple establishments in New York.) No church had ever been established in Rhode Island, Pennsylvania, or Delaware, nor, after English control, in New Jersey. In no colony was the Presbyterian church established, yet by the end of the colonial period it had surpassed the Anglican church in size and equaled the Congregationalist. The Baptists, who had caused the Puritans so much grief, were by this time equal in number to the Anglicans. Even the Quakers had increased their churches throughout the colonies to such an extent that they were the fifth most numerous Protestant denomination. As the colonies approached the Revolution, these five denominations—Congregational, Presbyterian, Anglican, Baptist, and Quaker—comprised about eighty-five percent of all the Protestant congregations. It is equally important, however, to remember that numerous other Protestant sects existed. In no other place in the Christian world were there so many different denominations. Many of America's immigrants had come from dissenting sects throughout Europe, creating an amazing collection of Protestants.

Considering the religious diversity, change was inevitable. By 1791, there were fourteen states in the union, and seven of those had religious establishments by law. However, not one of those was an establishment of a single, preferred church. After the American Revolution, even those states that enacted an establishment abandoned the Old World establishment of a single church and provided in their laws, instead, for public support of religion on a nonpreferential basis. The meaning of a religious establishment to post-revolutionary Americans was nonpreferential support for all churches, not the old meaning of public support for a single church.[1]

Eventually, disestablishment occurred in all of the states, with the tardiest being Massachusetts, which did not accomplish disestablishment until 1833. For students of the American Constitution, the legislative process of achieving religious liberty is most significant in the case of Virginia because of the participation of Jefferson and Madison, and because the Virginia law served as a model for others which followed.

The established Anglican church was very much a part of the social fabric of the Virginia aristocracy. A Virginian describing practices among the planter class observed that it was "a general custom on Sundays here, with Gentlemen to invite one another home to dine, after church; and to consult about, determine their common business, either before or after Service" at which time they discussed "the price of Tobacco, Grain, etc. and setting either the lineage, age, or qualities of favourite Horses." He also commented that is was "not the custom for Gentlemen to go into Church til Service is beginning, when they enter in a Body, in the same manner as they come out."[2] The established church thereby served not only religious needs but also provided business opportunities and evidence of social stature for the upper classes, and naturally most of that class supported a continued establishment. As one Virginian said, "Sure I am, that no *gentleman* would choose to go to Heaven otherwise than by the way of the established church."[3]

However, not all Virginians favored establishment. According to Thomas Jefferson, "the first republican legislature which met in 76. was crowded with petitions to abolish this spiritual tyranny."[4] Probably the loudest voices calling for disestablishment were those of the Baptists. In one of the Baptist petitions presented to the Virginia legislature, it is clear that they meant to see their rights recognized, no matter how difficult it might be. "We do not ask this, Gentlemen, as a favour which you have a privilege either to grant or withhold at pleasure, but as what we have a just claim to as freemen of the Commonwealth, and we trust it is your glory to consider yourselves not as the masters but servants of the people, whom you have the honor to represent, and that you will not fail in any instance, to recognize the natural rights of all your constituents."[5]

The first step in that direction was taken by the Virginia Convention with the passage of the Virginia Declaration of Rights on June 12, 1776. The original draft for the declaration was written by George Mason, a close neighbor and friend of George Washington. Although Mason was a supporter of the Church of England, his draft had called for complete toleration. James Madison urged something more than mere toleration, and so the section on religion was modified, although the rest of the declaration was adopted with only slight changes. Section XVI, which is the last of all the sections in the Declaration, provides:

> That religion, or the Duty which we owe to our Creator, and the manner of discharging it, can be directed only by reason and conviction, not by force or violence; and therefore all men are equally entitled to the free exercise of religion, according to the dictates of conscience; and that it is the mutual duty of all to practice Christian forbearance, love, and charity towards each other.

When asked during the convention whether the provision was meant to lay the groundwork for an attack upon establishment, Patrick Henry declared that it was not. Initially, it appeared that the legislature would not apply the declaration of religious freedom to existing laws, for as Thomas Jefferson complained, " . . . instead of taking up every principle declared in the bill of rights, and guarding it by legislative sanction, they passed over that which asserted our religious rights, leaving them as they found them. The same convention, however, when they met as a member of the General Assembly in October 1776, repealed all *acts of Parliament* which had rendered criminal the maintaining any opinions in matters of religion, the forbearing to repair to church, and the exercising any mode of worship."[6]

The repeal of these laws did not, however, disestablish the Anglican church. According to Jefferson, " . . . although the majority of our citizens were dissenters . . . a majority of the legislature were churchmen."[7] This Anglican majority involved Jefferson in what he described as "the severest contests in which I have ever been engaged,"[8] and it was nearly a decade between the passage of the Declaration of Rights authored by George Mason and the Virginia Act for Establishing Religious Freedom which Jefferson authored.

The first religious sect in Virginia to call for the separation of church and state was the Baptist, for this had been a part of their earliest beliefs. Initially, the Presbyterians had only urged their rights under the

English Act of Toleration, but eventually they joined the Baptists in arguing for church-state separation. The Methodists were, in the beginning, still within the Anglican church and thus a part of the establishment, but later they joined with the other dissenters. Added to these three were other groups such as the Quakers, Lutherans, and Mennonites, and among the voices calling for disestablishment were also people of no particular religious faith.

Dissenters made their opinions known to the legislature through the use of memorials, to which were attached petitions bearing the signatures of persons sharing the views expressed in the memorial. One of these petitions presented to the 1776 legislature came from "Dissenters from the Ecclesiastical Establishment," and contained about ten thousand names, a remarkable portion of the Virginia population. The petition pleaded, "Your Petitioners—having long groaned under the Burden of an ecclesiastical Establishment, beg leave to move your Honorable House, that this as well as every other yoke may be broken, and that the oppressed may go free."[9] The petition was not associated with any particular church organization, and considering the large number of names attached to it, the petition probably spoke for dissenters from several denominations, as well as for members of no church.

Many of the petitions, however, were sponsored by a church. The chief organization of the Presbyterians in Virginia was the Hanover Presbytery, and their memorial of October 24, 1776, although sponsored by that group, expressed the feelings of all the dissenting church groups.

It is well known, that in the frontier counties, which are justly supposed to contain a fifth part of the inhabitants of Virginia, the dissenters have borne the heavy burdens of purchasing glebes, building churches, and supporting the established clergy, where there are very few Episcopalians, either to assist in bearing the expense, or to reap the advantage; and that throughout the other parts of the country, there are also many thousands of zealous friends and defenders of our State, who, besides the invidious, and disadvantageous restrictions to which they have been subjected, annually pay large taxes to support an establishment, from which their consciences and principles oblige them to dissent: all which are confessedly so many violations of their natural rights; and in their consequences, a restraint upon freedom of inquiry, and private judgment.

In this enlightened age, and in a land where all, of every denomination are united in the most strenuous efforts to be free, we hope and expect that our representatives will cheerfully concur in removing every species of religious, as well as civil bondage. Certain it is, that every argument for civil liberty, gains additional strength when applied to liberty in the concerns of religion; and there is no argument in favour of establishing the Christian religion, but what may be pleaded, with equal propriety, for establishing the tenets of Mahomed by those who believe the Alcoran: or if this be not true, it is at least impossible for the magistrate to adjudge the right of preference among the various sects that profess the Christian faith, without erecting a chair of infallibility, which would lead us back to the church of Rome.[10]

The Anglicans were not silent through all of this, and perhaps the most vocal among them were the clergy. They argued that they had entered the ministry in reliance upon the economic support of the establishment. To change the law after they had prepared themselves for service to the church, they reasoned, would leave them without the security of the state support upon which they had relied in making their choice of profession. The effectiveness of the lobbying efforts of the clergy was assessed by James Madison: " . . . the clergy are a numerous and powerful body, have great influence at home [in England] by reason of their connection with and dependence on the Bishops and Crown, and will naturally employ all their art and interest to depress their rising adversaries; for such they must consider dissenters who rob them of the good will of the people, and may, in time, endanger their livings and security."[11]

During the decade of debates concerning religious liberty in Virginia, numerous laws were considered. The "free exercise of religion," which was promised in the Declaration of Rights did not automatically void existing laws involving religion, and the consideration of each law initiated a separate legislative battle. The dissenters' principal advocates in the legislature were Thomas Jefferson and James Madison, and with the consideration of each law, they gained a new set of allies, even some from among the Anglican majority. These alliances shifted, however, according to the proposal being considered.

The stages through which the struggle for religious liberty in Virginia passed during the legislative sessions from 1776 to 1779 were described by Jefferson: " . . . our opponents carried in the general resolutions of the commee [sic] of No. 19. a declaration that religious assemblies ought to be regulated, and that provision ought to be made for continuing the succession of the clergy, and superintending their conduct. And in the bill now passed was inserted an express reservation of the question Whether a general assessment should not be established by law, on every one, to the support of the pastor of his choice; or whether all should be left to voluntary contributions; and on this question, debated at every session from 76 to 79 (some of our dissenting allies, having now secured their particular object, going over to the advocates of a general assessment) we could only obtain a suspension from session to session until 79. when the question against a general assessment was finally carried, and the establishment of the Anglican church entirely put down."[12]

Using hindsight, Jefferson's statement that the establishment ended in 1779 is correct; however, the legislative battle concerning a general assessment raged for five more years, and during those years it was not at all certain that disestablishment was final. His description more accurately relates to the portion of the legislative struggles in which he was actively involved, for although Thomas Jefferson authored the Virginia Act for Religious Freedom, by the time of its passage he was serving the young nation in France, and James Madison was the one left in Virginia to champion the passage of the act. In Jefferson's absence, Madison was joined in sponsoring the act by Mason, Taylor, and George and W. C. Nicholas.

More accurately described, the legislative acts of 1779 were pivotal but not final. Without the efforts of legislative supporters, and more importantly, without the continuing deluge of petitions from the common people, the significance of the 1779 proceedings would have been eroded or lost. Two main complaints remained among the dissenters— first, the question of authority to perform marriage ceremonies, and second, the continued role of the vestries.

In a Baptist petition submitted in the fall of 1780, the petitioners complimented the legislature upon the work it had done but urged the need for more, particularly with reference to curing the abuses of the existing system for performing marriages. "[W]e your Memorialist, heartily approve of the Act that passed in your last Session which partly removes the Vestige of oppression; which 'till then hung over our heads, respecting the Ministers sallary Law: and as we hope to enjoy equal, Religious, as well as civil Liberty: while we demean our Selves as good Citizens, and peaceable Subjects of this Commonwealth—we your Memorialists therefore desire that an Act may pass, Declareing Mariges Solemnized by Dissenting Ministers, either by License, or publication; Valid in Law, for until such an Act shall take place; the Validity of Dissenters rights to officiate in the Same, is much disputed: as the following instances makes manifest of Ministers exacting the exhorbetant Sum of Sixty Pounds for that Service from two very poor people; and two Barrels of Corn from a Baptist, who applyed to his Minister who refused because the Licence was directed to a Minister of the Church of England . . . "[13]

The second issue about which dissenters complained concerned the vestries. Even after the vestries lost the power to lay assessments against all the citizens to pay ministers' salaries and church expenses, the vestrymen retained the responsibility of caring for the poor. The 1780 memorial from the Sandy Creek Baptist Association addressed this issue: "the Vestry-Law which disqualifies any person to officiate who will not subscribe to be conformable to the Doctrine and Discipline of the Church of England; by which means Dissenters are not only precluded, but also not represented, they not having a free voice, whose Property is nevertheless subject to be taxed by the Vestry, and whose Poor are provided for at the Discretion of those who may possibly be under the Influence of Party-Motives—And what renders the said Law a Greater Grievance is, that in some Parishes, so much Time has elapsed since an Election, that there is scarcely one who was originally chosen by the People, the Vacancies having been filled up by the remaining Vestrymen."[14]

With some limitations, both of these issues were settled to the satisfaction of the dissenters by the legislature in December of 1780. The last great challenge to disestablishment which remained was the question of a general assessment, the proceeds from which would be applied to all denominations, in effect, a multiple establishment.

The years of 1784 and 1785 called for all of Madison's skills as an advocate of religious liberty. He was well-suited for the challenge, for he brought not only political skills but also his years of theological studies to the task. Madison had studied for the ministry at Princeton under John Witherspoon, and after leaving school he continued to study theology. His passion for religious liberty was not antireligious but sprang from his impatience with religious persecution. As a young man of twenty-three, Madison had written to a college friend of the religious persecution in Virginia in 1774: "That diabolical, hell-conceived principle of persecution rages among some; and to their eternal infamy, the clergy can furnish their quota of imps for such business. This vexes me the worse of anything whatever. There are at this time in the adjacent country not less than five or six well-meaning men in close jail for publishing their religious sentiments, which in the main are very orthodox. I have neither patience to hear, talk or think of anything relative to this matter; for I have squabbled and scolded, abused and ridiculed, so long about it to little purpose, that I am without common patience."[15] Within a few years, Madison had found a way to achieve what his squabbling and scolding had not; in the Virginia legislature this impatient young man brought religious liberty to Virginia.

More than forty years after the struggle, Madison wrote to a descendant of George Mason, describing the events of that session: "During the session of the General Assembly 1784–5 a bill was introduced into the House of Delegates providing for the legal support of Teachers of the Christian Religion, and being patronized by the most popular talents in the House, seemed likely to obtain a majority of votes. In order to arrest its progress it was insisted with success that the bill should be postponed till the evening session, and in the meantime be printed for public consideration. That the sense of the people might be the better called forth, your highly distinguished ancestor Colonel George Mason, Colonel Nicholas also possessing public weight and some others thought it advisable that a remonstrance against the bill should be prepared for general circulation and signature and imposed on me the task of drawing up such a paper. The draft having received their sanction, a large number of printed copies were distributed, and so extensively signed by the people of every religious denomination that at the evening session the projected measure was entirely frustrated; and under the influence of the public sentiment thus manifested the celebrated bill 'Establishing Religious Freedom' enacted into a permanent barrier against future attempts on the rights of conscience as declared in the Great Charter prefixed to the Constitution of the State."[16] With this letter, Madison enclosed a copy of his Memorial & Remonstrance Against Religious Assessments.

This document, printed in full in Appendix A, deserves nearly as important a place in the history of religious liberty in America as the laws that were enacted to secure that liberty. Madison's eloquence stirred the emotions and voiced the opinions of such huge numbers of people that the legislature could not ignore their demands. Although the Memorial & Remonstrance does not have the stature of law, it does express the opinions of the man who authored the First Amendment to the Constitution of the United States, and it was significantly responsible for the passage of the Virginia Act for Establishing Religious Freedom. It should be required reading for anyone interested in religious liberty in America, and certainly for anyone proposing amendments to existing laws.

Madison stated his opposition to the bill providing support for teachers of the Christian religion in fifteen points:

1. "The Religion then of every man must be left to the conviction and conscience of every man; . . . in matters of Religion, no man's right is abridged by the institution of Civil Society, and that Religion is wholly exempt from its cognizance."

2. Religion is exempt from the authority of any Legislative Body. "The Rulers who are guilty of such an encroachment, exceed the commission from which they derive their authority, and are Tyrants. The People who submit to it are governed by laws made neither by themselves, nor by an authority derived from them, and are slaves."

3. " . . . it is proper to take alarm at the first experiment on our liberties. . . . Who does not see that the same authority which can establish Christianity, in exclusion of all other Religions, may establish with the same ease any particular sect of Christians, in exclusion of all other Sects?"

4. "Whilst we assert for ourselves a freedom to embrace, to profess and to observe the Religion which we believe to be of divine origin, we cannot deny an equal freedom to those whose minds have not yet yielded to the evidence which has convinced us."

5. Civil Magistrates are not competent judges of religious truth, and religion should not be an engine of civil policy.

6. Financial support "is not requisite for the support of the Christian Religion . . . for it is known that this Religion both existed and flourished, not only without the support of human laws, but in spite of every opposition from them."

7. "[E]cclesiastical establishments, instead of maintaining the purity and efficacy of Religion, have had a contrary operation."

8. "Rulers who wished to subvert the public liberty, may have found an established clergy convenient auxiliaries. A just Government, instituted to secure & perpetuate it, needs them not. Such a Government will be best supported by protecting every Citizen in the enjoyment of his Religion with the same equal hand which protects his person and his property; by neither invading the equal rights of any Sect, nor suffering any Sect to invade those of another."

9. An establishment destroys the religious asylum this country has offered. "It degrades from the equal rank of Citizens all those whose opinions in Religion do not bend to those of the Legislative authority."

10. It would have a "tendency to banish our Citizens."

11. "[I]t will destroy that moderation and harmony which the forbearance of our laws to intermeddle with Religion has produced amongst its several sects. . . . The very appearance of the Bill has transformed 'that Christian forbearance, love and charity,' which of late mutually prevailed, into animosities and jealousies, which may not soon be appeased. What mischiefs may not be dreaded, should this enemy to the public quiet be armed with the force of law?"

12. Establishment "is adverse to the diffusion of the light of Christianity."

13. "[A]ttempts to enforce by legal sanctions, acts obnoxious to so great a proportion of Citizens, tend to enervate the laws in general, and to slacken the bands of Society."

14. "[A] measure of such singular magnitude and delicacy ought not to be imposed, without the clearest evidence that it is called for by a majority of citizens."

15. Effect must be given to Article XVI of the Virginia Declaration of Rights allowing every citizen the free exercise of his Religion according to the dictates of conscience.[17]

Despite disestablishment of the Church of England in 1779, the bill providing for support for Christian teachers seemed likely to succeed because the money collected from the general assessment of the population was to be distributed to teachers among the various sects. Through such a plan of distribution, all sects stood to benefit financially under the proposed bill. The effect was in the nature of a multiple establishment. Therefore, some of the individuals and groups that had joined with Jefferson and Madison to fight establishment of a single church favored the general assessment, or multiple establishment, wherein the benefits would be shared. Assuming the leadership of the conservatives favoring the assessment was Patrick Henry.

Initially, the Presbyterian clergy were also among those favoring the bill. Madison found their reversal of position particularly disgusting as he explained to James Monroe in a letter dated April 12, 1785: "The only proceeding of the late Session of Assembly which makes a noise through the Country is that which relates to a General Assessment. The Episcopal people are generally for it, though I think the zeal of some of them has cooled. The laity of the other sects are equally unanimous on the other side. So are all the clergy except the Presbyterian who seem as ready to set up an establishment which is to take them in as they were to pull down that which shut them out. I do not know a more shameful contrast than might be found between their memorials on the latter and former occasion."[18] His criticism of them may have been excessive. Early in the proceedings, passage of the bill seemed certain, and it may have been prudence that led them initially to work with the prevailing mood rather than stubbornly to oppose what appeared inevitable. The language of the Presbyterian memorial is hardly enthusiastic: "Should it be thought necessary at present for the Assembly to exert this right of supporting religion in general by an assessment on all the people, we would wish it to be done on the most liberal plan. A general assessment of the kind we have heard proposed is an object of such consequence that it excites much anxious speculation among your constituients. We therefore earnestly pray that nothing may be done in the case inconsistent with the proper objects of human legislation or of the Declaration of Rights."[19] Whatever reason had prompted their original acceptance, by August 20th of that year, when Madison wrote to Jefferson in France, the Presbyterian clergy had withdrawn their support for the bill. Madison wrote that he was unsure whether they had done so because of "fear of their laity or a jealousy of the Episcopalians."[20]

Much of the support for the bill came from people who believed they saw a gradual weakening of religious faith. One such group from Amelia had petitioned the 1784 legislature that "your Petitioners have with much concern observed a general Declension of Religion for a number of Years past, occasioned in Part, we conceive by the late War, but chiefly by it not being duly aided and patronized by the civil Power; that should it decline with nearly the same rapidity in Future, your Petitioners apprehend Consequences dangerous, if not fatal to the Strength and Stability of Civil Government."[21] Another group, from Surrey, asked for state support for religion, saying, "It is with the most heartfelt concern that your Memorialists see the countenance of the civil power wholly withdrawn from religion, and Mankind left without the smallest coercion to contribute to its support."[22] Without the economic support of the state, they feared, religion would fail.

Madison sent a copy of his Memorial & Remonstrance to George Washington. Although Washington agreed with Madison that the bill should not be passed, he expressed his personal feelings that taxes in support of religion were not necessarily bad. "Although no man's sentiments are more opposed to any kind of restraint upon religious principles than mine are, yet I confess, that I am not amongst the number of those, who are so much alarmed at the thoughts of making people pay towards the support of that which they profess. . . . As the matter now stands, I wish an assessment had never been agitated, and as it has gone so far, that the bill could die an easy death; because I think it will be productive of more quiet to the State, than by enacting it into law, which in my opinion would be impolite admitting there is a decided majority for it, to the disquiet of a respectable minority."[23] Obviously, Washington personally agreed with the conservatives led by Patrick Henry, but politically he agreed with Madison.

In November of 1784, Madison and Henry debated the issue of a general assessment in the Virginia House. Patrick Henry and his conservative colleagues clearly owned the majority, and because of the conservative nature of the Senate it was believed that if a bill could be drafted quickly by the House and submitted to the Senate, it would pass that legislative body as well. A committee was appointed to draft a bill, and Henry was named chairman. The committee did its work, and in December the proposed bill was read and debated in the House. The legislative process called for the bill to be read three times before it could be passed. When the bill was called for the third and final reading on December 24th, a motion was made to postpone the reading until the following November, and the motion passed 45 votes to 38. It is important to note that between the November debates between Madison and Henry, and the December debates concerning the bill itself, Patrick Henry had been elected Governor and was therefore no longer present to oppose Madison. Henry's absence from the House may have contributed to Madison's success in gaining the postponement.

Lacking the votes necessary to defeat the bill, the opponents' achievement of a postponement was nevertheless a major victory, for it gave them an opportunity to rally the people behind the opposition. A resolution was passed that provided for copies of the bill, "together with the names of the ayes and noes, on the question of postponing the third reading of the said bill to the 4th Thursday in November next, be published in hand-bills, and 12 copies thereof delivered to each member of the General Assembly, to be distributed to their respective counties; and that the people thereof be requested to signify their opinion respecting the adoption of such a bill, to the next session of Assembly."[24] This, then, was the postponement to the "evening session" which Madison described in his letter to Mason's descendant. According to Madison, the opponents had decided to circulate a remonstrance against the bill as the most effective means of opposition. Their wisdom in selecting Madison as its author certainly contributed to its effectiveness.

The opponents of the bill knew they had some public support upon which to build, for during the 1784 session petitions had been received that opposed any general assessment bill. The citizens of Rockingham County had written, "That while we pay the greatest Deference to so venerable a Body we may be permitted Submissively to say it is our Humble Opinions that any Majestrait or Legislative Body that takes upon themselves the power of Governing Religion by human Laws Assumes a power that never was committed to them by God nor can be by Man. . . . "[25] From Rockbridge the people had also expressed their opposition, "That your Memorialists hoped after the happy termination of a long and dangerous War all denominations of Christians in this State would have enjoyed equal Privileges. . . . We have been also informed that it is in contemplation to have a Law passed this Session of Assembly to establish a general tax for the Support of the Ministers of the Gospel of all Denominations, with this reserve that each man may say to whom his quota shall be given—This scheme should it take place is the best calculated to destroy Religion that perhaps could be devised and much more dangerous than the establishment of any one Sect for whilst that Sect was corrupted by being independent of the will of the particular Societies or Congregations where they officiated for their Support the rest would remain pure or at least of Good Morals—But by a general tax all will be rendered so independent of the will of the particular Societies for their Support that all will be infected with the common contagion."[26]

During the months between the sessions, the opponents of the bill knew that they had to build upon this negative sentiment. George Washington had described the public opposition as being "a respectable minority." If the bill were to be defeated, the general populace had to make the Anglican legislators know that the majority of the common people opposed it. George Nicholas was especially skilled at rallying the people's opposition. The most important work, however, was done by the evangelical churches. The Presbyterian laity insisted upon a new memorial to replace the one submitted in October of 1784, which had voiced the clergy's acquiescence to the bill. The Baptists also prepared a new memorial.

When the legislative session reconvened in the fall of 1785, petitions opposing the bill were presented in such large numbers that Madison declared, "The steps taken throughout the Country to defeat the Genl. Assessment had produced all the effect that could have been wished."[27] Nearly all the petitions opposing the bill reflect the influence of Madison's remonstrance, some by paraphrasing its language and others by simply copying the words. Madison had written to Jefferson that copies of his Memorial & Remonstrance had "been sent through the medium of confidential persons in a number of the upper counties, and I am told will be pretty extensively signed."[28] Even he must have been surprised at the extent of its influence.

Petitions arrived not only from those who previously had remained silent. They also arrived from people who, upon reconsideration, had changed their minds. A petition from the Dinwiddie community admitted that its signers had done a complete reversal in opinion and "are now as decidedly opposed to a General Assessment as they were formerly in favour of it."[29]

The end result was, of course, that the bill for a general assessment to support Christian teachers failed, and in that same legislative session Jefferson's Act for Religious Freedom passed! In December of 1785, Jefferson's act was presented for its third reading, and the conservatives attempted the same tactic that had succeeded, ultimately, in defeating the General Assessment—they moved for a postponement until the following session. However, postponement was defeated and the bill passed the House by an overwhelming vote of 74 to 20.[30]

The final version was subjected to some amendments by the Senate. When the new version was first sent back to the House, it was rejected, but the Senate adhered to its amendments, and, after a conference, the House adopted the amendment, with amendments. Not to be outdone, the Senate amended the amendment of its amendment, and this was the version accepted by the House.

The significance of the passage of this act goes beyond its effect upon a single colony. Other colonies were writing their own Bills of Rights and looked to the example of Virginia. Many of the same men who served Virginia were serving important roles in the emerging nation. Most importantly, the role of James Madison in securing religious liberty for Virginia provides history with invaluable insight into the intentions of the author of the First Amendment. Even beyond America, other nations were examining the words this colony had chosen to express the religious freedom of her people. Jefferson reported to Madison that "The Virginia Act for religious freedom has been received with infinite approbation in Europe, and propagated with enthusiasm."[31] It had taken six years, from the time of its introduction by Jefferson in 1779 until its passage by the Virginia House in 1785, followed by Senate acceptance in January of 1786, for Virginia to establish religious freedom after ending the establishment of the Church of England.

The act may be separated into three parts. It begins with a summary of the evils that result from state intrusion into religious matters; it continues with the heart of the act: "That no man shall be compelled to frequent or support any religious worship, place, or ministry whatsoever, nor shall be enforced, restrained, molested, or burthened in his body or goods, nor shall otherwise suffer, on account of his religious opinions or belief; but that all men shall be free to profess, and by argument to maintain, their opinions in matters of religion, and that the same shall in no wise diminish, enlarge, or affect their civil capacities."[32] And, the act concludes with an attempt to restrict later legislators from tampering with the religious rights of Virginians.

Interestingly, the preamble, which warns against the ill effects of civil intrusion into religion, is at least five times as long as the substantive portion, and much of that opening language is directed at the historical abuses of legislators. It states: "That the impious presumption of legislators and rulers, civil as well as ecclesiastical, who, being themselves but fallible and uninspired men, have assumed dominion over the faith of others, setting up their own opinions and modes of thinking as the only true and infallible, and as such endeavoring to impose them on others, hath established and maintained false religions over the greatest part of the world and through all time."[33] The strength of such self-criticism is remarkable from a legislature that fought the passage of this act for six years. The full text of the act appears in Appendix B.

Although the wording of the act was almost entirely Jefferson's, a few of his words were deleted, all of which came from the declaratory portion rather than the substantive heart of the law. For a time, Jefferson was disappointed with these deletions, but soon he regained his pride in it. He wrote to Madison on December 16, 1786: "It is honorable for us, to have produced the first legislature who had the courage to declare, that the reason of man may be trusted with the formation of his own opinions."[34] That pride endured throughout his lifetime, for he left specific instructions that the inscription on his tombstone should bear the following words and no others: "Author of the Declaration of American Independence, of the Statute of Virginia for Religious Freedom, and Father of the University of Virginia." He did not include the fact that he was also President of the United States!

History should accord Jefferson high honor for having authored these important words, but without the skill and wisdom of his friend, James Madison, the statute would never have been enacted. Even more deserving of the credit for winning religious liberty for Virginia are the insistent Baptists who agitated for the separation of church and state, together with countless other dissenters who joined their cause, and the Anglican legislators who voted for religious liberty instead of their own self-interest.

12
THE FIRST AMENDMENT

A bill of rights is what the people are entitled to against every government on earth, general or particular, and what no just government should refuse or rest on inference.

—Thomas Jefferson to James Madison

The men who came together to write the Constitution of the United States of America were not carbon copies of one another with a single, national goal. They were first of all representatives of their individual states with the responsibility of protecting the particular interests of their constituents in the process of writing the Constitution. The miracle of the Constitutional Convention is that these men rose above their differences to create a document acceptable, eventually, to all thirteen states.

Not the least among their differences were matters of religion, both personally and with regard to the regions they represented. However, for their own self-interest, the framers of the Constitution knew that because they collectively represented so many religious viewpoints, it would be to their mutual benefit to keep out of the new government any religious tests for political office or any national religious establishment. Whether the framers were motivated by self-interest or by a genuine feeling of religious brotherhood, they recognized the importance of avoiding any religious entanglement in the Constitution.

Beyond the religious diversity of the framers themselves, their constituents reflected religious variety to an extent found in no other Christian nation. The framers of the Constitution could look to no European document for a precedent in dealing with such religious diversity, for none existed. Protecting the various cultural and religious backgrounds represented among the people was a uniquely American challenge.

On the second Monday in May, 1787, representatives from eleven states began the delicate process, involving both wisdom and compromise, of creating the United States Constitution. Eventually all but

Rhode Island participated. Remarkably, their mission was accomplished four months later, but as can be imagined, the labors had tested the endurance of the framers, and as they struggled with the final details, they were eager to be finished. When it was pointed out that no provision had been made for juries in civil cases, they decided to leave the matter for Congress to correct. George Mason agreed to this omission, especially if some "general principles" were included. As the author of the Virginia Declaration of Rights, he must have been anticipating some similar recitation for the United States Constitution. In fact, he stated his belief that such a declaration should be affixed to the Constitution, claiming that it would only take a few hours to draft it. Elbridge Gerry of Massachusetts moved for a committee to prepare a bill of rights, and the only man recorded as having spoken against it was Roger Sherman of Connecticut, whose objection was that he believed the bills of rights of the respective states, which were not repealed by the Constitution, were sufficient to protect the rights of the people, and therefore, inclusion of such a declaration in the federal constitution was unnecessary. Thereafter, the convention voted against Mason's proposal.

Their vote must be considered within the context of its timing. Mason's proposal came on Wednesday, September 12, while the framers awaited the printing of the report from the committee on style, and all that remained to be done was laboriously to compare the revised draft of the constitution reported by the committee with the proceedings referred to the committee. The men were tired and eager to be home. Despite Mason's assurance that a draft could be completed in a few hours, these politicians were astute enough to realize that approval of the draft could take much longer. The desirability of a bill of rights was not attacked; rather, one man simply expressed his opinion that it was not essential. The vote may reasonably be interpreted as more of a reflection of their desire to be finished than a decision regarding the propriety of a bill of rights, which could later be dealt with by Congress.

On Saturday, September 15, Edmund Randolph of Virginia made a final plea for a second convention, to be convened with the purpose of considering amendments proposed by individual state conventions. He stated that unless such a convention were planned, he could not sign the Constitution nor could he enthusiastically urge its ratification in his home state. Mason and Gerry, who had urged the selection of a committee to draft the bill of rights, also announced their disinclination to sign the Constitution without provision for a second convention to consider amendments. The other members were well aware of the difficulties they had experienced during the convention in reaching compromises and agreements, and they feared the difficulties of a second convention, whose members would have received specific instructions from their respective states concerning particular amendments. Therefore, they rejected Randolph's proposal. On Monday, September 17, 1787, the Constitution was signed by all the members present, except Mason, Gerry, and Randolph.

In order to be operative, the Constitution had to be ratified by nine of the thirteen states. Therefore, the labors of the members of the Constitutional Convention had only begun with its signing. There remained for them the task of urging its ratification in their respective states. They realized that their best hopes for ratification were to maintain the momentum begun by the publicity in connection with the convention and to work for prompt ratification.

Among the early opponents was George Mason. He prepared "Objections to the Constitution of Government formed by the Convention," and his first objection was the following: "There is no Declaration of Rights; and the Laws of the general Government being paramount to the Laws of Constitutions of the several States, the Declarations of Rights in the separate States are no Security. Nor are the people secured even in the Enjoyment of the Benefits of the Common-Law; which stands here upon no other Foundation than its having been adopted by the respective Acts forming the Constitutions of the several states."[1]

The constitutional opponents, or Antifederalists, adopted this omission as the centerpiece of their opposition. The lack of a bill of rights had great emotional appeal with the people, and with little effort the Antifederalists could represent its omission as some secret deception practiced by the Federalists against the American people. The sincerity of their concern is suspect, for as one Antifederalist wrote to another, "I am in doubts whether such a Bill would not of itself make the constitution far more dangerous than it now is."[2] Undoubtedly some of the opponents, such as Mason, were honestly fearful of the threat to personal liberties without the protections of a bill of rights, but for many of them it was just a means of manipulating public opinion, or as Alexander Hamilton expressed it, "the stale bait for popularity at the expense of the public good."[3]

Eventually the Federalists had to admit their tactical error in failing to include a Declaration of Rights. Once they were willing to admit their mistake, the principal argument of the Antifederalists was diminished. The new point of debate became whether the new Congress could be trusted to correct this omission if the Constitution were ratified without a bill of rights or whether amendments should be made a condition of ratification.

Thomas Jefferson, the author of the Declaration of Independence and the Virginia Act for Religious Liberty, was in France during the Constitutional Convention and the period of ratification which followed, but he stayed advised as well as possible. In a letter to a friend he wrote: "What I disapproved from the first moment also was the want of a bill of rights to guard liberty against the legislative as well as executive branches of government, that is to say, to secure freedom in religion, freedom of the press, freedom from monopolies, . . . "[4] He expressed that same concern to his friend, James Madison, who had been one of the most influential men at the convention and was one of the keys to its ratification.

Madison replied to Jefferson's concern by letter dated October 17, 1788, as follows: "My own opinion has always been in favor of a bill of rights; provided it be so framed as not to imply powers not meant to be included in the enumeration. At the same time I have never thought the omission a material defect. . . . "[5] Madison continued by explaining point by point his reasons for trusting ratification without a bill of rights.

1. Because I conceive . . . the rights in question are reserved by the manner in which the federal powers are granted.

2. Because there is great reason to fear that a positive declaration of some of the most essential rights could not be obtained in the requisite latitude. I am sure that the rights of conscience in particular, if submitted to public definition would be narrowed much more than they are likely ever to be by an assumed power. One of the objections in New England was that the constitution by prohibiting religious tests, opened a door for Jews, Turks & infidels. . . .

4. Because experience proves the inefficacy of a bill of rights on those occasions when its control is most needed. Repeated violations of these parchment barriers have been committed by overbearing majorities in every State. In Virginia I have seen the bill of rights violated in every instance where it has been opposed to popular current. Notwithstanding the explicit provision contained in that instrument for the rights of Conscience, it is well known that a religious establishment would have taken place in that State, if the Legislative majority had found as they expected, a majority of the people in favor of the measure; and I am persuaded that if a majority of the people were now of one sect, the measure would still take place and on narrower ground than was then proposed, notwithstanding the additional obstacle which the law has since created.

If Madison truly favored a bill of rights, why had he not applied his considerable influence during the convention to see that one was included? He was not alone in believing that the rights remained protected by the bills of rights of the individual states. He personally had struggled to assure religious liberty for his fellow Virginians, and he had reason to believe that the freedom they enjoyed under their state law was as broad as that enjoyed anywhere else in America, and perhaps in the world. By the silence of the Federal Constitution, perhaps he felt he was best able to protect that freedom in Virginia.

His fear that a declaration of the rights of conscience might be more narrowly drawn than desirable was clearly based upon his awareness of

New England attitudes. The Massachusetts Bill of Rights passed in 1780 began by stating that "It is the right as well as the duty of all men in society, publicly, and at stated seasons, to worship the Supreme Being . . . " and continued with "As the happiness of a people and the good order and preservation of civil government essentially depend upon piety, religion, and morality, and as these cannot be generally diffused through a community but by the institution of the public worship of God and of public instructions, in piety, religion and morality. Therefore . . . the legislature shall from time to time authorize and require . . . suitable provision, at their own [the city's] expense, for the institution of the public worship of God and the support and maintenance of public Protestant teachers of piety, religion and morality . . . [and] to enjoin upon all the subjects an attendance upon the instruction of the public teachers aforesaid."[6] Certainly the New England definition of freedom of conscience was far different from the freedom Virginians enjoyed.

Finally, Madison expressed to his friend his frustration with the effectiveness of the bill of rights in matters of conscience, an understandable frustration when it is remembered that the Virginia Declaration of Rights was passed in 1776 but that the religious establishment was continued until 1779. Madison must have been referring to the bitter legislative fight over the general assessment and the decade it took to achieve enactment of Jefferson's Bill for Religious Freedom.

Although Madison was a leader of the Federalists who served in the convention that drafted the Constitution without a bill of rights and a leader of the Federalists who urged its ratification without amendments, he was not an opponent of religious liberty. He may have allowed the omission for political reasons, but the feelings he expressed in his Memorial & Remonstrance about the importance of excluding the government from matters of religion had not changed.

Although Jefferson remained adamant in his position that a federal bill of rights was necessary, by May of 1788 he wrote to another friend that "For the present, however, the general adoption is to be prayed for."[7] George Washington also urged the ratification without amendments, saying "But to make such amendments as may be proposed . . . the condition of its adoption would, in my opinion, amount to a compleat rejection of it."[8]

By the time the Virginia convention met to consider ratification, eight other states had already ratified. The holdouts, in addition to Virginia, were New Hampshire, New York, South Carolina, and Rhode Island. Thus, Virginia had it within its power to be the key, ninth state to ratify and thus activate the Constitution. Madison led the forces for ratification, but he was opposed by his old ally, George Mason, joined by Patrick Henry. Either the conviction of his beliefs or the aggravation of opposing life-long friends like Madison and Washington had led Mason to an almost desperate stance, and the debates were long and heated. They were so long, in fact, that New Hampshire became the ninth state to ratify when their convention voted approval on June 21, 1788. New Hampshire wanted the honor of being the determining state for ratification, and they therefore recited the time of their vote, 1:00 p.m., in case Virginia were also to have ratified later during the same afternoon.

Virginia's vote was delayed until June 25, 1788, and was achieved when Madison defeated the opposition by convincing the Federalists to agree "to preface the ratification with some plain and general truths that cannot affect the validity of the act,"[9] that is, to include a desired statement of rights without making ratification conditional.

After Virginia ratified the Constitution, the remaining states did not immediately fall into line as expected. Two men were largely responsible for withholding their states' approval—Governor George Clinton of New York and Willie Jones of North Carolina. They continued to push for a convention to write the amendments, even though congressmen were being elected under the new Constitution. Eventually, New York ratified in July, North Carolina in November, and, most belatedly, Rhode Island ratified on May 29, 1790.

James Madison was able to continue his leadership role in the new nation by having been elected to the first Congress. He defeated James Monroe in a difficult race, which Madison won because of his campaign promise to work for amendments dealing with personal liberty, "particularly the rights of Conscience in the fullest latitude." Madison kept that promise and became the leading force in the writing of the federal Bill of Rights.

Five of the states had ratified subject to an understanding that a bill of rights would be added, and several states included a list of proposed rights with their ratifications.[10] New York and North Carolina, when they finally ratified, both submitted lists of rights, New York's list containing twenty-four! Since the Antifederalists had based their opposition to Constitutional ratification upon the lack of a bill of rights, it might have been assumed that they would lead the way in correcting this omission. In fact, they were lacking in agreement as to what specific rights were needed and generally indifferent toward those Madison proposed. Their actions seem to support the view that their expressions of concern over the protection of the people's rights during the ratification debates had been merely political tactics. It was left to a Federalist to urge the first Congress to enact the promised amendments, and James Madison willingly assumed that role.

Mindful of his own campaign promise and of the expressed desire of several states for amendments, and equally mindful of the criticism directed against the Federalists for not having included a bill of rights with the original Constitution, Madison addressed the House of Representatives on June 8, 1789, with these words:

> It appears to me that this House is bound by every motive of prudence, not to let the first session pass over without proposing to the State Legislatures, some things to be incorporated into the Constitution, that will render it as acceptable to the whole people of the United States, as it has been found acceptable to a majority of them. I wish, among other reasons why something should be done, that those who had been friendly to the adoption of this Constitution may have the opportunity of proving to those who were opposed to it that they were as sincerely devoted to liberty and a Republican Government, as those who charged them with wishing the adoption of this Constitution in order to lay the foundation of an aristocracy or despotism. It will be a desirable thing to extinguish from the bosom of every member of the community, any apprehensions that there are those among his countrymen who wish to deprive them of the liberty for which they valiantly fought and honorably bled. And if there are amendments desired of such a nature as will not injure the Constitution, and they can be ingrafted so as to give satisfaction to the doubting part of our fellowcitizens, the friends of the Federal Government will evince that spirit of deference and concession for which they have hitherto been distinguished. [11]

Ever the practical politician, Madison tried with those words to reconcile Federalist and Antifederalist, North and South, so that the Congress might rise above past disputes and regional self-interest to enact amendments that would enhance the Constitution, not diminish its effectiveness.

His desire to protect the rights of conscience to the "fullest latitude" was evident with his proposal of these words:

> The civil rights of none shall be abridged on account of religious belief or worship, nor shall any national religion be established, nor shall the full and equal rights of conscience be in any manner, or on any pretext, infringed.

This proposal was immediately sent to committee, and after several weeks' consideration the Select Committee, consisting of Madison and ten others, returned the following revision:

> No religion shall be established by law nor shall the equal rights of conscience be infringed.

The House debated the revised proposal on August 15, 1789, and their consideration of the matter was relatively brief. Others besides Madison who had participated in the Constitutional Convention's consideration of the need for amendments also were members of the new Congress. Roger Sherman, who was the only one recorded to have spoken against Mason's suggestion that a committee be appointed to draft a declaration of rights to accompany the Constitution, reurged his position that as Congress had no delegated authority to make religious establishment it was unnecessary to adopt this amendment. Elbridge Gerry, who had moved for a committee to draft amendments at the Constitutional Convention, suggested that the bill be changed to read, "that no religious doctrine shall be established by law." New York had included with its ratification a proposed amendment dealing with religion which provided, that no "religious sect or society ought to be favored or established by law in preference to others," and their representative in Congress, Peter Sylvester, expressed his concern that the proposal before the House might have a tendency "to abolish religion altogether." Representative John Vining suggested that the two parts of the bill be transposed, and Daniel Carroll of Maryland, a Roman Catholic, urged reasonableness, saying "[h]e would not contend with gentlemen about the phraseology, his object was to secure the substance in such a manner as to satisfy the wishes of the honest part of the community."[12]

Following these exchanges, Madison rose to speak. In answer to Roger Sherman, he said that some state conventions had worried that Congress might rely upon the "necessary and proper" clause of the Constitution to infringe rights of conscience or establish a national religion, and therefore, "to prevent these effects he presumed the amendment was intended, and he thought it as well expressed as the nature of the language would admit." As to his interpretation of the revised bill, "he apprehended the meaning of the words to be, that Congress should not establish a religion, and enforce the legal observation of it by law, nor compel men to worship God in any manner contrary to their conscience."

The New England attitude, about which Madison had expressed his concern to Jefferson, spoke in the voice of Benjamin Huntington of Connecticut. Although he expressed his respect for Madison's interpretation of the meaning of the bill, Huntington feared others might not interpret it so and that it might be used to threaten states like his own where religious establishment existed. Further, he did not like the idea of extending freedom of conscience to "those who professed no religion at all." In an effort to resolve Huntington's concern about application to established state religions, Madison proposed inserting the word "national" before "religion," but Gerry objected to any use of the word "national," because the Constitution created a federal form of government, not a national government. Madison argued that he did not mean to imply that the government was a national one, but he withdrew his suggestion nonetheless.

Representative Samuel Livermore had objected to the committee language and proposed instead, "Congress shall make no laws touching religion, or infringing the rights of conscience." His proposal was voted upon and passed by a vote of thirty-one to twenty. However, apparently without any debate on the matter, the House voted to change the bill to read: "Congress shall make no law establishing religion, or to prevent the free exercise thereof, or to infringe the rights of conscience," and this was the version sent to the Senate. (See Appendix C for the Report from the Annals of Congress of the House Debates on August 15, 1789.)

The Senate considered the matter on September 3, 1789, in secret, so that the only thing known of their debates is the final version of the bill which they sent back to the House. The Senate version read: "Congress shall make no law establishing articles of faith or a mode of worship, or prohibiting the free exercise of religion."

The House did not accept the Senate's version but rather requested a joint conference to consider the bill. It was this conference that chose the language which both the House and Senate later accepted:

> Congress shall make no law respecting an establishment of religion, or prohibiting the free exercise thereof.

It should be mentioned that on the same day that Madison proposed the language that was modified to become a part of the First Amendment, he had also proposed inserting the provision within the body of the Constitution itself, in Article I, Section 9, between clauses 3 and 4. This suggestion was rejected and Congress provided for religious freedom in the First Amendment.

James Madison is recognized as the man primarily responsible for the federal protection of religious liberty. His role began in Virginia, continued through the Constitutional Convention and its ratification, peaked during the drafting of the First Amendment, and survived thereafter in the application of the law. It is fortunate for history that Madison left so much evidence of his thinking regarding the relationship of church and state.

In a 1947 Supreme Court case, Justice Rutledge summarized the importance of Madison's role in these words:

> Ratification thus accomplished, Madison was sent to the first Congress. There he went at once about performing his pledge to establish freedom for the nation as he had done in Virginia. Within a little more than three years from his legislative victory at home he had proposed and secured the submission and ratification of the First Amendment as the first article of our Bill of Rights.
> All the great instruments of the Virginia struggle for religious liberty thus became warp and woof of our constitutional tradition, not simply by

the course of history, but by the common unifying force of Madison's life, thought and sponsorship. He epitomized the whole of that tradition in the amendment's compact, but nonetheless comprehensive, phrasing.[13]

In the years since the adoption of the First Amendment, much use has been made of the writings of the forefathers to determine just what was meant by those sixteen words. Of particular importance was their recognition of the unique diversity of the American people and the need to protect the rights of all within that diversity.

13
DIVERSITY

There is not a shadow of right in the general government to intermeddle
with religion. Its least interference with it, would be a most flagrant
usurpation.

> —James Madison, *Journals,* June 12, 1788

There can be no doubt of Madison's absolute belief that government
has no place in matters of religion, yet the above-quoted remark was
made in the year following the Constitutional Convention, during the
period when he was urging ratification without an amendment to protect religious liberty. Madison claimed that his "uniform conduct on
this subject" evidenced his constant warm support for religious freedom,
and it is therefore apparent that in his own mind he remained true to
the principles set down in his Memorial & Remonstrance, written in
1785. Since he had experienced no change of heart, what were his reasons for urging ratification without an amendment assuring freedom of
conscience? To Jefferson he had written that he felt the right had been
reserved in the grant of federal powers, that he feared a narrowly drafted
declaration, and that he questioned the efficacy of a bill of rights on the
question of religion. In his *Journals,* he stated a fourth reason: "Happily
for the states, they enjoy the utmost freedom of religion. This freedom
arises from that multiplicity of sects, which pervades America, and
which is the best and only security for religious liberty in any society.
For where there is such a variety of sects, there cannot be a majority of
any one sect to oppress and persecute the rest."[1]

This wealth of variety, he reasoned, was a national characteristic that
might not be present in individual states or localities. In a smaller area
one religion could dominate and oppress all others, and thus he warned
against local control of religious matters. "It is better that this security
should be depended upon from the general legislature, than from one
particular state. A particular state might concur in one religious project-
But the United States abound in such a variety of sects, that it is a

101

strong security against religious persecution, and it is sufficient to authorize a conclusion, that no one sect will ever be able to outnumber or depress the rest."[2] Thus, Madison explained why he felt the federal government was free from any threat of an establishment, even without a bill of rights to that effect, although states would not be.

During the ratification period, at the instigation of Alexander Hamilton, essays were written in support of the Constitution. The essay on Checks & Balances, appearing as #51 in the *Federalist Papers*, was written by Madison, and he restated the essential significance of diversity in the effective functioning of the new government.

> . . . in the federal republic of the United States Whilst all authority in it will be derived from and dependent on the society, the society itself will be broken into so many parts, interests and classes of citizens, that the rights of individuals, or of the minority, will be in little danger from interested combinations of the majority. In a free government the security for civil rights must be the same as that for religious rights. It consists in the one case in the multiplicity of interests, and in the other in the multiplicity of sects. The degree of security in both cases will depend on the number of interests and sects; and this may be presumed to depend on the extent of country and number of people comprehended under the same government.

An interesting parallel to Madison's opinion was expressed by the Reverend Ezra Stiles, a New England Puritan who led the opposition to an Anglican bishop and who served as president of Yale College. He said in his Discourse on the Christian Union, written in 1760, that, "Providence has planted the British America with a variety of sects, which will unavoidably become a mutual balance upon one another. Their temporary collisions . . . after a short ebullition, will subside in harmony and union, not by the destruction of either but in the friendly cohabitation of all. . . . Resplendent and all-pervading TRUTH will terminate the whole in universal harmony."[3] Writing to a fellow Congregationalist minister, he further said, "our great security is in the multitude of sects and the public Liberty necessary for them to cohabit together. In consequence of which the aggrieved of any communion will wither pass over to another, or rise into new sects and spontaneous societies."[4]

In 1831, a young Frenchman visited America and recorded his observations in a book entitled *Democracy in America*. Alexis de Tocqueville was amazed by the young nation, and the part religion played in America he found most remarkable. Accustomed to Old World practices, specifically those in France, where he had "almost always seen the spirit of religion and the spirit of freedom marching in opposite directions,"[5] he found America a complete contradiction. "The philosophers of the eighteenth century explained in a very simple manner the gradual decay of religious faith. Religious zeal, said they, must necessarily fail the more generally liberty is established and knowledge diffused. Unfortunately, the facts by no means accord with their theory. There are certain populations in Europe whose unbelief is only equalled by their ignorance and debasement; while in America, one of the freest and most enlightened nations in the world, the people fulfill with fervor all the outward duties of religion."[6]

Trying to understand why the philosophers had been wrong, at least with respect to America, de Tocqueville could not help but notice the extreme diversity present in America.

> The sects that exist in the United States are innumerable. They all differ in respect to the worship which is due to the Creator; but they all agree in respect to the duties which are due from man to man. Each sect adores the Deity in its own particular manner, but all sects preach the same moral law in the name of God. . . . [P]rovided the citizens profess a religion, the peculiar tenets of that religion are of little importance to its interests. Moreover, all the sects of the United States are comprised within the great unity of Christianity, and Christian morality is everywhere the same.
>
> It may fairly be believed that a certain number of Americans pursue a peculiar form of worship from habit more than from conviction. In the United States the sovereign authority is religious, and consequently hypocrisy must be common; but there is no country in the world where the Christian religion retains a greater influence over the souls of men than in America; and there can be no greater proof of its utility and of its conformity to human nature than that its influence is powerfully felt over the most enlightened and free nation of the earth.[7]

His observation that America at that time was principally a Christian nation was correct. Even as religious tolerance had crept into the colonies, it had first been extended only to other Protestants, then gradually to other Christians. Only the Rhode Island charter went so far as to welcome people of all faiths, providing that in that colony people could "freelye and fullye have and enjoye his and theire own judgments and consciences, in matters of religious concernments." No wonder Roger Williams caused such shock when he expressed his opinion that "It is the will and command of God that (since the comming of his Sonne the Lord Jesus) a permission of the most Paganish, Jewish, Turkish, or Antichristian consciences and worships, bee granted to all men in all Nations and countries."[8] The Hanover Presbytery was indeed enlightened to have included in their petition to the Virginia Assembly the statement that "there is no argument in favour of establishing the Christian religion, but what may be pleaded, with equal propriety, for establishing the tenets of Mahomed by those who believe the Alcoran."[9] While the American religious tradition was definitely Christian, nevertheless, the founding fathers provided no distinction or special privilege to members of any faith.

In fact, Thomas Jefferson expressed his belief that uniformity of belief was both impossible and undesirable to achieve. He warned against the dangers of government getting involved in enforcing certain opinions. "It is error alone," he said, "which needs the support of government. Truth can stand by itself. Subject opinions to coercion: whom will you make your inquisitors? Fallible men; men governed by bad passions, by private as well as public reasons. And why subject it to coercion? To produce uniformity. But is uniformity of opinion desireable? No more than that of face and stature. . . . "[10]

Jefferson continued with his assessment of the benefits of diversity and why governments must protect that diversity during times when religion seems least in danger of abuse. "Difference of opinion is advantageous in religion. The several sects perform the office of censor morum over each other. Is uniformity attainable? Millions of innocent men, women, and children, since the introduction of Christianity, have been burnt, tortured, fined, imprisoned; yet we have not advanced one inch towards uniformity. What has been the effect of coercion? To make one half the world fools, and the other half hypocrites. . . . Besides, the spirit of the times may alter, will alter. Our rulers will become corrupt, our people careless. A single zealot may commence prosecutor, and better men be his victims. It can never be too often repeated, that the time for fixing every essential right on a legal basis is while our rulers are honest, and ourselves united."[11]

Although de Tocqueville was from the Old World, he shared with the founding fathers the view that unity of church and state is disadvantageous to both. The things he saw while visiting America only reinforced that view. "[B]ut when a religion contracts an alliance of this nature, I do not hesitate to affirm that it commits the same error as a man who would sacrifice his future to his present welfare; and in obtaining a power to which he has no claim, it risks that authority which is rightfully its own."[12]

Diversity, therefore, not only gave rise to the need for religious liberty in America but also served as the best protection against a single national establishment. However, diversity alone could not be relied upon to protect minority sects in smaller localities, where the majority might impose its beliefs. The religious practice of the colonies evidenced the likelihood of the majorities to establish their particular church, and the experience in Georgia showed that this could happen even in a colony rich in religious diversity. The multiple establishments, such as New York employed, allowed majorities in smaller political subdivisions to determine the established church for their locality, but diversity afforded no protection to the minority sects within each locality.

The only absolute protection against the majority imposing its spiritual will upon the minority lay in complete separation of church and state. The First Amendment was enacted to ensure greater protection than would arise through the natural effects of religious diversity, and the application of the First Amendment's protections by politicians and judges has determined the extent of actual separation between church and state in America.

14
IMPLEMENTATION

I dare not look beyond my nose into futurity. Our money, our commerce,
our religion, our National and State Constitutions, even our arts and sci-
ences, are so many seed plots, of division, faction, sedition and rebellion.
—John Adams to Thomas Jefferson

Despite the prediction of John Adams that the nation's religions were
seed plots of rebellion, religious disputes have not grown the bitter fruits
of division and rebellion that he feared, although many disagreements
have sprouted since the First Amendment was written. Even in the
years soon after its enactment, difficulties were encountered in applying
the law.

In the spring of 1789, a few months before Congress labored over the
right words to use in protecting religious liberty in America, George
Washington did not hesitate to begin his term as president by recognizing God's presence in the making of America and in asking for His
continued blessing. Nor was he reluctant to declare his assurance that he
spoke for all of the citizens:

> It would be peculiarly improper to omit in this first official Act, my
> fervent supplication to that Almighty Being who rules over the Universe,
> who presides in the Councils of Nations, and whose providential aids can
> supply every human defect, that his benediction may consecrate to the
> liberties and happiness of the People of the United States, a Government
> instituted by themselves for these essential purposes: and may enable ev-
> ery instrument employed in its administration to execute with success, the
> functions allotted to his charge. In tendering this homage to the Great
> Author of every public and private good, I assure myself that it expresses
> your sentiments not less than my own; nor those of my fellow-citizens at
> large, less than either. No People can be bound to acknowledge and adore
> the invisible hand, which conducts the Affairs of men more than the
> People of the United States. Every step, by which they have advanced to
> the character of an independent nation, seems to have been distinguished
> by some token of providential agency. [1]

During the consideration by the Virginia Assembly of the general assessment for support of religious teachers, Washington had expressed his opinion that, "I am not amongst the number of those, who are so much alarmed at the thoughts of making people pay towards the support of that which they profess."[2] In 1797 he had written to an interdenominational group of clergymen in Philadelphia that he believed "*Religion* and *Morality* are the essential pillars of Civil society."[3] Upon resigning his commission at the close of the Revolutionary War, Washington addressed Congress with these words: "I consider it an indispensable duty to close this last solemn act of my official life by commending the interests of our dearest country to the protection of Almighty God, and those who have superintendance of them, to his holy keeping."[4] George Washington clearly perceived God as ever present in the conduct of affairs of the new nation and did not pretend to separate his religious from his political life.

That is not to say that Washington did not favor religious freedom, and throughout his public life he stated the importance of each man worshipping as he pleased. During the first autumn of his presidency, shortly after Congress had accepted the language to protect that liberty, Washington sent his reply to an address from a five-state meeting of Quakers. He wrote, "Government being, among other purposes, instituted to protect the persons and consciences of men from oppression, it certainly is the duty of rulers, not only to abstain from it themselves, but according to their stations, to prevent it in others." Washington continued, "The liberty enjoyed by the people of these States, of worshipping Almighty God agreeably to their consciences, is not only among the choicest of their *blessings,* but also of their *rights.* While men perform their social duties faithfully, they do all that society or the state can with propriety demand or expect; and remain responsible only to their Maker for the religion, or modes of faith, which they may prefer or profess."[5] There are countless examples of Washington's belief "that every man, conducting himself as a good citizen, and being accountable to God alone for his religious opinions, ought to be protected in worshipping the Deity according to the dictates of his own conscience."[6]

However, with regard to the First Amendment, Washington's emphasis was clearly upon the "free exercise" portion of the law, which he vigorously endorsed, rather than in prohibiting any establishment, which, as he had admitted in Virginia, he did not find particularly alarming. Accordingly, it was Washington who set the precedent of proclaiming the first Thanksgiving Day under the new Constitution, with these words:

> Whereas it is the duty of all Nations to acknowledge the providence of Almighty God, to obey his will, to be grateful for his benefits, and humbly to implore his protection and favor, and Whereas both Houses of

Congress have by their joint Committee requested me to recommend to
the People of the United States a day of public thanks-giving and prayer to
be observed by acknowledging with grateful hearts the many signal favors
of Almighty God, especially by affording them an opportunity peaceably
to establish a form of government for their safety and happiness.

Now therefore I do recommend and assign Thursday the 26th day of
November next to be devoted by the People of these States to the Service
of that great and glorious Being, who is the beneficent Author of all the
good that was, that is, or that will be. That we may then all unite in
rendering unto him our sincere and humble thanks, . . . [7]

Once the precedent had been established, later Presidents found it
difficult not to follow. Even James Madison, who had shown his courage in supporting religious liberty against popular sentiment, continued
the precedent begun by Washington. He expressed his feelings about
having issued Executive Proclamations for days of thanksgiving and fasts
in a letter written in 1822, after his years as president. "There has been
another deviation from the strict principle in the Executive Proclamations of fasts and festivals, so far, at least, as they have spoken the language of injunction, or have lost sight of the equality of all religious
sects in the eye of the Constitution. Whilst I was honored with the
Executive Trust I found it necessary on more than one occasion to follow
the example of predecessors. But I was always careful to make the Proclamations absolutely indiscriminate, and merely recommendatory; or
rather mere designations of a day, on which all who thought proper
might unite in consecrating it to religious purposes, according to their
own faith & forms."[8]

Thomas Jefferson, on the other hand, could not personally reconcile
the prohibition against religious establishment contained in the First
Amendment with the chief executive issuing a proclamation designating
a day as set aside for religious activities. During the second year of his
presidency, Jefferson received an inquiry from a group of Baptists concerning the designation of a day of fasting for the nation. Jefferson used
their correspondence as an opportunity to address the question of the
propriety of such proclamations. Before sending his reply, Jefferson prudently sought the counsel of Attorney General Levi Lincoln. The following is extracted from Jefferson's letter to Lincoln: "It furnishes an
occasion, too, which I have long wished to find, of saying why I do not
proclaim fastings and thanksgivings, as my predecessors did. . . . I
know it will give great offence to the New England clergy; but the
advocate of religious freedom is to expect neither peace nor forgiveness
from them."[9]

The letter that Jefferson sent to the Danbury Baptist Association on
January 1, 1802, contains the phrase that has so often since been used
with reference to the First Amendment, "a wall of separation between
Church and State." The full text of Jefferson's letter to the Baptists of

Danbury is contained in Appendix D, but the portion that dealt with the issue of executive proclamations is as follows:

> Believing with you that religion is a matter which lies solely between man and his God, that he owes account to none other for his faith or his worship, that the legislative powers of government reach actions only, and not opinions, I contemplate with sovereign reverence that act of the whole American people which declared that their legislature should 'make no law respecting an establishment of religion, or prohibiting the free exercise thereof,' thus building a wall of separation between Church and State. Adhering to this expression of the supreme will of the nation in behalf of the rights of conscience, I shall see with sincere satisfaction the progress of those sentiments which tend to restore to man all his natural rights, convinced he has no natural right in opposition to his social duties.[10]

It is interesting that Jefferson used a phrase that has often been cited in support of curtailing governmental intrusion in matters of religion in reference to a practice that has not been curtailed. Jefferson's stand against presidential proclamations did not reverse the precedent.

Although the strong imagery evoked by Jefferson's "wall of separation" has engrafted that language onto most writings dealing with the First Amendment, Madison used nearly the same expression in a letter he wrote in 1832. In that letter, Madison acknowledged that judges face difficult decisions under the law. "I must admit moreover that it may not be easy, in every possible case, to trace the line of separation between the rights of religion and the civil authority with such distinctness as to avoid collisions and doubts on unessential points. The tendency to a usurpation on one side or the other, or to a corrupting coalition or alliance between them, will be best guarded against by an entire abstinence of the Government from interference in any way whatever, beyond the necessity of preserving public order, and protecting each sect against trespass on its legal rights by others."[11] Judges today who have faced the delicate task of applying the First Amendment to real situations, especially when the free exercise portion of the law seems to conflict with the prohibition against establishment, might agree that their task is more of a fragile tracing of a line than it is the obvious building of a wall. Regardless of imagery, however, both Jefferson and Madison insisted upon the crucial importance of maintaining the separation of church and state.

Another deviation from the strict principle of separation about which Madison expressed his disapproval was the appointment of congressional chaplains who were paid from public funds. He wrote, " . . . it was not with my approbation, that the deviation from it took place in Congress, when they appointed Chaplains, to be paid from the National Treasury. It would have been a much better proof to their Constituents of their pious feeling if the members had contributed for the purpose, a pittance from their own pockets."[12]

Even in their own lifetimes, the founding fathers who possessed the wisdom to include religious liberty in the First Amendment did not always possess the objectivity to apply it to themselves! It is complicated to separate church and state in a nation where religious faith has played such a significant, if not the key role throughout, yet that separation has allowed religion to march alongside the growth of America. That delicate teaming of separate elements was noted by de Tocqueville when he wrote: "Religion in America takes no direct part in the government of society, but it must be regarded as the first of their political institutions; for if it does not impart a taste for freedom, it facilitates the use of it. Indeed, it is in this same point of view that the inhabitants of the United States themselves look upon religious belief. I do not know whether all Americans have a sincere faith in their religion—for who can search the human heart?—but I am certain that they hold it to be indispensable to the maintenance of republican institutions. This opinion is not peculiar to a class of citizens or to a party, but it belongs to the whole nation and to every rank of society."[13] Although he wrote these words in 1832, he would probably find it true today that most Americans believe much of the nation's political strength lies in the spiritual strength of its citizens. He would find it less true, however, that religion takes no direct part in government or that people believe separation protects religious liberty.

Many people today may never have considered the viewpoint expressed by Madison when he described the experience in Virginia by saying: "It was the Universal opinion of the Century preceding the last, that Civil Government could not stand without the prop of a Religious establishment, and that the Christian religion itself, would perish if not supported by a legal provision for its clergy. The experience of Virginia conspicuously corroborates the disproof of both opinions. The Civil Government, tho' bereft of everything like an associated hierarchy, possesses the requisite stability and performs its functions with complete success; whilst the number, the industry, and the morality of the Priesthood, and the devotion of the people have been manifestly increased by the total separation of the Church from the State."[14]

In his old age, John Adams wrote to his friend Jefferson, "[W]e may say that the Eighteenth Century, notwithstanding all its errors and vices, has been, of all that are past, the most honorable to human nature. . . . But what are we to say now? Is the Nineteenth Century to be a contrast to the Eighteenth? Is it to extinguish all the lights of its predecessor?"[15] Perhaps the founding fathers would be amazed that the Constitution and Bill of Rights have served so long and so well, and although they deserve much credit for the writing of those documents, so also the United States Supreme Court deserves much credit for the preservation of the ideals those laws represent.

15

THE UNITED STATES SUPREME COURT

No higher duty, no more solemn responsibility, rests upon this Court than
that of translating into living law and maintaining this constitutional
shield deliberately planned and inscribed for the benefit of every human
being subject to our Constitution—of whatever race, creed or persuasion.
—Justice Hugo Black

The United States Supreme Court was born with the Constitution in
Article III, but its character awaited later formation. The Constitution
established "one supreme Court" but provided very little definition. The
first steps in defining the federal court system were taken by the Congress of 1789 with the passage of the Judiciary Act. Two days after its
passage, President Washington presented his nominations for the Supreme Court, but not without some difficulty. The Court was originally
perceived as having so little significance in the new government that
some of the president's original choices declined the honor of serving on
the Court.

The first members were Chief Justice John Jay of New York, and
Associate Justices John Blair of Virginia, William Cushing of Massachusetts, James Iredell of North Carolina, John Rutledge of South Carolina,
and James Wilson of Pennsylvania. Three of these men had served their
states at the Constitutional Convention and all of them were known to
be strong supporters of the Constitution. Their first meeting was held in
the Royal Exchange Building in New York City on February 2, 1790,
and the importance of the meeting was considered so minor that not all
of the justices even attended. During the Court's first decade, there were
some important decisions rendered out of a total of about fifty cases
decided, but the power and prestige of the Court had not fully evolved.

That evolution surged forward with the appointment of John Marshall as chief justice in 1801. He served the Court until 1835, and
during those thirty-four years he provided much of the definition that
the Constitution had omitted. In the process, Marshall also did a great
deal to define America, imposing a strong national government over

111

what had been a loose union of proud, and largely independent states. The ambiguity and absence of definition in the constitutional provisions regarding the Court allowed Marshall and other justices to gradually build its power and prestige without attracting particular attention, resulting in a stronger federal court system than would probably ever have gained the approval of all the states at the Constitutional Convention.

By the end of Marshall's life, the Court had assumed its position of equal dignity with the executive and legislative branches of government, and although there have been years during the past century and a half when its reputation and influence have waned, the Court has maintained the power Marshall asserted. Despite the respect with which the Court is regarded by most Americans, very few citizens really understand the manner in which the Court functions. It would be impossible in a single chapter to fully explore the structure of the United States Supreme Court, but the next pages will summarize the functioning of the Court to the extent necessary to better understand its role in interpreting and applying that portion of the First Amendment dealing with religion.

In considering the actual powers of the Supreme Court, the symbolic powers it also possesses must not be ignored, for its influence over the American people may be as significant as the legal effect of the Court's decisions. America has few popular philosophers, and the words of Supreme Court justices have often been quoted as expressing the American conscience. One writer described the role of the Court as it applies to the common citizen as follows: "That court is commissioned to interpret to us our own purposes, our own meanings. To a self-governing community it must make clear what, in actual practice, self-governing is. And its teaching has peculiar importance because it interprets principles of fact and of value, not merely in the abstract, but also in their bearing upon the concrete, immediate problems which are, at any given moment, puzzling and dividing us."[1] That is to say that while the Court does its job in the legal sense, it also serves the concerns of the rest of the population by showing them how the laws they have written through their representatives are working, or not working. As another analyst put it, "We accept the Court as a symbol in the measure that, while performing its appointed tasks, it manages at the same time to articulate and rationalize the aspirations reflected in the Constitution."[2]

When legislators, on both the state and federal levels, are writing laws, they are dealing with immediate problems of concern to their constituents. They are trying to find solutions on a near term basis, and, not incidentally, trying to please enough of their constituents with the solution they adopt to gain reelection. Supreme Court justices, on the other hand, are appointed, according to Article III of the Constitution, for life, subject only to good behavior, and this results in a different perspective with respect to the laws enacted by the legislatures. Supreme Court Justice Learned Hand commented on this difference by saying, "Judges are perhaps more apt than legislators to take a long view, but that varies so much with the individual that generalization is hazardous."[3] Nevertheless, the training and experience of judges and lawyers, relying on a body of law which has evolved over centuries, is more apt to emphasize the long-term effect than the short-term solution. This distinguishes them from legislators as much or more than the consideration of having or not having to face the voters on election day.

Regardless of their role on the Supreme Court, justices are people, each with his or her own attitudes and values. Justice Hand addressed the effect of individual personalities on issues before the Court by saying, "No doubt it is inevitable, however circumscribed his duty may be, that the personal proclivities of an interpreter will to some extent interject themselves into the meaning he imputes to a text, but in very much the greater part of a judge's duties he is charged with freeing himself as far as he can from all personal preferences, and that becomes difficult in proportion as these are strong."[4] It is only natural that when people disagree with a decision rendered by the Court, they accuse the justices of ruling according to personal prejudices and preferences rather than in accordance with the law. Understanding how the Court functions should help you to decide whether the justices who have interpreted the First Amendment over the years have freed themselves of personal preferences in interpreting its sixteen words dealing with religion.

Supreme Court Justice Felix Frankfurter explained the difficulty in discerning the individual thoughts of the persons who serve as justices on the Court because of the manner in which opinions are written. He said, "The obvious map to the minds of the justices—the opinions of the Court—is deceptive precisely because they are the opinions of the Court. They are symphonies, not solos."[5] While this analogy is correct when all of the justices join in one opinion, there is provision for solo voices in the writing of Supreme Court opinions. When a case is considered by the Court, the Chief Justice, if he is among the majority, assigns a justice to write the majority opinion. If all of the justices join in that one opinion, it is the only one written. However, if a justice agrees with the decision of the majority but not the reasoning behind the decision, he or she may write a concurring opinion. This means that the concurring opinion is counted as having voted with the majority in the decision rendered, but the basis for his or her vote was not necessarily the same as that of the majority. Finally, if a justice disagrees with the majority decision, he or she may write a dissenting opinion. Obviously, the dissenter was against the decision rendered by the majority. Justices who do not write separate opinions may join in the opinion of any of the three types of opinions—majority, concurring, or dissenting. Only the majority opinion has the force of law, but the concurring and dissenting opinions often are relied upon to aid in understanding the thinking of the Court in reaching its decision, and many times they foretell the direction in which the Court may be headed in deciding related cases. Sometimes the dissenting view, a few years later, becomes the majority opinion.

Most Americans ignore the significance of the number of justices voting with the majority when a decision is handed down by the court. They react only to the decision itself, the bottom line so to speak. However, it is not difficult to see that a 9–0 decision with all of the justices joining in the majority opinion is much stronger and less likely to be subsequently altered than a 5–4 decision in which four separate concurring opinions were written and four justices dissented. That means that only the author of the majority opinion fully accepted the reasoning it expresses, although the four justices who concurred agreed with the decision itself. Obviously, such a decision is very vulnerable to being modified or overruled if a later case dealing with the same issue is heard by the Court. One of the concurring justices may change his or her mind or a new justice may have been appointed since the last case was heard. Therefore, the manner in which each justice voted and how many justices chose to write separate opinions or join in an opinion other than the majority opinion indicates the strength of the decision. In addition, when Supreme Court cases are quoted, writers sometimes fail to identify whether the quote is taken from the majority or a concurring or dissenting opinion, but only the majority opinion states the law to be applied from the case. Concurring or dissenting opinions sometimes find greater public acceptance, and with the arrival of new members on the Court, may become the majority view when a new case is heard. As Justice Oliver Wendell Holmes said, "The history of the Supreme Court is not the history of an abstraction, but the analysis of individuals acting as a Court who make decisions and lay down doctrines, and of other individuals, their successors, who refine, modify, and sometimes even overrule the decisions of their predecessors, reinterpreting and transmuting their doctrines. In law, also, men make a difference."[6]

Unlike the Congress, which may introduce bills dealing with any subject of concern to the country, the Supreme Court can only consider issues that are presented to it in the form of actual cases. The previous paragraph explained that the Court may change its opinion, but any change must await the presentation of an actual case dealing with that issue. Until such a case comes before the Court, the old decision remains the law, even though the present members of the Court may disagree with the prior ruling.

Among the types of cases heard by the Court are those involving the United States Constitution. In the very beginning, there was the belief that since the three branches of the government—executive, legislative, and judicial—were equal, they therefore shared the responsibility to protect and interpret the Constitution. Gradually, the Supreme Court established itself as the sole interpreter. There remain differences of opinion, however, concerning the extent to which interpretation should be taken. On the one hand are those who believe the powers of the Court should be strictly construed so that the justices do not intrude into the legislative territory in writing policy. Opposing this strict view are those who believe that the Court must keep the Constitution alive by reinventing it to accommodate present-day situations. It would be impossible for the Court to function without a certain degree of policymaking resulting from its decisions, but it must balance that need with respect for the legislative branch of the government. Interpretation relies primarily upon three methods: plain meaning, legislative intent, and precedent.

If the words of the Constitution are clear and specific, and they address the exact situation presented in the case, the Court will apply the plain meaning of the law. In fact, very few cases of this sort ever reach the Supreme Court because few litigants disagree over matters of obvious legal interpretation, and if they do disagree, lower courts quickly dispose of the matter. The cases that come before the Supreme Court are more complicated.

If the meaning of the words is not so obvious, the Court tries to determine what the legislature meant when it wrote the law and to give effect to the legislative intent. It is for this reason that the writings of James Madison have been so important to the Court in interpreting the First Amendment. In relying upon the expressions of Madison's views concerning the subjects of religious freedom and establishment, the Court has sought to discern the legislative intent of the authors of the First Amendment. Madison is consulted as a member of the Congress that passed the amendment, and more specifically, as its author and sponsor, and his words are of more significance than those of other historical figures of that period who were not a part of the legislative process in the writing and passage of the First Amendment.

A third means of interpreting the Constitution is through an examination of precedent opinions. If a case comes before the Court that involves issues that have never been considered before, it is called a case of first impression, but few cases are without precedent. Instead, the law has been built, case by case, over the centuries, and when judges consider a new case, they look to the past to see what has been said by judges ruling on these same issues in prior cases. It is for this reason that an understanding of any decision, including First Amendment cases, must begin with a review of prior cases dealing with that issue. While it is possible for the Supreme Court to overrule a precedent opinion, they are very reluctant to do so, and they must be convinced of the necessity. This reluctance derives from the justices' respect for the wisdom of their predecessors and also from the need for continuity in the law. People need to be able to depend upon the meaning of a law and not to feel concerned that the law will change each time a new justice is appointed to the Court. Chief Justice John Marshall spoke of the need for permanence with these words: "That the people have an original right to establish, for their future government such principles as, in their opinion, shall most conduce to their own happiness, is the basis on which the whole American fabric has been erected. The exercise of this original right is a very great exertion; nor can it, nor ought it, to be frequently repeated. The principles, therefore, so established, are deemed fundamental: and as the authority from which they proceed is supreme, and can seldom act, they are designed to be permanent."[7] The Chief Justice who immediately followed Marshall was Roger Taney. In an 1849 opinion, he spoke of the Court's responsibility to balance the need for permanence with the need for appropriate modifications of interpretation. He said that the Supreme Court's " . . . opinion upon the construction of the Constitution is always open to discussion when it is supposed to have been founded in error, and that its judicial authority should hereafter depend altogether on the force of the reasoning by which it is supported."[8] Clearly, the Court will not overrule precedent lightly, but we shall see that in a pair of cases heard within three years of each other, the so-called Flag Salute Cases,[9] the Court did not hesitate to set aside an opinion which they no longer believed was correct. Prior precedent is generally honored, but the Court will not be bound by it, whether it is ancient or new, if the Court believes it is wrong.

From this brief discussion, it is clear that the Supreme Court does not have unlimited power to detour the Constitution in some false direction dictated by the personal whim of one justice or group of justices. First of all, there must be an actual case with the issue to be determined present in the facts of the controversy. Second, the justices act as a team, working together to arrive at a majority decision, but allowing independent opinions if a single, common view cannot be reached. While the majority opinion states the law, the concurring and dissenting opinions restrict the ability of one justice or group of justices to dominate the Court. Third, if the Constitution has a plain meaning, that must be applied. Fourth, if the legislative intent is discernible, it will be given effect. This is not true, however, in the case of statutes that are found to be unconstitutional. Finally, the Court is overwhelmingly guided by centuries of legal precedent.

As the highest court in America, the Supreme Court naturally gets the tough cases, the cases in which the facts are complicated and lower courts have found few precedents to guide them. As Chief Justice John

Marshall said, "The judiciary cannot, as the legislature may, avoid a measure because it approaches the confines of the Constitution. We cannot pass it by because it is doubtful. With whatever doubts, with whatever difficulties a case may be attended, we must decide it if it be brought before us. We have no more right to decline the exercise of jurisdiction which is given, than to usurp that which is not given."[10] A century and a half later, Chief Justice Earl Warren quoted those words as the concept that guided him as well.

One of the problems that the Supreme Court faces today is that America has changed a great deal since the Constitution was written, and it is impossible to determine the founding fathers' legislative intent with reference to the application of the Constitution to certain situations because such a situation would never have been within the contemplation, or even the imagination of the legislative body that wrote the Constitution. As Chief Justice Warren said, "The problems that confront the Court in these days are so complex and their special circumstances are so far beyond the vision of even the wisest of the Founding Fathers that it would be impossible to find specific words in precedent cases to justify every decision reached. The Founding Fathers were aware of this. They contemplated expansion of the Union under changed conditions and wrote the Constitution as broadly as possible to permit adjustment to such changes."[11] It is when the Court makes these "adjustments" that its critics claim abuse of judicial power and argue that the present Court is bound by the intent of the original authors of the Constitution.

Chief Justice Hughes, who served during the decade of the nineteen thirties, expressed the impossibility of such restriction upon interpretation. He said, "It is no answer to say that this public need was not apprehended a century ago, or to insist that what the provision of the Constitution meant to the vision of that day it must mean to the vision of our time. If by the statement that what the Constitution meant at the time of its adoption it means to-day, it is intended to say that the great clauses of the Constitution must be confined to the interpretation which the framers, with the conditions and outlook of their time, would have placed upon them, the statement carries its own refutation."[12] Justice Holmes also commented upon the responsibility to carry forward the work of the original framers when he said, " . . . we must realize that they have called into life a being the development of which could not have been foreseen completely by the most gifted of its begettors. It was enough for them to realize or to hope that they had created an organism; it has taken a century and has cost their successors much sweat and blood to prove that they created a nation."[13] To those who demanded that the Court remove itself from policymaking and simply apply the law of the Constitution as written, Holmes answered, " . . . the provisions of the Constitution are not mathematical formulas having their essence in their form; they are organic living institutions transplanted from English soil. Their significance is vital not formal; it is to be gathered not simply by taking the words and a dictionary, but by considering their origin and the line of their growth."[14] Chief Justice Rehnquist, on the other hand, is extremely cautious in this regard. He has said, "to go beyond the language of the constitution, and the meaning that may be fairly ascribed to the language, and into the consciences of individual judges, is to embark on a journey that is treacherous indeed."[15]

When the Supreme Court makes what Chief Justice Warren called an adjustment to change, people who agree with the decision applaud the wisdom of the Court. Those who disagree threaten impeachment and seek a way around the decision. Chief Justice Burger described some available options. "It is clear that when Congress disagrees with the judicial interpretation of a statute, Congress can enact a new statute that supersedes that judicial interpretation. Congress has done this many times in our history. Similarly, in four instances Congress and the state legislatures have overridden a Supreme Court opinion through constitutional amendment. Furthermore, when appointments are made to the Supreme Court, it is surely not unnatural that presidents try to appoint, subject to Senate confirmation, justices who they hope will interpret the Constitution 'properly.' "[16]

Overriding an opinion by means of a constitutional amendment presents a formidable task. First of all, the Congress is reluctant to tamper with the Constitution. Second, the requirement of a two-thirds majority in each house of Congress presents a difficult obstacle, and likewise, Article V of the Constitution requires application by two-thirds of the state legislatures for Congress to call a convention for the purpose of proposing an amendment. Finally, however, the greatest impediment to overriding a Supreme Court decision dealing with the Bill of Rights is that such an amendment would obviously affect the liberties those first ten amendments were written to protect. There is extreme reluctance to limit the protections of liberty assured by the Bill of Rights, and no constitutional amendment has ever done so.[17]

There is another means that might be employed by Congress to defeat the Court's power over a particular subject, and although it has often been threatened and sometimes even attempted, it has never been successfully used by Congress. That is the removal of subject matter jurisdiction from the Court. Although untested, Congress probably has the power to limit the Court's jurisdiction over a certain category of cases, such as cases involving the issue of public school prayer, and this power could be exercised without the two-thirds majority required of a constitutional amendment and presentment to the states for ratification. Why, then, have such attempts failed?

The answer, of course, would have to come from the members of Congress who refused to support such efforts, but their reasons might be found in the strong statement issued by the Senate Committee on the Judiciary in 1937 when President Roosevelt attempted to enlarge the number of justices on the Supreme Court and pack it with appointees whose philosophies were akin to his own. The Senate committee said, "Shall we now, after 150 years of loyalty to the constitutional ideal of an untrammeled judiciary, duty bound to protect the constitutional rights of the humblest citizen against the Government itself, create the vicious precedent which must necessarily undermine our system? . . . Let us, of the Seventy-fifth Congress, in words that will never be disregarded by any succeeding Congress, declare that we would rather have an independent court, a fearless court, a court that will dare to announce its honest opinions in what it believes to be the defense of liberties of the people, than a court that, out of fear or sense of obligation to the appointing power or factional passion, approves any measure we may enact. We are not the judges of the judges. We are not above the Constitution."[18]

Another reason may lie in the fact that removal from the federal Supreme Court would not place the power in Congress but rather would allow state judiciaries, over whom Congress has no control, to decide these cases. As the United States Supreme Court said in 1855: "[O]ur national union would be incomplete and altogether insufficient for the great ends contemplated, unless a constitutional arbiter was provided to give certainty and uniformity, in all of the States, to the interpretation of the constitution and the legislation of congress; with powers also to declare judicially what acts of the legislatures of the States might be in conflict with either."[19] Or, as the Supreme Court said even earlier, in 1816: "Judges of equal learning and integrity, in different states, might differently interpret a statute . . . or even the constitution itself. . . . The public mischiefs that would attend such a state of things would be truly deplorable. . . ."[20]

When the school prayer amendment he favored was defeated in 1984, Jesse Helms announced on the Senate floor, "There is more than one way to skin a cat, and there is more than one way for Congress to provide a check on arrogant Supreme Court Justices who routinely distort the Constitution to suit their own notions of public policy."[21] One of the ways Senator Helms had already tried was Senate Bill 481, which he introduced on February 16, 1981, and which read in part, " . . . the Supreme Court shall not have jurisdiction to review, by appeal, writ of certiorari, or otherwise, any case arising out of any State statute, ordinance, rule, regulation, or any part thereof, or arising out of any act interpreting, applying or enforcing a State statute, ordinance, rule, or regulation, which relates to voluntary prayers in public schools and public buildings."[22] The Helms bill failed.

Most legal commentators agree that Congress may possess the power to limit subject matter jurisdiction, as Senator Helms and others have tried to do. The Court discussed the power of Congress to limit its power to hear certain cases in *Ex parte McCardle:*[23] "We are not at liberty to inquire into the motives of the Legislature. We can only examine into its power under the Constitution; and the power to make exceptions to the appellate jurisdiction of this court is given by express words. What, then, is the effect of the repealing Act upon the case before us? We cannot doubt as to this. Without jurisdiction the court cannot proceed at all in any cause. Jurisdiction is the power to declare the law, and when it ceases to exist, the only function remaining to the court is that of announcing the fact and dismissing the cause." *McCardle* dealt, of course, with removal of appellate jurisdiction by Congress and not with the limitation of subject matter jurisdiction. The disinclination of Congress to use that power, as a means to circumvent the more difficult requirements of amendment, shows legislative respect for the balance of power among the three branches of government established by the Constitution—executive, legislative, and judicial. "Frequent, unreflective resort to the jurisdiction-limiting power would reduce to little more than a transient whisper the now powerful voice of the Court. . . . "[24] As one law professor said, "Some members of Congress undoubtedly have deep and principled objections to one or another of the Court's decisions, and others must find themselves the objects of intense political pressure to act against the Court. But these bills propose a gross breach of the institutional premises by which we have chosen to govern ourselves, and no legislator should succumb to their temptation."[25]

There is a further restraint upon the Court which has not been mentioned. Although the justices retain their seats upon the Court for life and do not have to face the American voter, the effect of the public's reaction to the decisions of the Court is significant. The justices are not subjected to the pressure from special interest groups and lobbyists to which legislators are subjected, but the Court cannot entirely ignore the American mood. The Court has no enforcement branch, and obviously its decisions would stand for nothing if the nation refused to comply and there were no enforcement methods to effect compliance. As an example, federal troops were employed to enforce compliance with the Supreme Court decision on desegregation but the order for their deployment came from the president and not from the Court. In the school prayer cases, the Supreme Court has had to rely upon the support of local school boards, classroom teachers, and administrators, and in some cases even today the decisions are ignored. For the most part, however, Americans do obey the law, even when its application by the Court is initially unpopular. One writer observed, "From time to time it has been said that the Court—by its decisions about slavery, about the New Deal, or about educational equality—has made trouble for the nation. It would be more accurate to say that the American people have made trouble for themselves by listening reverently and obediently to men who remind them of their past, who prefer legality to popularity. The uncanny American reverence for law has made possible the uncanny power and dignity of the American Supreme Court."[26]

When Supreme Court decisions are considered within the historical context of the times in which they were rendered, it can almost always be seen that there was a movement within the nation toward the decision. That historical context usually accounts for the case ever having arrived before the Court. Clearly, not every American agreed with the decisions on desegregation or legal counsel for the indigent or school prayer when they were written, but enough Americans did agree that the Court found public support and cooperation in enforcement.

Sometimes attendance to public opinion is essential to the Court's decision. For instance, the Eighth Amendment to the Constitution prohibits "cruel and unusual punishment" without attempting to describe just what that is. Types of punishment that found public support in seventeenth-century America, such as cutting off ears and thrusting irons through the tongue, would surely constitute cruel and unusual punishment to today's public. The death penalty is frequently attacked as being cruel and unusual, but the American public has not yet demanded that the Court declare it so. More often, the support of the public is sought not out of legal necessity, as in the case of the Eighth Amendment, but to insure more willing compliance with the law.

Desegregation was certainly easier in those communities in which the citizens complied with the Court's decision out of respect for the law than in those communities in which compliance was enforced by federal troops. For this reason, the Supreme Court considers public reaction and makes certain gestures to gain greater public acceptance. Obviously, the vehicle for such gestures is the Court's opinion. For example, the chief justice may have assigned a southern justice to write the majority opinion of an early case dealing with a racial issue. In the school prayer case, *Engel v. Vitale,* the opinion was written by Justice Black, a former Alabama Baptist Sunday school teacher. Sometimes the chief justice will assign the majority opinion to himself to lend the prestige of his position to the decision. Often, concurring opinions will be written to explain what the decision does not mean and to reassure the public, as was done in the case of *Abington School District v. Schempp,* prohibiting required Bible reading in public schools. Thus, although the Supreme Court does not answer to the popular will, it is not insensitive to the public sentiments of the times.

When a president has the opportunity to appoint several justices, he can influence the direction of the Court. As an example, between 1937 and 1943, President Roosevelt appointed eight members to the Court, with one position having to be filled twice. As a result, the previous 40 years of economic ultraconservatism were replaced with a period of economic liberalism. The fact remained, however, that while a common philosophy with regard to one issue was established through appointments made for that purpose, divergence of viewpoints appeared among the justices on other issues. In the case of the Roosevelt appointments, a uniformity of thought on economic issues resulted, but great division existed with respect to civil liberties. Even with the great potential for predisposing the Court which the president has by means of his political appointments, it nevertheless remains virtually impossible for him to pack the Court with justices sympathetic to his philosophy on all issues.

Sometimes the past actions of a nominee to the Court do not accurately predict how that person will vote upon issues he or she considers as a Supreme Court justice. Speaking of the one-man, one-vote issue with which he had been involved as both the 3-term governor of California and later as chief justice, Earl Warren said, "In California I went along with the thought that we should leave well enough alone. It simply was a matter of political expediency. But I saw the situation in a different light on the Court. There you have a different responsibility to the entire country."[27] That responsibility to all the American citizens, of whatever faith or lack of faith, led the Warren Court to some very controversial decisions in matters of religion.

16
INTERPRETING THE FIRST AMENDMENT

Our Chief Justices have probably had more profound and lasting influence on their times and on the direction of the nation than most Presidents have had.
> —Richard Nixon, nominating Chief Justice Burger

When a long overview of Supreme Court cases is taken, a pattern of emphasis upon certain cases during the tenure of particular justices emerges, and the obvious impact of the Warren Court was in the area of civil rights. When President Eisenhower nominated Earl Warren as chief justice in 1953, he surely anticipated a cautious justice, seasoned by his years as governor of California. Instead, Warren led the Supreme Court boldly into the field of civil liberties, an area that had been of only minor concern to the Court until the mid-1930s.

The first ten amendments to the Constitution, commonly referred to as the Bill of Rights, only were intended to protect citizens from unjust federal laws. That is why during the ratification debates the Federalists initially relied upon the separate bills of rights of the individual states and did not urge including such protections in the federal Constitution. When the federal Bill of Rights was adopted, it did not apply to unjust state and local laws. After the Civil War, the 14th Amendment was adopted. It provides, in part, that "No state shall make or enforce any law which shall abridge the privileges or immunities of citizens of the United States; or shall any state deprive any person of life, liberty or property, without due process of law; nor deny to any person within its jurisdiction the equal protection of the laws." Near the beginning of the twentieth century the Court began to explore the effect of the 14th Amendment upon state laws, but the extension of its effect was rather confined until near the time of the Second World War. Perhaps the examples of the abuse of civil liberties provided by the governments in Germany and Russia turned public sentiment in America toward insuring greater protection of the rights expressed in the first ten amendments. On the Court, the attitude began to shift in the late 1930s, but it was the Warren Court that made the application of the Bill of Rights to the states by means of the 14th Amendment nearly complete.

In searching for precedent cases dealing with religion prior to the twentieth century, few are to be found. However, in 1878 a case was decided by the Supreme Court that involved the question of whether a person might safely ignore a law because it was contrary to his religious belief. The facts involved a Mormon who had ignored the federal criminal laws relating to bigamy because his religion approved the taking of more than one wife. The Court held that a person could not "escape punishment because he religiously believed the law which he had broken ought never to have been made."[1]

That old case illustrated very well the two elements involved in the free exercise portion of the First Amendment. It provides that Congress shall make no law prohibiting the free exercise of religion, and the Mormon's defense had been that he was simply exercising his religion and therefore could not be punished for breaking the law, against bigamy, that would restrict his free exercise of faith. The Court, then and since, held that free exercise of religion involves both belief and action. With respect to belief, there can be no limitation. People are absolutely free to believe whatever they choose. However, when they act upon that belief, they expose themselves to certain limitations. The Court will protect Americans from undue infringement of even their actions that are related to religious beliefs, but the protection cannot be absolute because once people begin to act upon their faith they affect others by their conduct.

Another old case, decided in 1872, involved a conflict between two church groups that had originally formed one congregation.[2] The dispute was over ownership of the original church property. The Court stated the rule that if a dispute is over a matter that is "strictly and purely ecclesiastical in its character," the courts must not intrude, for such a matter should be left to the church to decide. In the case before it, the Court rendered a decision, finding that when one group separated itself from the prior membership it abandoned any claim to the property of the church. While the specific ruling was important to the litigants, the rule that did not control the facts before the Court was more important to others reading the case, namely that churches will not be bothered by the courts with respect to internal matters.

The second portion of the First Amendment dealing with religion provides that Congress shall make no law respecting an establishment of religion. The Court had held that this prohibition is more than merely a limitation upon setting up an established church, as the early colonists did, because it prohibits any law "respecting an establishment." Something less than an actual establishment may nevertheless be found to respect an establishment, and as a result it is prohibited. As in the case of the feuding congregations, the law must always strive to remain outside matters of a purely religious nature, for any intrusion may be construed as a law respecting an establishment.

Cases may be grouped together as involving the separation of church and state. However, in order to understand the legal issues presented by those cases, three separate concepts must be recognized—religious beliefs, religious actions, and matters respecting an establishment. While more than one of the three may be present in a particular case, the concepts are distinct and involve different legal principles.

Sometimes laws seeming to have nothing to do with religion are found to have the effect of encroachment on religious liberty. Following World War I several states prohibited the teaching of German, laws that would not appear upon first reading to affect religion. In practice, however, many Lutheran parochial schools used German extensively in their teaching programs. When the Nebraska law containing this prohibition came before the Supreme Court in 1923, it was found to be unconstitutional.[3] Two years later, an Oregon law which made a more direct attack upon parochial schools came before the Court.[4] The state law required parents of children between eight and sixteen years of age to send them to public schools. The Court found the Oregon law unconstitutional, adding specifically " . . . this court has gone very far to protect against loss threatened by such actions." Both of these cases predate the Court's active involvement in civil rights cases, yet the Court acted to protect the parental right to educate their children in parochial schools, which included religious instruction.

Although it was not until the middle of the twentieth century that the real emphasis upon civil liberties occurred, the trend had already begun when these cases were heard. In a 1929 case involving a forty-nine year old Quaker woman who was refused citizenship because she declined to promise to bear arms for the United States in a future war because of her pacifist beliefs, Justice Oliver Wendell Holmes said, "Some of her answers might excite popular prejudice, but if there is any principle of the Constitution that more imperatively calls for attachment than any other it is the principle of free thought—not free thought for those who agree with us but freedom for the thought that we hate. I think that we should adhere to that principle with regard to admission into, as well as to life within, this country."[5] Ten years later, in writing a majority opinion, Justice Harlan Stone included a comment by way of a footnote that the Court should give "more exacting judicial scrutiny" to policies that infringe upon civil liberties. That footnote signaled the direction which the Court was eventually to take,[6] but the shift in the direction of the Court with respect to civil liberties acquired even greater national import with the pivotal case of *Cantwell v. Connecticut.*[7]

In *Cantwell* the Supreme Court declared that: "The fundamental concept of liberty embodied in that Amendment [the 14th] embraces the
liberties guaranteed by the First Amendment. The First Amendment
declares that Congress shall make no law respecting an establishment of
religion or prohibiting the free exercise thereof. The Fourteenth Amendment has rendered the legislatures of the states as incompetent as Congress to enact such laws." With those words the doors of the federal
courts were opened to those who wished to challenge state laws concerning the rights of individuals, and Americans responded by filing cases
involving a great variety of religious issues.

The Court anticipated the difficulty inherent in applying the dual
aspect of the First Amendment when it said in the *Cantwell* case, " . . .
the Amendment embraces two concepts,—freedom to believe and freedom to act. The first is absolute but, in the nature of things, the second
cannot be. Conduct remains subject to regulation for the protection of
society." By extending the First Amendment to the states through the
Fourteenth, the Court involved the federal courts in determining
whether state legislators have properly exercised the state's need to regulate without having abused the freedom to believe of the individual
citizens.

Further, the difficulty of protecting individual beliefs in a nation with
so great a religious diversity among its citizens was also recognized by
the Court in the *Cantwell* opinion: "In the realm of religious faith, and
in that of political belief, sharp differences arise. In both fields the tenets of one man may seem the rankest error to his neighbor. . . . But
the people of this nation have ordained in the light of history, that, in
spite of the probability of excesses and abuses, these liberties are, in the
long view, essential to enlightened opinion and right conduct on the
part of the citizens of a democracy. . . . Nowhere is this shield more
necessary than in our own country for a people composed of many races
and of many creeds."

Interestingly enough, among the numerous cases that were filed following the *Cantwell* decision, many dealt with religion and education. A
pair of cases dealing with the issue of saluting the American flag illus-
trates the shift in the Court during this important historical period. The
second case, decided in 1943, overruled the one decided only three years
earlier on essentially the same facts.[8] The setting in both cases was a
public school classroom and the students' refusal to salute the flag was
based upon their religious beliefs as Jehovah's Witnesses. In the 1940
case, by a seemingly strong 8 to 1 decision, the Court upheld the local
school board's expulsion of the two children who refused to salute the
flag, a brother and sister. However, during the three years between the
two decisions, the Court had placed First Amendment freedoms in a
"preferred position," which meant that those freedoms would not be in-

fringed unless there was "a clear and present danger of a kind the state is empowered to prevent and punish."[9] Therefore, when the second flag-salute case was heard, three of the majority justices from the earlier case changed their opinions and two new justices disagreed with the opinions of their predecessors on the Court. By a new 6 to 3 majority, the Court decided that people could not be forced to participate in a symbolic ceremony such as saluting the flag. In writing the majority opinion, Justice Robert Jackson said, "If there is any fixed star in the Constitutional constellation, it is that no official, high or petty, can prescribe what shall be orthodox in politics, nationalism, religion, or other matters of opinion or force citizens to confess by word or act their faith therein. If there are any circumstances which permit an exception, they do not now occur to us."

There were other significant cases dealing with religion decided by the Court during the 1940s. One of the most important was a case involving a New Jersey statute that allowed local school districts to make rules and contracts to provide for the transportation of children to and from schools.[10] Relying upon that law, one township board of education authorized reimbursement to parents who utilized public transportation to get their children to school, and such reimbursement was made regardless of whether the school the children attended was public or parochial. The issue before the Supreme Court was whether the state statute and its application by the township authorizing reimbursement to parents of children attending parochial schools violated the Constitution. The Court held that the law was not unconstitutional, saying: "The State contributes no money to the schools. It does not support them. Its legislation, as applied, does no more than provide a general program to help parents get their children, regardless of their religion, safely and expeditiously to and from accredited schools." The opinion cited Thomas Jefferson's Wall of Separation letter to the Danbury Baptists in emphasizing the importance of maintaining the separation of church and state, even though the Court found the specific New Jersey economic interaction between the board of education and parents of parochial students constitutional.

Another pair of cases heard four years apart dealt with the issue of arranging for religious instruction for children attending public schools. The first case, decided in 1948, involved religious classes taught during regular school hours in the school building by denominational teachers.[11] The Court found this arrangement unconstitutional, saying: "Here not only are the State's tax-supported public school buildings used for the dissemination of religious doctrines. The State also affords sectarian groups an invaluable aid in that it helps to provide pupils for their religious classes through use of the state's compulsory public school machinery. This is not separation of Church and State. . . . " The facts of the second case, decided in 1952, modified the arrangements for religious instruction so that students who wished to receive religious instruction were allowed to leave the school buildings during the school day upon the written request of their parents, at which time they could receive the instruction at their own churches. Students who did not request to be excused for religious instruction or devotional exercises were required to remain in school. The Court found this arrangement constitutional, saying: "The program may be unwise and improvident from an educational or a community viewpoint. . . . Our individual preferences, however, are not the constitutional standard . . . the public schools do no more than accommodate their schedules to a program of outside religious instruction."[12] The Court referred to its decision of four years earlier by distinguishing the facts of the two cases and refusing to apply the earlier decision to the facts presently before the Court: "But we cannot expand it to cover the present released time program unless separation of Church and State means that public institutions can make no adjustments of their schedules to accommodate the religious needs of the people. We cannot read into the Bill of Rights such a philosophy of hostility to religion."

A group of cases decided in 1961 also reflect the Court's unwillingness to apply the law in such a way as to show hostility towards religious practices. These cases challenged the Sunday closing laws of various states. In every case, the laws were upheld, the explanation for which was well stated by the Court in a case involving the Maryland law.[13] "People of all religions and people with no religion regard Sunday as a time for family activity, for visiting friends and relatives, for late-sleeping, for passive and active entertainments, for dining out and the like. . . . We do not hold that Sunday legislation may not be a violation of the 'Establishment' Clause if it can be demonstrated that its purpose—evidenced either on the face of the legislation, in conjunction with its legislative history, or in its operative effect—is to use the State's coercive power to aid religion." Thus, the Court upheld the right of the state to set aside a special day for people to use as they pleased, which use might include religious activities, but the Court warned against the state using such laws to coerce church attendance or other religious activities. As in the cases involving religious instruction for public school students, the Court stated its approval of accommodation but disapproved compulsion by the state.[14]

Another case decided in 1961 dealt with the applicability of the First Amendment's protection to people who held no particular religious belief. The question before the Court was whether a Maryland constitutional provision that "no religious test ought ever to be required as a qualification for any office of profit or trust in this State, other than a declaration of belief in the existence of God" was violative of the First and Fourteenth Amendments.[15] The Court found that it was, saying, " . . . neither a State nor the Federal Government can constitutionally force a person 'to profess a belief or disbelief in any religion.' Neither can constitutionally pass laws nor impose requirements which aid all religions as against non-believers, and neither can aid those religions based on a belief in the existence of God as against those religions founded on different beliefs." Always a nation of great religious diversity, America has grown even more diverse with immigration from all areas of the world and the creation of new sects as well. The Court was only recognizing that religious diversity and extending it the same protections afforded those of more traditional faiths. Maintaining the importance of the state not intruding in matters of personal beliefs, however, the Court also upheld the rights of non-believers. This is, of course, consistent with Madison's view that "Whilst we assert for ourselves a freedom to embrace, to profess and to observe the Religion which we believe to be of divine origin, we cannot deny an equal freedom to those whose minds have not yet yielded to the evidence which has convinced us."[16] In 1965 the Court applied the same reasoning to the test for obtaining recognition as a conscientious objector.[17] The Court held that the test "is whether a given belief that is sincere and meaningful occupies a place in the life of its possessor parallel to that filled by the orthodox belief in God of one who clearly qualifies for the exemption."

Indisputably, the American Constitution and Bill of Rights as interpreted by the United States Supreme Court have made room in this nation for people of all faiths and people of no religious faith. In striving to respect the dual aspect of the First Amendment the Court has attempted to accommodate religious practices, and to enforce a state neutrality toward religion, without hostility. In 1962 the Warren Court was asked to balance the diversity of religious beliefs of America's students in the public schools with the desire of the state legislature of New York to mandate a spoken prayer, and the reverberations from that decision have never completely subsided.

THE SCHOOL PRAYER CASE: *ENGEL V. VITALE*

When the positive content of faith has been bleached out of a prayer, I am
not too concerned about retaining what is left.
                        —Dr. Franklin Clark Fry, President of the
                        Lutheran Church in America, 1962

Without citing a single case as authority for its opinion, the Supreme
Court decided on June 25, 1962, that a short, nondenominational
prayer recited in New York public schools was an unconstitutional practice. Only one justice dissented from the majority. The case was Engel
v. Vitale, but it is commonly known as the School Prayer decision.[1]

Public reaction was immediate and loud. Yet many of the people voic-
ing the greatest outrage spoke out against it without having read the
opinion. One Atlanta clergyman reacted by claiming the decision was
"the most terrible thing that's ever happened to us," only to admit after
making this claim that he did not really know what the opinion said.[2]
A Connecticut minister called Chief Justice Warren the anti-Christ, and
from his pulpit he urged Warren's impeachment, in support of which
six hundred seventy-four members of his congregation joined in signing
a petition.[3] A South Carolina Congressman proposed a bill to require
that the words "In God We Trust" be inscribed above the bench of the
Supreme Court, to remind the justices that "there is an Authority higher
than that of the Supreme Court of the United States."[4]

The prayer that caused all of this legal turmoil was written by the
New York State Board of Regents in an attempt to utilize language that
would be inoffensive to all faiths. As the former chancellor of the Regents said at the time of the Court's decision, "We didn't have the
slightest idea the prayer we wrote would prove so controversial. At the
time, one rabbi said he didn't see how anybody could take offense."[5]
The words chosen by the Regents were these: "Almighty God, we acknowledge our dependence upon Thee, and we beg Thy blessings upon
us, our parents, our teachers and our Country." The Board of Education

in New Hyde Park, New York instructed the principal to begin each school day with a spoken recitation of this prayer by the students. The parents of ten pupils reacted by bringing the lawsuit which eventually found its way to the Supreme Court.

Lawrence Roth was the father of two sons who attended New Hyde Park public schools. In opposition to the prayer, he and other parents first objected to the school board, but the practice continued. The next step was a challenge in the courts. Roth advertised in a local paper for other parents who would be willing to join him in bringing suit, and initially, fifty parents came forward. By the time of the trial, however, only five remained. The lower courts upheld the right of New York to use the Regent's prayer, so long as students were not compelled to join in the recitation.

The Supreme Court disagreed. The majority opinion, written by Justice Black, began with these words: "We think that by using its public school system to encourage recitation of the Regents' prayer, the State of New York has adopted a practice wholly inconsistent with the Establishment Clause." The opinion continued, " . . . the constitutional prohibition against laws respecting an establishment of religion must at least mean that in this country it is no part of the business of government to compose official prayers for any group of the American people to recite as a part of a religious program carried on by government." The remainder of the relatively short opinion cited history in support of the decision rather than relying upon legal precedent. Referring to our forefathers, the Court remembered, "These people knew, some of them from bitter personal experience, that one of the greatest dangers to the freedom of the individual to worship in his own way lay in the Government's placing its official stamp of approval upon one particular kind of prayer or one particular form of religious services." The opinion recognized that a democracy afforded some protection, but warned that the majority of America's citizenry should no more dictate religious practices than should a single ruler. "Our Founders were no more willing to let the content of their prayers and their privilege of praying whenever they pleased be influenced by the ballot box than they were to let these vital matters of personal conscience depend upon the succession of monarchs."

The Court anticipated that the decision would be greeted with charges that it was antireligious and hostile to religion, although the justices were probably unprepared for the vigor with which such charges were made. In the opinion itself, the Court declared that the decision should not be interpreted as showing a hostility toward religion or toward prayer. Nothing, the Court said, could be more wrong. "These men [the Founding Fathers] knew that the First Amendment, which tried to put an end to governmental control of religion and of prayer, was not written to destroy either. They knew rather that it was written to quiet well-justified fears which nearly all of them felt arising out of an awareness that governments of the past had shackled men's tongues to make them speak only the religious thoughts that government wanted them to speak and to pray only to the God that government wanted them to pray to. It is neither sacrilegious nor antireligious to say that each separate government in this country should stay out of the business of writing or sanctioning official prayers and leave that purely religious function to the people themselves and to those the people choose to look to for religious guidance." The full text of the opinions in *Engel v. Vitale* is contained in Appendix E.

Despite the historical basis for the decision that was elaborated by the Court, many Americans concluded that the Court was composed of godless men. In his *Memoirs,* Chief Justice Warren remembered the public reaction during this time. "We were also heavily attacked by many people, particularly legislators, when we decided compulsory prayer in public schools to be unconstitutional. I vividly remember one bold newspaper headline saying, 'Court outlaws God.' Many religious denominations in this same spirit condemned the Court."[6] Senator Robert Byrd of West Virginia was among those legislators critical of the Court. "Can it be that we, too, are ready to embrace the foul concept of atheism," Byrd asked; "Is this not in fact the first step on the road to prompting atheistic and agnostic beliefs? . . . Somebody is tampering with America's soul. I leave to you who that somebody is."[7] Another southern senator, Herman Talmadge of Georgia, objected to the decision reached by the Court in the school prayer case, as well as other contemporary decisions. "For some years now the members of the Supreme Court have persisted in reading alien meanings into the Constitution of the United States . . . they have sought, in effect, to change our form of government. But never in the wildest of their excesses . . . have they gone as far as they did yesterday."[8] A congressman from Alabama joined his anger about the school prayer decision with his anger towards another Supreme Court decision that was unpopular among many of his southern constituents when he said, "They put Negroes in the schools and now they've driven God out of them."[9]

Although there were many personal attacks maligning the spiritual beliefs of the justices, according to a Princeton historian of their time, most of the justices were profoundly religious men.[10] Earl Warren, Jr. said of his father, "My father was the most religious man I ever knew. He was raised on the Bible."[11] Justice Hugo L. Black, who wrote the majority opinion, and Chief Justice Warren were both Baptists. Of the remaining members of the majority Tom Clark, John Marshall Harlan, and William O. Douglas were Presbyterian and William J. Brennan, Jr. was Roman Catholic. Douglas was a minister's son and Clark had served for years as an elder in his church. Two justices, Frankfurter, a Jew, and

White, an Episcopalian, did not participate in the decision. The lone dissenter, Potter Stewart, was also Episcopalian.[12] In recalling his brother justices and the decision they had made, Earl Warren said, "The majority of us on the Court were religious people, yet we found it unconstitutional that any state agency should impose a religious exercise on persons who were by law free to practice religion or not without state interference. Among other things, this assured that conflict between religious factions could be avoided."[13]

Justice Douglas joined with the majority, but he also wrote a separate concurring opinion nearly as long as the majority opinion itself. In his concurring view he expressed his dissatisfaction with many American practices in which strict separation of church and state was not maintained, such as prayers in Congress and the use of taxpayers' money to reimburse parents for costs of transportation to parochial schools, which the Court had upheld. Douglas's concurring opinion, not the majority view, formed much of the basis for concerns such as those expressed by the Reverend Billy Graham: "This is another step toward the secularization of the United States. Followed to its logical conclusion, we will have to take the chaplains out of the armed forces, prayers cannot be said in Congress, and the President cannot put his hand on the Bible when he takes the oath of office. The framers of our Constitution meant we were to have freedom of religion, not freedom from religion."[14] Cardinal Spellman of New York expressed similar concern: "I am shocked and frightened that the Supreme Court has declared unconstitutional a simple and voluntary declaration of belief in God by public school children. The decision strikes at the very heart of the Godly tradition in which America's children have for so long been raised."[15]

In fact, these concerns were addressed in a footnote of the majority opinion. It read: "There is of course nothing in the decision reached here that is inconsistent with the fact that school children and others are officially encouraged to express love for our country by reciting historical documents such as the Declaration of Independence which contain references to the Deity or by singing officially espoused anthems which include the composer's professions of faith in a Supreme Being, or with the fact that there are many manifestations in our public life of belief in God. Such patriotic or ceremonial occasions bear no true resemblance to the unquestioned religious exercise that the State of New York has sponsored in this instance." Unfortunately, most people skip over footnotes, and many of the published reports of the decision omitted any reference to this footnote. Intended to allay such fears as those expressed by religious leaders such as Graham and Spellman, the footnote was instead ignored.

There were cries for impeachment and for amendments to the Constitution. Former President Herbert Hoover urged, "The Congress should at once submit an amendment to the Constitution which establishes the right to religious devotion in all governmental agencies—national, state or local."[16] On the day following the announcement of the decision two amendments were submitted in Congress, and in the days that followed, nearly one hundred fifty were proposed. State governors passed a resolution only eight days after the decision during their annual Governors' Conference which read: "Be it resolved that the conference urge the Congress of the United States to propose an amendment to the constitution of the United States that will make clear and beyond challenge the acknowledgment of our nation and people of their faith in God and permit the free and voluntary participation in prayer in our public schools." Only Governor Nelson Rockefeller of New York refused to support the resolution, saying: "I shall abstain from the endorsement of any hasty action by the Governors relating to amendment of the United States Constitution."[17]

After the initial uproar, the furor faded. Two months after the decision, a polling of Protestant and Jewish leaders reflected support for the decision; however, the Roman Catholic leadership continued to deplore the decision. Protestant and Jewish clergymen and laymen in the Kansas City area issued a statement saying, "The worship of God is by nature a voluntary expression and ought not to be associated with the coercive functions of the state."[18] Even in the days immediately following the announcement of the decision there had been voices raised in support. *Christian Century* magazine editorialized: "The High Court has not outlawed prayer. . . . The only thing the court has outlawed is transgression by any official, including educational officials, of the proper separation between church and state."[19] A Los Angeles rabbi warned, "It is important that people not be misled by distorted statements about the decision. The Supreme Court has nowhere in its decision denied belief in God, prayer, religious songs, Bible reading, or any other religious belief or practice."[20] A New York congressman supported the Court even though the law it overturned was from his home state, saying: "All parties agreed that the prayer was religious in nature. This being so, it ran contrary to the First Amendment—which is well grounded in history and has served to save the United States from religious strife."[21] The United States Commissioner of Education, a Mormon, said: "Religion is something that should be private, and prayer a private practice."[22] A *New York Times* editorial acknowledged that those opposing the school prayer were a minority, but reminded readers, "the Constitution was designed precisely to protect minorities."[23]

Potter Stewart, standing alone in his dissent, denied the relevance of historical events that had occurred centuries ago. Rather, he said, the Court should have looked to the "history of the religious tradition of our people, reflected in countless practices of the institutions and officials of our government." Certainly one such practice in mid-twentieth-century America was prayer in public schools, for not only New York sanctioned school prayer. Twenty-four states at that time permitted or required prayers in their public schools. A national survey of public school super-intendents taken the year before *Engel v. Vitale* was decided revealed that 76% of the schools provided their teachers with materials to help in teaching about religion; Gideon Bibles were distributed in 42.74% of the schools; about half of the schools had homeroom devotionals in at least some of the schools within the superintendent's system and chapel exercises were held in 22% of the schools. Bible reading was conducted in 41.74% of the schools.[24] One Tennessee court in 1956 had even up-held what it considered "simple ceremonies" but which, in fact, com-bined Bible reading, Christian hymns, and the Lord's Prayer.[25] This was the educational environment into which the Supreme Court decision was thrust.

Many of the schools vowed to defy the Court. In the Long Island, New York area from which the *Engel v. Vitale* case had come, eight school district superintendents stated their intention to ignore the rul-ing. In Atlanta, the deputy superintendent of public schools said, "We will not pay any attention to the Supreme Court ruling."[26] In Pennsyl-vania, one school official declared, "What the hell! It's illegal, but they can't put us in jail. All they can do is get an injunction."[27]

Other schools devised ways to maneuver around the Court's ruling, without directly defying it. In Illinois a kindergarten teacher who had used a simple children's prayer in her classroom deleted the single refer-ence to God and continued her use of the verse. The students recited: We thank you for the flowers so sweet; We thank you for the food we eat; We thank you for the birds that sing; We thank you for everything. The federal court found the use of the verse unconstitutional, although the court admitted that the plaintiffs who had filed suit seemed to be making a legal issue out of something of little real significance. In rul-ing for the plaintiffs, the court nevertheless said, "Certainly, this verse was as innocuous as could be insofar as constituting an imposition of religious tenets upon nonbelievers. The plaintiffs have forced the consti-tutional issue to its outer limits. We are reminded, however, of what the Supreme Court said in *Schempp:* '[I]t is no defense to urge that the reli-gious practices here may be relatively minor encroachments on the First Amendment. The breach of neutrality that is today a trickling stream may all too soon become a raging torrent.' "[28]

Although some schools ignored the decision, eventually most altered their educational practices to conform with the ruling. Surveys taken six years apart found that 33.2% of the reporting schools had conducted regular devotional services in 1960, but by 1966 only 8% did so; devotional Bible reading had dropped from 41.8% to 12.9% during those same years.[29]

President John F. Kennedy offered the American people a simple solution for getting around the Supreme Court opinion. During a press conference held soon after the *Engel v. Vitale* decision was announced, the president was asked: "Mr. President, in the furor over the Supreme Court's decision on prayer in the schools, some members of Congress have been introducing legislation for constitutional amendments specifically to sanction prayer or religious exercises in the schools. Can you give us your opinion of the decision itself and of these moves of the Congress to circumvent it?"

President Kennedy replied: "I haven't seen the measures in the Congress and you would have to make a determination of what the language was and what effect it would have on the first amendment. The Supreme Court has made its judgment, and a good many people obviously will disagree with it. Others will agree with it. But I think that it is important for us if we are going to maintain our constitutional principle that we support the Supreme Court decisions even when we may not agree with them."

"In addition," the president continued, "we have in this case a very easy remedy and that is to pray ourselves. And I would think that it would be a welcome reminder to every American family that we can pray a good deal more at home, we can attend our churches with a good deal more fidelity, and we can make the true meaning of prayer much more important in the lives of all of our children. That power is very much open to us. And I would hope that as a result of this decision that all American parents will intensify their efforts at home, and the rest of us will support the Constitution and the responsibility of the Supreme Court in interpreting it, which is theirs, and given to them by the Constitution."[30]

In effect, that is what occurred. None of the justices was impeached and no constitutional amendment was passed. The national respect for the Supreme Court endured, and the American people adjusted to the school prayer ruling. The interest in passing a constitutional amendment allowing spoken prayer in school waned for the time being. However, in the very next term the Supreme Court was asked to consider a pair of cases involving Bible reading in public schools.

18

THE BIBLE READING CASES:
ABINGTON V. SCHEMPP

The Court's historic duty to expound the meaning of the Constitution has encountered few issues more intricate or more demanding than that of the relationship between religion and the public schools.

—Justice William Brennan

Insulated from the wrath of the American voter by their lifetime appointments to the Supreme Court, the justices are, nevertheless, sensitive to public opinion. Having endured the public outcry following the *Engel v. Vitale* decision, the Court was given the opportunity just one year later to explain itself. That opportunity came in the form of a pair of cases involving required Bible reading in public schools. Lest they be misunderstood and accused of ungodliness once again, Justice Tom C. Clark in writing for the majority expressly stated: " . . . it might well be said that one's education is not complete without a study of comparative religion or the history of religion and its relationship to the advancement of civilization. It certainly may be said that the Bible is worthy of study for its literary and historic qualities. Nothing we have said here indicates that such study of the Bible or of religion, when presented objectively as part of a secular program of education, may not be effected consistently with the First Amendment." Having made that clear, the majority ruled, nevertheless, that the required Bible reading in the cases before the Court was unconstitutional.

The cases before the Court involved the laws of two different states—Pennsylvania and Maryland. Both involved opening the school day with readings from the Bible and both allowed students to be excused from participation upon parental request. [1]

The Schempp family, who challenged the Pennsylvania law, were Unitarians who regularly attended religious services. Mr. Schempp testified at the trial that he had not exercised his parental right to request that his two children be excused from the Bible readings for fear that to do so would expose them to the ridicule or distrust of their classmates and teachers. He perceived the American social climate at that time as one in which religious objections tended to be associated with atheism and communism. It was his fear that to separate his children from the objectionable religious activity would be interpreted as un-American and possibly as immoral. The Schempps symbolized the religious minority subjected to ceremonies imposed by the religious majority.

Madalyn Murray and her son, William, represented a different minority. Avowed atheists, the Murrays challenged the Maryland law. They based their objection upon the law's threat to "their religious liberty by placing a premium on belief as against non-belief." The Murrays took issue with having their freedom of conscience subjected to the rule of the majority. They claimed that the ceremony implied that belief in God was the source of all moral and spiritual values, thereby rendering suspect the values of non-believers. According to the Murrays, the Bible reading sessions promoted doubt and questioned the morality, good citizenship, and good faith of non-believers such as themselves.

In upholding the challenges brought by the Schempps and the Murrays, the Supreme Court was more mindful of the effect of its opinion upon the American public than it had been the previous year. This time the majority opinion generously cited supporting legal precedent, in contrast to the opinion of the previous year which had cited not a single case. From the precedent cases cited, the Court extracted the principal of governmental neutrality in matters of religion. To introduce this concept, the opinion quoted from a century-old case in which the dissent was written by Judge Alphonso Taft, the father of a Supreme Court chief justice. In his dissent Judge Taft had said, "The government is neutral, and, while protecting all, it prefers none, and it disparages none."[2]

Explaining the concept of neutrality, the majority opinion in *Schempp* said, "[It] stems from a recognition of the teachings of history that powerful sects or groups might bring about a fusion of governmental and religious functions or a concert or dependency of one upon the other to the end that official support of the State or Federal Government would be placed behind the tenets of one or of all orthodoxies. This the Establishment Clause prohibits. And a further reason for neutrality is found in the Free Exercise Clause, which recognizes the value of religious training, teaching and observance and, more particularly, the right of every person to freely choose his own course with reference thereto, free of any compulsion from the state." The Court went ever further by defining a test for examining questionable state laws. "The test may be stated as follows: what are the purposes and the primary effect of the enactment? If either is the advancement or inhibition of religion then the enactment exceeds the scope of legislative power as circumscribed by the Constitution." Both the Pennsylvania and the Maryland laws were found to have exceeded the proper legislative powers.

The Court also addressed the fact that the majority of the population might approve the unconstitutional laws.[3] Even if such public approval were to exist, the Court declared that the Constitution prohibits the majority from using the machinery of the State to practice its beliefs. Quoting from a 1943 Supreme Court opinion, the majority said, "The very purpose of a Bill of Rights was to withdraw certain subjects from the vicissitudes of political controversy, to place them beyond the reach of majorities and officials and to establish them as legal principles to be applied by the courts. One's right to . . . freedom of worship . . . and other fundamental rights may not be submitted to vote; they depend on the outcome of no elections."[4]

The majority in this case consisted of eight justices, but of those eight, four wrote concurring opinions. As he had a year before, Douglas wrote a concurring opinion complaining of other violations in strict separation of church and state. The other two concurring opinions were written by William Brennan, the Court's only Roman Catholic, and Arthur Goldberg, the Court's only Jew. Harlan joined in Goldberg's concurring opinion. The participants in this historic case, on both sides of the bench, illustrate the very diversity that the Amendment was designed to protect. Once again, as he had the previous year, Stewart wrote the only dissenting opinion.

In his *Memoirs*, Chief Justice Warren referred to a conflict a century before in Philadelphia in which "bloody strife, murder, and arson were rampant because of a controversy over whether the Protestant or Catholic Bible should be used in public school devotions,"[5] and expressed his belief that the Supreme Court opinions protected the nation from a repetition of such strife.[6] Clearly the Court did not confine itself to legal precedent in deciding these cases but rather was enormously influenced by historical events. In concluding the majority opinion, Justice Clark wrote, "The place of religion in our society is an exalted one, achieved through a long tradition of reliance on the home, the church and the inviolable citadel of the individual heart and mind. We have come to recognize through bitter experience that it is not within the power of government to invade that citadel, whether its purpose or effect be to aid or oppose, to advance or retard. In the relationship between man and religion, the State is firmly committed to a position of neutrality."

Unlike public reaction to *Engel v. Vitale* a year earlier, when the *Schempp* decision was rendered in 1963, the reaction of the public and the press was more restrained. The Dean of the Episcopal Cathedral in Chicago explained the difference in his own reaction in this way: "Unlike last year when I reacted emotionally, illogically, and non-intellectually, this decision doesn't disturb me."[7] The passage of the year between the two decisions had allowed religious leaders and laymen to consider the Supreme Court's reasoning, and most Protestant denominations and Jewish groups had concluded that the Supreme Court was correct in its ruling. As the secretary of the American Baptist Convention said in his testimony before the House Judiciary Committee, "compulsory Bible reading and prayer in the public schools is not only a danger to the freedom of nonbelievers, it is also a threat to the religious well-being of the believer."[8] The same viewpoint was expressed by a leader in the Presbyterian church who said, "My experience is uniformly that where there is careful study of the issues involved—in contrast to an initial and unconsidered emotional reaction—a substantial body of thoughtful church-member opinion sees the dangers inherent in the practice of devotions in the public schools."[9] Thus, having had a year to consider the issues and having the benefit of a fuller explanation in the Court's second opinion, most Americans accepted the second ruling without alarm.

The acceptance was not universal, however. The denomination raising the greatest objection to the decision remained the Roman Catholic church. In addition, great opposition came from Protestant groups in the South. Governor Wallace of Alabama declared that if the Supreme Court tried to stop Bible reading in any Alabama school, he would personally go to the school and read from the Bible. He instructed the state school board to ignore the Supreme Court opinion. One year after the decision, six states required religious services in the public schools by state law—Alabama, Arkansas, Delaware, Florida, Georgia, and Idaho. In nine other states, Bible reading was continued in most public schools as a matter of tradition, though not mandated by state law. These nine states were Indiana, Kansas, Mississippi, North Carolina, Oklahoma, South Carolina, Tennessee, Texas, and Virginia.[10] One study surveyed the varience in the percentage of public schools in which Bible reading occurred between 1960 and 1966 by region, and in every region the reduction was significant; however, in the South nearly half the schools reporting continued Bible reading after the Schempp decision. Specifically, in the East the percentage dropped from 67.6% to only 4.3%, in the Midwest from 18.3% to 5.2%, in the West from 11.0% to 2.3%, but in the South from 76.8% to 49.5%.[11]

The people who opposed the decisions continued to call for a constitutional amendment, with organized support coming from such groups as the American Legion and Kiwanis International. Among the proposed resolutions introduced in Congress, one of the most vigorously supported was that offered in 1963 by Representative Frank J. Becker of New York.[12] It read:

> Nothing in this Constitution shall be deemed to prohibit the offering, reading from, or listening to prayers or biblical Scriptures, if participation

therein is on a voluntary basis, in any governmental or public school, institution, or place.

Nothing in this Constitution shall be deemed to prohibit making reference to belief in, reliance upon, or invoking the aid of God or a Supreme Being in any governmental or public document, proceeding, activity, ceremony, school, institution, or place, or upon any coinage, currency or obligation of the United States.

Nothing in this Article shall constitute an establishment of religion.

During the consideration of the resolution by the House Judiciary Committee, various religious and political leaders testified. A Baptist spokesman opposed the amendment, saying, "Some persons have said that these devotional exercises may be the only time some children are exposed to religious ideas and to the Bible. If these devotional exercises are to be religious education, then this is not a business in which the state should be engaged. That is the responsibility of the church, and the church should not depend on the state to do the church's work." In his testimony in support of the amendment, Governor Wallace of Alabama found it fantastic that school children were prohibited from participating in a simple invocation at the beginning of a school day. He said: "That right has been nullified by the United States Supreme Court by decree as sweeping and as deadly as any ever issued by any dictatorial power on the face of this earth. . . . It is a part of the deliberate design to subordinate the American people, their faith, their customs and their religious tradition to a godless state."[13]

The Becker proposal never got out of committee. Resolutions were proposed by senators as well as congressmen. Senator Everett Dirkson of Illinois, joined by forty-three other senators from both parties, introduced a resolution that provided:

Nothing contained in this Constitution shall abridge the right of persons lawfully assembled, in any public building which is supported in whole or in part through the expenditure of public funds, to participate in nondenominational prayer.

None of the House or Senate resolutions was successful, and it was not until 1980 that the voice of an incumbant American president was added to those calling for an amendment. In 1984, opportunity was allowed for a full Senate debate.

19
SENATE DEBATES: THE PERSONAL SIDE

It is time for the people, through their Congress and the State legislatures, to act, using the means afforded them by the Constitution. The
amendment I propose will remove the bar to school prayer established by
the Supreme Court and allow prayer back in our schools.
—President Ronald Reagan, remarks to Congress, 1982

Religious freedom has flourished in America because enough of us in difficult times have taken the risk of resisting those who would regulate it.
The risk we take in this most recent effort at Government control and
regulation is slight compared to the risks taken by those who struggled to
reach these shores so that they could pray if they wished, when they
wished, and how they wished.
—Senator Carl Levin, 1984

While not truly a cross section of the American people, the members
of the Senate nevertheless represent all of the fifty states, and in their
individual viewpoints they share, or at least advocate, the opinions of
many of their constituents. A close analysis of the Senate debates of the
school prayer amendment affords more than the opportunity to examine
the political process. Their arguments, though perhaps more eloquent,
nevertheless encapsulate the arguments, both pro and con, informally
debated in classrooms, pulpits, living rooms and bars across the nation.
Of course, many of the arguments are premised upon objective and
logical examination of the issue. However, the disclosures of personal
experiences may be among the strongest arguments. Certainly the magnitude of the school prayer amendment led senators to reveal personal
feelings rarely expressed in the Capitol. In the following chapters the
advocates, both favoring and opposing a constitutional amendment, are
represented by the senators who argued that issue in 1984. Their arguments are separated into two chapters, the first presenting the personal
reasons expressed by the senators for their particular positions on the
issue and the second presenting the objective, legalistic and historical
arguments made by the senators.[1]

142

For those senators more concerned with re-election than with the Constitution or their own consciences, their 1984 vote on the school prayer amendment was simple. As Senator Baucus of Montana recognized, "This vote would be very easy for me if I were only thinking about politics. I, like everyone else, have seen the public opinion polls. I, too, have received thousands of phone calls and letters urging me to support the amendment. But I was not elected just to make political votes. I was elected to make informed, thoughtful, prudent, and judicious votes on difficult questions."[2] Fortunately for America, there were senators whose intellects and emotions led them to both sides of this complex issue, and for two weeks during March of 1984, the United States Senate debated whether there should be an amendment to the Constitution which would allow group prayer in American public schools.

The Amendment was proposed by President Ronald Reagan, and on March 5, 1984 Senate Majority Leader Howard H. Baker, Jr. opened the debates by reading these words:

> Nothing in this Constitution shall be construed to prohibit individual or group prayer in public schools or other public institutions. No person shall be required by the United States or by any State to participate in prayer. Neither the United States nor any State shall compose the words of any prayer to be said in public schools.[3]

Senator Robert C. Byrd of West Virginia recognized the historic role of President Reagan in proposing the amendment. "He is the first Chief Executive to propose an amendment to the United States Constitution correcting the judicial trends of the past two decades. He is the first Chief Executive to focus the attention of this country upon the issue of school prayer . . . Thanks to President Reagan, we are now, after two decades at least able to debate this matter on the floor of the world's most deliberative body. That is significant progress, no matter what ultimately happens to any individual proposal."[4]

As the debates began, Senator John C. Danforth of Missouri, an Episcopal priest, reminded his colleagues, "I also think that it is important, though, for us to recognize that there are two sides to this and that both sides are held by very devout people, and that their religious sensitivities are involved in it."[5] Senator Lowell P. Weicker, Jr. of Connecticut, who spoke strongly in opposition to the amendment throughout the debates, despite the sponsorship of the Republican president, warned his colleagues against using the issue politically. "So, for those that would bring it into politics, they demean our political system, our Constitution, and our ideals. Let us judge ourselves on many issues, but even as among ourselves and as a member of a political system, let us respect each other for our faiths and not engage in any verbal religious civil war."[6]

With some obvious exceptions, the senators honored the call for mutual respect, and the final vote was not aligned according to political party. Although Senator Daniel J. Evans of Washington complained that the debates were not "debates in the historic sense, but rather a series of statements given to a largely empty Chamber,"[7] their words, nevertheless, expressed the emotionalism and the philosophical challenge of the school prayer issue. The debates revealed both the personal and the public side of these men.[8] With their words and their votes, these one hundred senators decided whether to begin the process of enacting an amendment to the Constitution.

The difficulty of that process was remarked upon by many of the senators during the debates. As Senator Gary Hart of Colorado said, "the framers of our Nation's Constitution made the Amendment process intentionally difficult. They wanted to insure that only those amendments consistent with the Constitution's core values, only those amendments designed to guarantee the security and survival of a free people would become part of our national charter."[9] Senator Orrin G. Hatch of Utah cited the following statistics: "There have been more than 10,000 proposed amendments to the Constitution during the history of our country; of these only 33 have come through the legislative process and of the 33 there are only 26 which have become amendments to the Constitution."[10] Of particular relevance to the consideration of the school prayer amendment was Oregon Senator Bob Packwood's reminder that, "Only four times in the history of this country have we passed constitutional amendments to overturn a decision of the Supreme Court."[11]

Senator Daniel Patrick Moynihan of New York warned, "Amendments should be made only for the most pressing reasons and only in the most clear-cut instances."[12] To emphasize the gravity of a constitutional amendment, Senator Evans reviewed the twenty-six amendments that had been made to the United States Constitution. "Ten of those, of course, were adopted along with the Constitution as our bill of rights and, of course, we are subjecting one of those to potential change now. Two of them canceled each other, prohibition and the repeal of prohibition. The 14 remaining are of two types: One is ministerial or organizational. The establishment, for instance, of a two-term limitation for a President, and several constitutional amendments which have repeatedly changed the succession of the Presidency. The other type is those which deal with fundamental rights or responsibilities of citizens. Eight of the fourteen are organizational in scope. Only six amendments in the 195 years of our history have been those relating to fundamental rights and responsibilities. And what are they? The 13th Amendment which abolished slavery; the 14th amendment which came along just behind it stating that citizenship rights were not to be abridged by the several

States, the so-called interstate commerce clause, and it arose out of the Civil War; the 16th amendment, which I suspect some would repeal if they had the chance, establishing the income tax for this Nation; and the 15th, the 19th, and the 26th, all expanding the right to vote, the first to those of all races, the second to women, and the third to 18 year olds. I think that leads us to the first question we should approach in this debate. Does this or any of the several current proposals fit the historical mold of those few but great amendments which have been adopted to our Constitution?"[13]

After analyzing the issue, Senator Evans answered his own question. "I do not believe it ranks with the other six amendments."[14] Other senators feared tampering with the existing First Amendment protections of religious freedoms. With humor, Senator Dale Bumpers of Arkansas expressed his common sense approach. "[N]ext to the Holy Bible, the Constitution of the United States is the most sacred document in existence, so far as I am concerned. When it comes to amending the Constitution of the United States I belong to the 'wait-just-a-minute club.' "[15]

Senator Arlen Specter of Pennsylvania expressed the same caution, especially when the amendment is one proposed as an attempt to circumvent the judiciary. "That is my concern that amendments to the Constitution of the United States be approached with great care because of the texture of our constitutional Government, which provides that the Constitution be interpreted by the Supreme Court of the United States, which has through history become our national moral conscience. It is my view that we should look with great caution at amending the Constitution in response to specific Supreme Court decisions."[16]

Often during the debates senators would quote from writers outside of Congress. In addressing the gravity of tampering with the existing Constitution, Senator Moynihan quoted from a statement signed by students and teachers of constitutional law. These constitutional scholars warned, " . . . we oppose changes in the Bill of Rights. We recognize that no provision of the Constitution is totally immune from repeal or alteration through amendment. But we also know that the Bill of Rights, which protects our fundamental freedom, derives its strength precisely from its unique ability to inspire a reverence so deep that Americans have refrained from changing it since it was made part of our Constitution nearly two centuries ago."[17]

Senator Mark O. Hatfield of Oregon also expressed his concern that an amendment would jeopardize the precious freedoms already enjoyed under the present Constitution. "There is nothing wrong with the first amendment in its present form. It has served us well. While we may individually disagree on various Supreme Court decisions from time to time let us pause carefully before we fundamentally alter the balance that already exists."[18]

Those supporting the amendment also emphasized the sanctity of the Constitution. However, they perceived the need for the amendment not because of deficiencies in the Constitution itself but because of misinterpretation of the Constitution by the courts. As Senator Baker explained early in the debates, "Our purpose is to neutralize the antireligious bias in America's public schools which has flowed from a series of court decisions over the past two decades."[19] Echoing this same theme on the last day of debates, Senator Ernest Fritz Hollings of South Carolina said, "For make no mistake—these court decisions make hostility to religion official Government policy."[20]

The urgent need for an amendment to allow group prayers in public schools was summarized by Senator James A. McClure of Idaho. "In today's world, the schools have an enormous influence on a child's perception of what is right. Our children are our future and we cannot falter in our determination to provide the right atmosphere in which moral character can prosper. In our complicated society, children need prayer now more than ever."[21]

On both sides of this issue, Senators perceived threats to the nation. Fighting these threats with the strongest weapons they possessed, their words, they often revealed personal beliefs not ordinarily disclosed by politicians.

When he introduced the proposed amendment to the Senate, Majority Leader Baker remarked that his father-in-law, Senator Everett Dirksen, had begun the effort to reverse the effects of the Supreme Court decisions shortly after those landmark decisions were rendered.[22] Similarly, Senator Alan Fooi Simpson of Wyoming recalled that his father had co-sponsored the original school prayer amendment with Senator Dirksen, and related that his mother had admonished him to continue the good work of his father.[23]

The uniquely personal nature of these debates was summed up by Senator Patrick J. Leahy of Vermont when he said, " . . . in my statement on Senate Joint Resolution 73, I probably gave one of the longest speeches that I have given in 10 years in the Senate. It is one of the very few times that in a speech in the Senate I refer to my own personal feelings and to my own personal beliefs. It is one of the things that normally do not have to become part of the political world that we live in."[24] As a parent as well as a senator, Leahy expressed his concern. "I care very, very much about the specific content of the prayers that are offered in my own family. . . . I can imagine the questions they [my children] would have when they found the school board or the Government was telling them to say different prayers than their own parents and their own church had taught them. This is a very, very serious issue to me as a parent. The issue comes down very specifically to this: Somebody else is going to tell my children how to pray."[25]

Senator Leahy was concerned about his children receiving directions regarding prayer. Senator John Glenn of Ohio was equally concerned about giving such directions to others, when he said, "I am a Christian and an elder in the Presbyterian Church. My father and mother were both elders in the Presbyterian Church before me. In the home where I grew up, and in the small town of New Concord, Ohio, religion was a vital part of our life. In later years, I taught Sunday school. I believe firmly in my religion and I have tried to pass along these beliefs to my children. But however strongly I may feel, I do not believe that I have any right to force a Presbyterian Protestant prayer on a child of Catholic, Jewish or any other faith in public school."[26]

Senator Daniel K. Inouye of Hawaii evoked a particularly poignant image as he related his own experience during a debate in the Hawaii Territorial Legislature in 1947. The issue being debated was whether to place crosses over the graves at Punchbowl National Cemetery. As commander of the Disabled American Veterans of the Territory, Inouye had spoken against using crosses. He recalled, "I knew of many men buried there who were not Christians. I felt it would have been wrong for Government to impose its will without the consent of those men. The crosses would have been touching and dramatic, but I think today Punchbowl Cemetery is even more beautiful with each stone having engraved on it a cross, a Star of David, Buddhist prayer-wheel, a symbol from an eastern religion, or nothing at all. The power of Government cannot add to or surpass such eloquent expression; it can only threaten it."[27]

Senator Danforth occupied the unique position during the debates of being both senator and Episcopal priest. "I want to express my reluctance, even embarrassment, to stand on the floor of the Senate, quote Scripture and talk about religious beliefs. I am sensitive to the fact that the people of Missouri elected me to be their Senator, not their pastor. They elected me to serve all of them, regardless of their religious beliefs or lack of religious beliefs."[28]

Perhaps the most moving personal testimony during the debates came from Senator Jeremiah Denton of Alabama, a former prisoner of war. To his colleagues he revealed, "I confess to my colleagues that I am intensely motivated personally by situations in which individuals are deprived of the right of prayer. When I was a prisoner of war in North Vietnam, prayer was what sustained my life and that of my fellow prisoners. Silent prayer was important, group prayer was especially important, and vocal prayer was most important. . . . When I personally know how important the free speech and prayer are to individual survival, I cannot help but be disturbed by arguments that vocal prayer in our schools is offensive to freedom."[29]

These personal disclosures, often made at considerable emotional as well as political cost, reveal the accuracy of Senator Danforth's observation: "[T]he debate on school prayer is not between the godly and the ungodly. For strongly held religious reasons, people have arrived at opposite conclusions on the pending amendment."[30]

Unfortunately, there were those, both within and without the Senate, who could not accept the idea that men of faith might oppose the amendment. Senator Weicker received the following telegram during the debates: "You are doing a great job. Keep up the good work. Have room for you and yours. Your pal, Satan."[31] Reacting with good humor instead of anger, Senator Weicker noted that the telegram originated in Elmhurst, Illinois and commented, "That means that those of us in Washington, Connecticut, et cetera, need have no fear so long as Satan stays in Elmhurst, Illinois."[32]

Some of the name-calling came from within the Senate itself. In concluding his remarks, Senator John P. East of North Carolina aligned the proponents of the amendment with the founding fathers and the opponents with a noted atheist, saying, "I stand with those two gentlemen [Jefferson and Madison], and I think it is good company, and it sure beats Madalyn Murray O'Hair."[33]

Opponents of the amendment recognized that their position would be misconstrued. Senator Slade Gorton of Washington acknowledged that reality when he said, " . . . we will soon be asked to cast a vote which we know will be misunderstood by those who believe that a no vote means that we do not appreciate the issue or that we are not committed to addressing it. That is simply not the case."[34] Senator Christopher J. Dodd of Connecticut also acknowledged this misconception, noting "the simplistic and mistaken notion that those who oppose this constitutional amendment do so because they lack reverence for the significance or spiritual worth of prayer. Quite the contrary is the case. In fact, I believe that the very recognition of the sacred, personal, transcendant nature of communications with the Almighty leads one directly to a position of opposition to the amendment before us."[35]

In trying to emphasize that opposition to the amendment was not evidence of a lack of personal faith, Senator Weicker quoted from a statement by a group of Christian and Jewish clergy. These religious leaders explained, "We have taught them [our children] to pray and we don't want government teaching them. Prayer is for the parents to teach and not the board of education. Prayer is for the church and synagogue to teach and not the government. We don't want some board of education committee watering down our faith as it toils to write a prayer which offends no one. . . . Prayer is our business, the concern of a religious people. Keep the long arm of government out of our discourse with God and leave the First Amendment alone!"[36]

Senator William S. Cohen of Maine concluded his remarks with this plea. "I respect the religious commitment of those individuals who endorse this legislation, and I know that there is probably nothing that I can say to sway the views of those who strongly disagree with me. I only ask that they try to understand why I and thousands of deeply religious Americans believe that this amendment is unnecessary and unwise, and that they respect the fact that we do so not in any attempt to restrict religious freedom but rather because of a strong conviction that in opposing this amendment we are protecting the religious liberty of all Americans."[37]

Despite such eloquent efforts on the part of the opponents to the amendment to explain their opposition, misunderstandings were inevitable, and it took considerable political courage to face the criticism that ensued. Senator Jeff Bingaman of New Mexico commented on the impact of such criticism when he said, "Some of the supporters of the prayer amendment who have called my office have accused me and others opposed to this amendment of being instruments of Satan and false Americans for our position on this issue. It is my job to make decisions according to the facts, my conscience, and the best and most careful judgment that I can make about what is best for this country. And I would far rather be on the receiving end of such messages than have a 6-year-old child be on the receiving end of such messages because he or she chose not to pray in the manner decreed in a particular town or school."[38]

A great deal of the debate time of those opposed to the amendment was spent declaring their own personal faith. Those who supported the amendment spent less time expressing their own religious beliefs because their faith was more easily presumed. Public opinion played a significant role in the Senate debates, and the political survival of many of the amendment's opponents depended upon convincing the voters back home that their opposition to the amendment did not reflect a lack of personal faith. Senator Specter addressed the political dilemma each member of the Senate faced. "It is obviously hard for someone who looks to the majority to stay in office, which all of us elected officials must do, to give the same attention and consideration to the rights of the minority."[39]

Part of the political jeopardy Senators faced in opposing the amendment arose because of public misunderstanding. Senator Baucus explained, "Substantively and politically this would seem to be an easy issue. When Americans are asked whether they support school prayer, they answer overwhelmingly 'yes.' At first glance that's what these constitutional amendments seem to be about. That's what I thought at first, and I'm sure the thousands of well-intentioned Americans who support these amendments feel that way too. But when I examined these amendments more carefully, I found that much more is at stake. The school prayer constitutional amendment proposed by President Reagan pits our two religious traditions against one another. The proposal tries to make us choose between our support for religion and our support for religious freedom. That is the dilemma we face."[40]

Senator Mack Mattingly of Georgia in his support of the amendment expressed the simplistic view, saying: "[T]here was no vote among the American people to remove prayer from public schools. Had there been, prayer would never have been prohibited."[41]

Even Senator Weicker, who led the opposition, agreed with the amendment's advocates that public opinion favored the amendment. He admonished his colleagues, however, that they could not legislate on the basis of public opinion. He reminded them that certain civil rights legislation would never have passed if Congress had been bound by public opinion. He cited current public opinion on the issues of the equal rights amendment and abortion to emphasize that his colleagues did not feel bound by public opinion on those issues. "Let us understand that the job of a U.S. Senator and the President of the United States is a matter of leadership and not a matter of finding out where the percentages lie."[42]

Midway through the debates, Senator Danforth reported to his colleagues, "In the past week I have noticed something quote remarkable that has happened in my office with respect to telephone calls coming into the office. Whereas a week or so ago, almost 100 percent of the phone calls that came in on the school prayer issue were in favor of a constitutional amendment, in the past few days a shift has occurred and now it is probably somewhere in the neighborhood of 50-50."[43]

In addition to their mutual concern for present day public opinion, senators on both sides of the issue expressed their concern for fidelity to the principles of the founding fathers. Each side objected to the other side's reliance upon history for support. Senator Hollings, who favored the amendment, declared, "Those who fight so vehemently in opposition to this amendment misunderstand our Constitution, misunderstand our basic rights, misunderstand the country's history, and misunderstand what America is all about."[44] On the opposite side of the issue in his opposition to the amendment, Senator Metzenbaum declared, "This amendment ignores the history of our country as a place to which millions of people fled in order to be able to practice their religions in freedom and dignity. This amendment flies in the face of the great lessons we have learned from 200 years of American experience."[45]

Irreconcilably, both sides relied upon Jefferson and Madison for support of their opposing positions. Senator Howell Heflin of Alabama appealed, "We must restore the original understanding of the establishment clause that James Madison intended when he drafted the first amendment—that there shall be no national religion—not that our country should favor non-religion over religion."[46] Senator Hatch accused the opponents of misconstruing Madison's words, saying, "Either Mr. Madison was a scoundrel and a hypocrite in acting inconsistently with his stated principles, or else he does not fall quite into the model of an 18th century ACLU-civil libertarian as described by my friend from Maryland," referring to Senator Mathias.[47]

Senator Mathias had called Senator Hatch to task for relying upon half a sentence spoken by Madison, without including the meaning of the full sentence. Mathias explained to his colleagues that he had studied Madison's writings at length. "Because of my long acquaintance with James Madison through his writings, I find it intriguing that the proponents of this resolution, which would grant to the States the power to establish official forms of prayer, should quote, of all people, James Madison, as if they would expect his approval, as if they would seek through his writings as [sic] posthumous endorsement of their purpose."[48] Senator Weicker expressed his irritation with use of the words of Jefferson and Madison in support of the amendment more bluntly, "I am afraid you are going to have to find your authority elsewhere. It does not lie in those two men."[49]

Many of the senators made reference to religious history as the basis for their positions regarding the amendment. Senator Weicker warned, "Thousands of years ago, the debate centered on whether the object of devotion should be the Sun or Moon, animals or ancestors. Religion has evolved considerably over that time, as has politics. The intervening centuries have shown us that no greater mischief can be created than to combine the power of religion with the power of government. Theocracy, the union of the two, has given rise to tyrants and inquisitions."[50] Senator Melcher of Montana reminded his colleagues, "No school child can be told what, when, or how to pray. That is form, and historically religions and nations have split both hairs and heads in arguing religious forms."[51] Most of the senators, however narrowed the world view and focused their attention upon religious history in America.

Daily, throughout the two weeks of the debates, senators implored their colleagues to remember the lessons of history. Senator Packwood concluded his remarks in opposition to the amendment with this request: "All I ask, as we debate this issue, is that we remember that history, we cherish it, we protect it, we preserve it, and we pass it on to our daughters and to our sons a bit more secure than we received it from our parents."[52] Senator Leahy of Vermont concluded his remarks similarly. "We vote on big issues and we vote on little issues in the Senate. We should stop and think for a moment that we are only 100 who have the great responsibility to 275 million Americans. What we could do in this vote is to send a signal that we are willing to turn our backs on a 200-year tradition grounded in our Constitution."[53] In speaking of the founding fathers and his respect for their wisdom, Senator Alan

Cranston of California said, " . . . many of them were deeply religious. They were also fervent patriots who saw clearly that the greatest threat to religious freedom in their emerging country lay in the historical inclination of Government to define and control what a person's experience of God should be. These patriots envisioned a nation in which the sanctity of religious thought and religious expression would be inviolate. Their wording of the Constitution set the stage for what had never before existed in civilization: a nation that so respected the individual's relationship with God that Government was explicitly denied the power to define, inhibit, or influence what that relationship would be or how it would be carried out. Mr. President, the language of the first amendment is one of the greatest spiritual contributions of any assemblage of patriotic nationalists in the history of the world."[54]

In supporting the amendment senators also expressed their respect for America's history. However, they saw that history quite differently. In the opening day of the debates, Senator Hatch summarized his historical viewpoint. "In summary, whatever one's views on the wisdom of public school prayer, the idea that such prayer is in violation of the first amendment is inconsistent with the ultimate text of this amendment, the clear intentions of its framers, and the long-standing policies of State and local governments from the outset of our Nation's existence."[55]

His remarks in support of the amendment were followed by those of Senator Jesse Helms of North Carolina, a long time supporter of the need for school prayer. "[I]t is abundantly clear that the banning of voluntary school prayer is an aberration in our history—an alien graft on the American body politic that has taken hold only because of raw power flagrantly exercised by Federal judges against the natural rights and traditional liberties of the people."[56]

Thus, both sides looked to history for guidance, but they interpreted its lessons differently. Senator Moynihan voiced his opinion that, "the historical context in which the establishment clause of that amendment was adopted has somehow become remote from us. At times, even a body as steeped in tradition as the U.S. Senate can become ahistorical."[57]

Whatever the reasons for their differing views of history, the differences remained, and the Senate was left with the need to consider other arguments to resolve the question of whether to pass the school prayer amendment. Apart from all the disclosures of personal beliefs, the analysis of public opinion, and the interpretations of history, the debates narrowed to a few simple themes. Principally, the opponents of the amendment urged that no single student is denied individual freedom to pray under existing law and that any amendment would sacrifice individual religious freedom to achieve group uniformity. The advocates of the amendment urged the need for group prayer to rebuild the moral and spiritual fiber of America. Senator Cranston asked the question, "What is at issue is whether Government is wise enough to determine what is prayer, who shall enter into it, how, and where."[58] The opponents of the amendment cried out in reply "No!" but the supporters shouted back "Yes!"

20

SENATE DEBATES: THE ARGUMENTS

If those arguing about this issue in the Chamber cannot themselves agree, then what sort of chaos is going to be visited on every school board, teacher, and child in this country?

—Senator Jeff Bingaman, 1984

After asking rhetorically whether Government possessed the wisdom to implement public school prayer, Senator Cranston answered his own question, saying: "To my mind these are issues to be addressed not by the Congress, but by individuals and their churches in communion with their conscience and with God."[1] For many Senators their response to the amendment was determined by their pragmatic assessment of the impossibility of implementing school prayer. As Senator Inouye said, "I find it difficult to imagine a Government imposed system of prayer which would accommodate this rainbow of belief yet remain meaningful. Instead, what I fear, and what I more easily envision, is that the politicizing of prayer and the desecularizing of public education would result in divisions and confusion which ultimately does far more harm than good."[2] Senator Moynihan theorized various methods of devising a public prayer that would not offend any religion and concluded, "It will not work. The early founders of the Nation understood why it would not—because there is too diverse a set of religious views, today more diverse than in the 1770s and 1780s when the Constitution and the Bill of Rights were written and enacted."[3] On the final day of the debates, Senator John Heinz of Pennsylvania reminded his colleagues, "What we have gone through these past two weeks is proof of the difficulty, if not impossibility, of permitting group, vocal prayer without transgressing our strong tradition of religious tolerance and freedom."[4]

Several senators warned that efforts to draft an inoffensive prayer could only lead to prayer lacking any real substance. Senator Weicker observed, "Indeed, the more innocuous and the more politically acceptable in the secular sense, the more objectionable from a religious point

154

of view." He objected that, " . . . by the time we are through with all this we are going to have a 'To Whom it May Concern' prayer."[5] Senator Metzenbaum expressed the same concern by quoting from columnist George F. Will: " . . . prayer that is so general and so diluted as not to offend those of most faiths is not prayer at all. True prayer is robust prayer. It is bold prayer. It is almost by definition sectarian prayer. . . . when government acts as liturgist for a pluralistic society, the result is bound to be a puree that is tasteless, in several senses."[6] Senator Bill Bradley of New Jersey agreed. "I cannot imagine a prayer, acceptable to everyone, that would reflect the richness of each faith's tradition,"[7] and Senator Cohen expressed a like fear that the effort to omit objectionable language "would trivialize prayer."[8]

Supporters of the amendment denied the impossibility of implementing the amendment and disregarded the concerns about empty words, entrusting instead the ability of local communities to resolve these problems. Senator Hatch explained, "Under Senate Joint Resolution 73, there would be no uniform national policy on school prayer; rather, the decision would be up to countless local officials and school administrators across the country. These are the public officials closest to the American people and most directly reflective of their values and sense of right and wrong. There is virtually no evidence that these individuals were insensitive to the interests of all our school children prior to the 1962 and 1963 Supreme Court decisions. There is no evidence that they would not be equally tolerant and respectful of minority rights as they were prior to that time. There is no evidence that the average American in this country is any less sensitive to minorities, any less tolerant of those with whom they disagree, and any less committed to preserving the values of our Constitution than are Federal judges here in Washington and elsewhere."[9] In his message to the Congress, President Reagan had also emphasized local control of implementation. "If school authorities choose to lead a group prayer, the selection of the particular prayer—subject of course to the right of those not wishing to participate not to do so—would be left to the judgment of local communities, based on a consideration of such factors as the desires of parents, students and teachers and other community interests consistent with applicable state law."[10] Senator Denton urged, "We can realize that the fine points of one, several, or many good ways describing how prayers could be offered cannot all be spelled out in the simple language of a constitutional amendment, and they need not be. We can afford to trust local wisdom and fairness to prevail."[11] Senator Steven D. Symms of Idaho emphasized the importance of removing the Federal government from the matter. "What the administration bill will do is remove the further consideration of the issue from the Federal level. The individual States and local school districts would once again be empowered to decide the question of religious conduct in their own schools." He asked, "Why not place our trust in the hands of those close enough to the issue to deal responsibly with it? Have we completely lost our respect for—and trust in—the American character and sense of fairplay that has made us the great nation we are today? Must Congress continue to be embroiled in the daily moral affairs of the American people?"[12]

Opponents of the amendment warned of the negative consequences to religious liberty if control were to be placed in local communities. First of all, they feared the animosities that would erupt. Senator Hart prophesied, "This amendment is so vague as to promise great strife and divisiveness in the years ahead in every community in our Nation. Nothing would do more harm to national unity than the passage of this constitutional amendment."[13] Senator George Mitchell of Maine made a similar prediction. "Our citizens come from all over the world. They are of many races and they practice many different religions. That diversity which could have weakened us, could even have torn apart our concept of nationhood, has not. Indeed, it has been one of the sources of our national strength. It is to preserve that diversity that we must reject this amendment, for we in this country are not immune to racial and religious conflict."[14] Senator Bradley disagreed with the theory that by removing Federal and State officials from the prayer selection process problems would be averted. He asked, "If the State does not write the prayers, either directly or by local school boards or teachers, who will? If this amendment passes, not even classroom teachers would be able to exercise effective authority over the choice of prayers. That opens up the troubling prospect that members of the community with serious religious commitments of their own, will see these prayer readings as opportunities to advance their own doctrines. And that, in turn, threatens to plunge the schools into precisely the kind of devisive denominational politics from which the Bill of Rights currently protects us."[15]

In addition to fearing the devisiveness of the amendment, the opponents feared the potential for domination by a strong majority. As Senator Packwood predicted, "There is no way, Mr. President, that you can have any kind of organized prayer that is not eventually going to, probably directly but certainly indirectly, reflect the predominant religious strain in the community. I think it is almost inevitable."[16] Senator Bingaman explained why religion should never be the subject for majority rule. "[I]t is true we are a democracy; we do transact most of our business in government by majority rule. Outside of government is the marketplace, where supply and demand, price, packaging, and fashion prevail. But we have set certain rights and privileges above these forces. At the beginning of our history we deemed these rights too important, too fundamental, too critical to preserving the prerogatives of the individual in relation to government to leave them to the whims of the marketplace and the twists and turns of political passion. By their very nature, the first amendment freedoms of religion and speech are not susceptible to majority rule. They were created specifically to protect the minority, the unpopular, the unusual faith or idea, because it was understood that if we did not, we would be no different from the sectarian persecutions we left behind us in Europe."[17]

Senator Howard M. Metzenbaum of Ohio pointed out the interesting fact that even predominant faiths are minorities in certain parts of America. "[E]very American is in a very real sense a member of a religious minority. The religious majority in this country changes from region to region, town to town, and neighborhood to neighborhood. Mormans are a majority in Utah, but a minority when they move out of that State. Catholics and Jews are numerous in our major cities, but less so in rural areas and much of the South." In light of that fact, he asked, "Do we really want to see a situation in this country in which the local majority imposes its prayer and its style of worship upon the children of the local minority? . . . The whole idea of imposing a prayer upon all is intolerable and profoundly un-American."[18]

For those who found it difficult to envision how such domination could be particularly threatening to mainstream America, Senator Packwood reminded them of the example of Antelope, Oregon. "[S]everal years ago, there was located near Antelope a religious sect, the Rajneesh . . . They have taken over the town of Antelope, for all practical purposes. . . . These are, by and large, people with college degrees, in their late twenties and thirties, some of them with families. What if they decide to become teachers in the schools of that area and the prayer they are going to offer is the prayer of their religion? Do you think there will be any outcry from those in this country who support this prayer amendment? You bet there will, because they did not intend for a non-Christian prayer to be the prayer to be offered in public schools."[19]

Senator Bumpers pointed out to his colleagues, "Throughout our world the bloodiest conflicts at this very moment are between religious groups. We see it in Lebanon, we see it in Ireland, and in a deadly battle to the death between Iran and Iraq." He emphasized that America's Constitution protects Americans from such strife. "It is essential to the inner strength of this Nation, and we have each one felt secure because we knew our religious preference was protected by that great document, next to the Holy Bible the most sacred, our Constitution, and the most sacred part of that, the first amendment."[20]

Senator Carl Levin of Michigan described the significance of government making decisions concerning religious ritual. "[T]he greatest protection of our own freedom to worship when and how we choose depends precisely on how strongly we defend our neighbors' right to worship as they choose." He mentioned such rituals as prayer shawls, skullcaps, and beads, and then referred his colleagues to the statement in the committee report accompanying one of the proposed school prayer amendments. "The committee calls such sacred gestures, rituals, and ornaments 'incidental physical displays' and 'incidental forms of conduct' and states that the decision whether or not such sacred rituals and religious practices should be allowed would be within 'the purview of state and local authorities.' That should sound ominous to all lovers of religious freedom. How extraordinarily casually this amendment and its legislative history relegate our religious practices and freedoms to the hands of the state. No Government authority should be granted such power over religious practices in America, where religious freedom has found a true homeland."[21]

In responding to such concerns, Senator Hatch emphasized the importance of remembering the religious rights of the majority as well as protecting the rights of the minority. "Unlike reading, writing, and arithmetic, there is, of course, no single right way to revere one's Creator, yet it is undeniably true that our civilization places a high value upon acknowledging the role of a Supreme Being having created our world and having infused its inhabitants with his spirit. Those who reject this understanding are free to believe as they choose; they are not free, however, to require that the majority redefine the values of their civilization. They are not free to be less tolerant of the rights of the majority than the majority is tolerant of their rights."[22]

To Senator Hatch and the other supporters of the amendment, all the difficulties in drafting an acceptable prayer and the threats to minority religious freedoms were dwarfed by the overwhelming need to return group prayer to the classroom. As Senator William V. Roth, Jr. of Delaware observed, "I do not think it is coincidental that the decline in the moral climate in this Nation and the breakdown of the family unit has come at a time when God was banned from our country's schools."[23] Senator Charles E. Grassley of Iowa perceived this same connection. "While I do not suggest that all that has transpired is the result of the Supreme Court's taking prayer to God out of the classroom, I do believe that there is a link between the removal of religious belief and practice from our educational institutions and the diminution of our society's moral strength."[24] In full agreement was Senator Helms: "It is no mere chance coincidence that the decline in American public education has roughly parallelled the banning of school prayer by the Supreme Court in the early 1960s."[25] Senator Denton noted that, "I believe that our public school students perceive the banning of prayer on the school ground as state hostility toward religion." He stated his belief that, "To regard schools as helping to shape the world view of our children and then to censor religion and prayer cannot help but bring about a world without religion. Our children in their most important formative years are in essence being instructed that God is not relevant, or that religion is a lie."[26]

The opponents of the amendment responded to these comments with the principal opposition argument of the debates. Throughout the entire two weeks of Senate argument, Senator Weicker asked again and again, "[T]ell me, tell the body where a child cannot pray in the United States today, where a child, not an institution, not a school, not a class, tell me where it is under our present laws, under the present Constitution, under the court decisions of this land, under the laws of this land, where can a child not pray?"[27] The answer to the question, according to Senator Weicker and other opponents of the amendment, is that a child is already absolutely free to pray under existing law.

Senator Leahy answered those pleading for the return of prayer to the classroom through enactment of an amendment with these words: "Mr. President, each of these proposals restores what was never taken away. It is giving us back something that we never lost. Each Member of this body and each inhabitant of this Nation is free to practice his or her religion without restraint. Probably no other country in the world gives such total freedom to practice one's own religion as does the United States. But, unfortunately, it is the wish of some to have the Government direct that practice. And that direction will, in itself, restrain the very freedom the proponents say they are out to protect."[28]

Upon one issue both sides agreed. Speaking for the proponents of the amendment, Senator Hatch said: "Of course, the Government cannot outlaw a student praying to himself when he or she chooses. . . . The issue . . . is voluntary group prayer, voluntary group prayer accompanied by school authorities. That is the issue we are debating here."[29] On the final day of the debates, Senator Cohen, who opposed the amendment, repeated this same theme from his opposing perspective. "No Supreme Court decision, nor any lower court decision, has ruled against the right of an individual to pray in public schools. . . . No court has attempted, nor would it be able, to take prayer and religion out of the public schools. The courts have simply mandated that the Government shall not be in the business of sponsoring and conducting religious exercises for school children. In other words, the Government cannot constitutionally direct or sponsor the time, content, or manner of student prayer. However, any student can now engage in voluntary prayer, silent or vocal, so long as that prayer is not coercive to others and does not disturb educational activities. Purely private, voluntary prayer is and always has been permitted."[30] Voluntary prayer for the individual, therefore, was not the issue. The issue motivating the amendment was group prayer in the classroom.

Senator Weicker summed up the position of the opponents to the amendment thusly, "And the issue before us today is precisely this: Is prayer to remain a personal act of devotion, a one-on-one relationship between an individual and his or her God, or is it to be an official function of the State? And putting school in front of the word 'prayer' does not make it any less Government prayer. Indeed, the two are interchangeable. School is an arm of Government . . . "[31] Senator Weicker read to his colleagues a statement from a group of Christian and Jewish clergy. "It has been said in recent days by politicians and clerics that God has been excluded from the public schools and that by amending the Constitution, we must put God back into the public schools. This is blasphemy. God cannot be kept out of our schools by mere mortals, not even by the Supreme Court."[32]

For the supporters of the amendment, the omnipresence of God in the classroom and the right of individual students to pray to Him was not enough. They urged the crucial need to restore American morality through group public school prayer. Among the many Senators sounding this theme was Senator Paul Laxalt of Nevada. "Prayer in public schools has long been considered a desirable means of imparting constructive social and moral values to schoolchildren and encouraging the practice of self-reflection."[33] In accord was Senator Howell Heflin of Alabama. "Prayer has traditionally been a part of the education of our schoolchildren. America is, and always has been, a God-fearing nation, and the strength of our nation lies in our schools, churches, and spiritual convictions. . . . As we address the issue of prayer in our schools, we must also insure that the faith in God which contributed to the founding of our Nation and is symbolized every day in the operations of our Government is not subject to further legislative or court interference."[34]

Other supporters emphasized the Judeo-Christian values of America. Senator Roger W. Jepsen of Iowa urged, "Our Nation's single most precious resource is our youth. It is well that they be not only properly trained, but properly exposed and introduced to the absolute value system that we have had throughout the history of this country—that which is based on Judeo-Christian principles."[35] On the opening day of the debates Senator Hatch urged the same argument. "Education properly understood must include the teaching of the moral character as well—the learning of values. Further, I am not in the slightest bit hesitant to suggest that the values of our civilization—Western civilization, Judaeo-Christian civilization, liberal civilization—should be primary among these values. These values are good values; they are responsible values; they are values which have proven compatible with the flowering of the most prosperous, the most free, the most tolerant, the most compassionate societies in the history of a largely impoverished, unfree, intolerant, and harsh world. These values are those in which the overwhelming majority of people in this country are proud and confident."[36]

Senator Helms explained why he perceived a need for beginning each school day with group prayer in these words. "Thus, in order to learn at all, it is first necessary for the pupil to see that there is something beyond self which is good and worthwhile and which merits the effort to find out about. . . . And this is exactly where beginning the school day with a prayer comes in. By pausing a few moments and lifting one's heart and mind up to the Lord, the pupil has conveyed to him, in an unmistakable way, the idea that there is something outside of self, that God is the ordering Power and intelligence behind the universe, that he and the things he creates are good, and that therefore efforts to learn about the created order are worthwhile. Thus, through the very act of praying, a solid basis for learning is established."[37]

The opponents of the amendment saw such explanations as revealing that the true intention of supporters was not to provide a means whereby students who already enjoyed a strong religious faith could practice that faith, but rather, a means whereby students without personal beliefs, or whose beliefs differed from the Judeo-Christian majority, could be exposed to a religious experience at school. Senator Leahy observed, "[A]t some point we are going to have to wake up in this country. We should not turn over to the Government every single aspect of our life. At some point we are going to have to realize we have the major responsibility for our own children, for our own family."[38] Senator Edward M. Kennedy of Massachusetts did not question the worthy motives of the supporters but warned against their overstepping constitutional bounds. "The Separation of Church and State can sometimes be frustrating for women and men of deep religious faith. They may be tempted to misuse Government in order to impose a value which they cannot persuade others to accept. But once we succumb to that temptation, we step onto a slippery slope where everyone's freedom is at risk."[39]

Senator Packwood also discussed the risk of employing laws to impose religious values. "[W]hen we decide that, for the sake of all of us, the prayers of some of us will be imposed on the rest of us who do not like those prayers, then we are then starting down the road to compulsion, conformity and eventual disillusion and failure. . . . God did not speak to any one of us and make us perpetually, eternally right. When we think God did and when we are in a position of power already, then we are so dangerous. Because if we assume we are right and if you disagree you must be wrong, then it is just a short step to the 'end justifies the means.' "[40] The opponents of the amendment urged that the end that the supporters envisioned, a strengthening of America's moral and spiritual values, was not justified by the means they sought to employ to achieve it. To emphasize that point, Senator Bingaman reminded his colleagues of a scene from Robert Bolt's play, A Man for All Seasons. "Sir

Thomas More, in an eloquent defense of the rule of law that protects the rights of each of us, says to his son-in-law: 'What would you do? Cut a great road through the law to get after the Devil?' And Roper responds, 'I'd cut down every law in England to do that!' And More responds: 'Oh? And when the last law was down, and the Devil turned round on you—where would you hide, Roper, the laws all being flat? This country's planted thick with laws—and if you cut them down—do you really think you could stand upright in the winds that would blow then?' "[41]

The threats to the nation that the supporters of the amendment perceived were those that arose from a lessening of spirituality in America. They could not see the threat from a moment of group prayer at the start of a school day, and several senators expressed that view. Senator Hatch said, "I genuinely do not know how a period of morning prayer in our schools could hurt anyone. I genuinely believe, on margin, that school prayer will promote greater diversity, pluralism, and respect for the viewpoints and the beliefs of others."[42] Senator Denton agreed. "I just cannot see how, when a little kid stands up and says a prayer in his or her own words, not structured, not necessarily written, that it is going to offend another kid when that kid respects the first kid and when the second kid stands up and says his or her prayer the next day. I just do not see the harm coming from that."[43] Senator Proxmire urged the same position. "But prayer—a bad influence? You have to be kidding. Every prayer I have ever heard from whatever source has been good for my soul. After all what do prayers do? They talk to our conscience. And what do they tell us? They tell us to be kind and gentle and loving. They teach us to help others. They teach us to forgive our enemies, and to try to understand those who disagree with us. . . . If praying has evil or harmful consequences, I would like to hear what they are."[44]

If Senator Proxmire was listening, many of his colleagues who opposed the amendment were only too willing to identify the harmful consequences of praying, at least in the context of the school prayer amendment.

As an Episcopal priest, Senator Danforth was well equipped to express his objections with generous biblical and denominational references. First of all, he urged the sacred nature of prayer. "Prayer is a relationship with the transcendent, with the holy . . . then it follows that prayer should not be cheapened. It should not be trivialized. . . . It could be concluded that a classroom period of prayer for school children from diverse religious backgrounds might sooner inspire boredom, or even giggling, than reverence." Second, he emphasized that the representations that God had been removed from America's classrooms and depended upon an amendment to allow His return were offensive in themselves. "To many religious people, God is not dependent on the Supreme Court or the Congress. Objects may be kept out of the classroom, chewing gum for example. God is not chewing gum. He is the Creator of heaven and earth." Third, he explained, "Advocates of school prayer seem to say that all prayer is good, regardless of its content, that all prayer is equally efficacious, that the fact of prayer is important, not the content. This point of view would be flatly rejected by religious opponents of the proposed amendment. To them, the content of prayer is of very great concern." Finally, he warned of the following danger if the amendment were passed. "Because many religious people are intensely interested in the content of prayer and are unwilling to concede that one prayer is as good as any other, they are anxious that they retain control of their children's religious training. Parents can determine the churches their children attend. Parents can guide religious education within the home. But many parents have no practical alternative to sending their children to public school and no control whatsoever over the identity or religious beliefs of their children's teachers. Under our Constitution, religion cannot be a test of public employment. A school board is not permitted to deny employment on the ground that a teacher is a Baptist or a Roman Catholic, or a Scientologist or a follower of the Reverend Moon. But, under the Constitution as it now stands, a parent can insist that the teacher keep his religious opinions to himself. This would not be so under the proposed amendment."[45]

Many senators pointed to the influence of teachers as well as peer pressure. Senator Dodd said, "In theory, it may be possible for grade school or junior high school students to demur and excuse themselves from joining in a prayer led by their teachers and followed by the majority of their classmates. As a practical matter I doubt very many third or seventh graders have that measure of self-confidence and intellectual fortitude. Discipline in the classroom may not be what it once was, but the teacher remains a formidable authority figure and peer pressure is an extraordinarily powerful force for children and adolescents."[46] Senator Leahy agreed: "[T]he proposition that the prayer would be voluntary should reassure no one. Teachers have a special duty with the very young. They are the trustees and delegates of the community and its parents to pass on not only knowledge, but the spirit that makes that knowledge live. Children look up to teachers as special people and hate to disappoint them. When a teacher leads an exercise—either prayer, or a discussion of an important chapter in a schoolbook—the average child will want very much to participate. An order from a parent to excuse himself or herself is a problem for the child, whether it is followed or not."[47] Senator Inouye urged the same theme. "It is argued that any such devotional exercises could do no harm because they would be entirely voluntary. But what, I wonder, would be the impact on a young child who, in personal conscience or by parental belief, must be singled out or identified as different? I am not a psychologist, but I question whether such pressures, or the hypocrisy bred by indirectly coerced participation, would truly be harmless."[48] Senator Cohen urged his colleagues to recall the pressures of childhood. "Perhaps as adults, with childhood far behind us, many of us have forgotten what it is like to be children who typically have a tremendous need to be liked and accepted by their peers. Given the power of peer pressure among children, there is no way to assure that participation in organized group prayer could ever be truly voluntary. I do not believe that children, particularly very young children, should be placed in the difficult and awkward position of having to choose between adhering to their religious beliefs or compromising those beliefs in order to conform to a practice that may be acceptable to a majority of their classmates."[49] As Senator Mathias characterized it, "The amendment before the Senate would not protect the full and equal rights of conscience. It would do nothing to restrain government's hand from even the gentlest touch on the developing beliefs of a young child. To the contrary, it would provide a license to the States to infringe these rights."[50]

Near the end of the debates, Senator Metzenbaum answered the argument of the supporters that the voluntary nature of the school prayer amendment protected minorities with a practical analysis of the options a child would face. "The group prayer sessions these amendments would present to religious minorities would give them three distasteful choices: One, to give in to peer pressure and please the teacher by joining in prayers they find religiously or personally offensive. Two, to refuse to join in and risk the hostility and ridicule of others. Three, to leave the room and be considered by the other children as 'different', 'weird' or worse. The practical effect of this amendment would be to pressure children into joining prayers in which they do not believe."[51]

The personal experiences of Senator Proxmire may have resulted in every prayer he heard having been good for his soul, but Senator Weicker reminded his colleagues, "In my generation and those before mine, we looked upon group prayer as some sort of warm little event in the course of our school day. Yet, if you were Jewish, if you were a Muslim or a Hindu or anything but Christian and Protestant, it was a very uncomfortable moment."[52]

In supporting the amendment, Senator Grassley responded to such concerns with a concern of his own. "I share the concerns which some of my colleagues have expressed about the peer pressure that may be visited upon some students who do not wish, for whatever reason, to engage in prayer in school. But I stress to them that this unjustified pressure should not have the opposite effect—of prohibiting prayer by the State merely because of adolescent sensitivities."[53]

As the debate drew to a close and the final vote approached, Senator Gorton remarked, "I do not believe that there is one among us who has not come to appreciate more than ever, in the course of this debate, what a remarkable document the U.S. Constitution is."[54]

Senator Weicker, who had led the opposition, urged in closing, "[W]hen this debate is over, let us leave the field—and I mean both up here in the Senate and down at the other end of Pennsylvania Avenue—with pride in the fact that each one of us put forth our best efforts on behalf of our conviction and principles."[55]

Senator Baker reminded his colleagues that passage of a constitutional amendment requires a two-thirds majority vote, for which he appealed with these words, "[T]he hour is at hand to stop talking and to start voting. The time has come to cast our votes, either to restore the neutrality of the States in the free exercise of religion, or to officially affirm an anti-religion bias in our schools which I believe a series of court decisions has created."[56] At 3 p.m. on March 20, 1984, Senate Joint Resolution 73 was read for the third time and a roll call vote was taken. Fifty-six senators voted "yea" but forty-four cast "nay" votes, and although the majority favored the amendment, it was not the two-thirds majority required for passage, and the amendment failed.[57]

21
EQUAL ACCESS LEGISLATION

There is more than one way to skin a cat, and there is more than one way for Congress to provide a check on arrogant Supreme Court Justices who routinely distort the Constitution to suit their own notions of public policy.

—Senator Jesse Helms, 1984

The counting of Senate votes on the school prayer amendment was hardly complete when Senator Helms rose to issue this challenge. "[T]o all the parents of children in the public schools and all other citizens who want to restore our great American tradition of voluntary school prayer, I say: we have just begun to fight. Round 1 is over, but so long as I am in the U.S. Senate there will be many more rounds to come."[1]

Throughout the debates, senators on both sides of the issue had expressed support for equal access legislation. When the school prayer amendment was defeated, Senator Roger W. Jepsen of Iowa, who had voted for the amendment, reminded them, "I strongly urge my colleagues to consider the next step in restoring the right to the free exercise of religion in schools. I refer to legislation insuring equal access to school facilities for voluntary religious activities."[2] Senator Jeremiah Denton of Alabama, who had also favored the school prayer amendment, joined in urging the Senate to direct its attention to passage of the equal access bill. "The equal access approach clarifies the right of religious public school students voluntarily to meet on an extracurricular basis, during noninstructional time, on the same basis as other student groups such as the Chess Club or the Drama Club. Under the equal access approach, public schools that have created a forum must treat all student groups alike under a content neutral policy."[3]

During the school prayer debates, one of the most articulate opponents of its passage was Senator Patrick J. Leahy of Vermont. Yet, in the midst of his opposition he had taken the time to say, "There are problems concerning religion and the schools that I think can be dealt with by Congress. There is concern that religious clubs or groups are not

166

given equal access to school facilities during noninstructional hours. If a school has a forum open to all clubs, the phrase 'all clubs' should include religious clubs and if those clubs choose to pray during a meeting that is their private business. I would support legislation to provide for equal access in schools with open forums, providing it had sufficient safeguards to prevent misunderstanding or misuse by those whose intent was to bring official prayer back to the classroom."[4]

Another outspoken opponent of the school prayer amendment was Senator Mark O. Hatfield of Oregon, yet in the early days of the debates he reminded his colleagues of his co-sponsorship of equal access legislation. "Instead of concentrating upon a school prayer amendment, I urge my colleagues to devote their energies to rooting out ridiculous barriers that have been erected to forbid voluntary meetings of students who seek to meet and pray in nondisruptive ways." He explained why he favored legislation over a constitutional amendment. "As the original sponsor of equal access legislation that was introduced on September 17, 1982, I want the Senate to know that I am adamantly opposed to the idea of including equal access language in a constitutional amendment for it undercuts the very heart of my legislation. A student's right to gather together with others for prayer and religious discussion is inherent in the first amendment right now. It comes under the protections of free speech and the freedom of association when an open forum is established by the school. . . . Instead of ill-conceived constitutional amendments, let us proceed to a simple statute that provides a judicial remedy to aggrieved high school students."[5]

The Constitution and its amendments deal with fundamental American rights and responsibilities, utilizing language broad enough to be adaptable to countless situations and generations of Americans. Because the Constitution expresses such fundamental values, it is not easily amended and the process is intentionally difficult. Legislation, on the other hand, is intended to meet day-to-day needs of the country. The words are carefully chosen to address specific situations, and because situations change, legislation is capable of changing with the country's needs. Therefore, senators who opposed the school prayer amendment were willing to vote for legislation drafted to address a particular situation such as equal access. As Senator Hatfield explained, legislation could be enacted within existing constitutional law to meet specific national needs, without overturning the constitutional protections or the case law interpreting the Constitution which has evolved over the years.

Senator Lowell Weicker contrasted the need for permanence in the Constitution with the ability for drafting legislation to meet changing needs according to current wisdom. "The Constitution stands against the passions of the time."[6] To explain his meaning, he used the proposed school prayer amendment as an example and continued: "What do you think this amendment would have consisted of had it been written 50 years ago? Do you think it would have been silent prayer? Do you think it would have been no instruction as to the verbiage in the prayer? Or even if you are on the other side of this issue from me, would you agree with me it would have been a Christian prayer and it would have been a Protestant prayer 50 years ago? That is why you leave the Constitution alone."[7] The religious passions of the times during the past two centuries might have sanctioned school prayers unacceptable today. Such changing passions do not belong in the Constitution.

In other words, the Constitution defines the values of the nation while legislation addresses immediate problems. Senators who had been unwilling to tamper with the traditional religious values expressed in the First Amendment were quite willing to support legislation directed toward the immediate problem of equal access, and on August 11, 1984, less than five months after the defeat of the school prayer amendment, the equal access bill became law.

The version that eventually passed had evolved from Senate Bill 1059 introduced by Senator Jeremiah Denton on February 3, 1983, with certain changes modified from a portion of Senate Bill 815 introduced by Senator Mark Hatfield. Thus, the opponents and proponents of the school prayer amendment joined together in drafting and passing the legislation that is known as the Equal Access Act, the full text of which appears in Appendix F.

The heart of the act is contained in its first paragraph, which says: "It shall be unlawful for any public secondary school which receives Federal financial assistance and which has a limited open forum to deny equal access or a fair opportunity to, or discriminate against, any students who wish to conduct a meeting within that limited open forum on the basis of the religious, political, philosophical, or other content of the speech at such meeting."[8] Much of the remainder of the act is devoted to defining and explaining the terms used in the opening paragraph.

Before the act is applicable to a school, that school must have established a limited open forum. As the Senate Committee on the Judiciary reported in its analysis of the bill, "It does not require schools to allow students to engage in extracurricular activities; it merely prohibits discrimination against extracurricular religious speech or activities in those cases where a school has decided generally to allow its students to engage in extracurricular activities. . . . The Act applies only to schools that implement a policy or practice that generally permits students or groups of students to engage in voluntary extracurricular activities. If a school does not have such a policy or practice, the Act does not apply."[9]

There are numerous safeguards built into the act to insure that the religious activities are voluntary and student initiated. The act is only applicable during noninstructional time, which includes before and after school, lunch periods, study hall, homeroom or specially allocated activity periods, and teachers are expressly prohibited from participating in the meetings. Teachers may attend to maintain discipline and student well-being and to assure that students are participating voluntarily. Teachers must not, however, endorse or influence the religious content of the meetings. As for attendance by people from outside the school, their presence is not prohibited, but outsiders may not direct or regularly attend the meetings. The objective of the act is to allow students to exercise their religious freedom without opening the door to religious influence from outsiders and teachers.

During the hearings on the bill, the senators heard testimony from several high school students. The legislative history of the act summarizes their testimony in this way: "Students who testified before the Committee did not seek State advancement of their religious beliefs. They sought merely the school's passive acquiescence—leaving them to pray and discuss matters that concern the religious aspect of their lives. In essence, these students want the government passively to acknowledge that they have religious interests, just as others are 'benefitting' from their school's recognition that they are interested in sports, journalism or the theatre."[10] The committee specifically commented upon the sophistication and maturity of the students who testified.

Not only was the equal access legislation a result of Senate compromise and public demand. It was also a response to developing case law. In 1969, during the Vietnam War, the Supreme Court decided a case that upheld the First Amendment rights of students with regard to freedom of expression. A group of junior and senior high school students had chosen to wear black arm bands as a protest of American involvement in the war. The Court found that students do not "shed their constitutional rights to freedom of speech or expression at the schoolhouse gate," and that students could express their opinions on controversial issues, so long as it was done "without materially and substantially interfer[ing] with the requirements of appropriate discipline in the operation of the school and without colliding with the rights of others."[11]

The Supreme Court specifically considered the equal access issue in 1981, as it applied to college students.[12] A state university had denied access to a group of students who wished to use school facilities for religious worship and discussion, even though the university recognized over one hundred student organizations and had a stated policy of encouraging the activities of student organizations. Eight justices concluded that the university's refusal to grant student religious groups was unjustifiable. Only one justice dissented.

In the majority opinion, Justice Powell acknowledged, "We are not oblivious to the range of an open forum's likely effects. It is possible—perhaps even foreseeable—that religious groups will benefit from access to University facilities. But this Court has explained that a religious organization's enjoyment of merely 'incidental' benefits does not violate the prohibition against the 'primary advancement' of religion." The consideration of the benefits as incidental was based upon two factors. "First, an open forum in a public university does not confer any imprimatur of State approval on religious sects or practices. As the Court of Appeals quite aptly stated, such a policy 'would no more commit the University . . . to religious goals,' than it is 'now committed to the goals of the Students for a Democratic Society, the Young Socialist Alliance,' or any other group eligible. Second, the forum is available to a broad class of nonreligious as well as religious speakers. . . . " The majority was careful to express the limitations of its holding. "Our holding in this case in no way undermines the capacity of the University to establish reasonable time, place, and manner regulations. Nor do we question the right of the University to make academic judgments as to how best to allocate scarce resources or 'to determine for itself on academic grounds who may teach, what may be taught, how it shall be taught, and who may be admitted to study.' Finally, we affirm the continuing validity of cases . . . that recognize a university's right to exclude even First Amendment activities that violate reasonable campus rules or substantially interfere with the opportunity of other students to obtain an education."

Only Justice White dissented from the majority view. He began by emphasizing, "The Establishment Clause, however, sets limits only on what the State may do with respect to religious organizations; it does not establish what the State is required to do. . . . I believe the States to be a good deal freer to formulate policies that affect religion in divergent ways than does the majority." Beyond that, however, Justice White argued that there are many situations in which freedom of speech has had to yield to the Establishment Clause and that were it otherwise, "the Religion Clauses would be emptied of any independent meaning in circumstances in which religious practice took the form of speech." He cited as examples the Supreme Court decision of one year before in which a state statute requiring the posting of a copy of the Ten Commandments on classroom walls was found unconstitutional,[13] as well as the earlier school prayer and Bible reading cases.[14] He reasoned, "If the majority were right that no distinction may be drawn between verbal acts of worship and other verbal acts, all of these cases would have to be reconsidered. Although I agree that the line may be difficult to draw in many cases, surely the majority cannot seriously suggest that no line may ever be drawn. If that were the case, the majority would have to uphold the University's right to offer a class entitled 'Sunday Mass.' Under the majority view, such a class would be—as a matter of constitutional principle—indistinguishable from a class entitled 'The History of the Catholic Church.' "

The majority opinion opened the way for equal access legislation, although a few senators questioned whether legislation was really necessary in light of the Court's decision. However, the opinion dealt with college students, and, therefore, its effect upon high school students was unsettled. Lower federal courts hearing cases involving high school students were unsure of the applicability of the Supreme Court opinion involving university students, and different lower courts rendered opposing opinions. The executive director of the Christian Legal Society testified regarding the practical effect in the nation's schools of such confusion among the courts. "[N]o inquiry comes to us more commonly than those that indicate uncertainty and confusion on the part of school administrators and school teachers on precisely such questions. Decisions of the courts which have very properly barred the use of the machinery of the school and its teachers to advance religious causes have been confusing to many school administrators as to whether or not they must affirmatively discriminate against such expression even when totally initiated by students and independent of school structures and programs."[15] Many schools concluded that they would be better safe than sorry and banned virtually all religious speech. The congressional committee urged the need for legislation to resolve the dilemma faced by the schools.

Not all of the opponents of the school prayer amendment favored equal access legislation. Senator Charles Mathias of Maryland believed that Congress should have left the matter to the courts. Senator Howard M. Metzenbaum of Ohio agreed, and he warned, "this legislation runs a great risk of encouraging activities that will be counter to the Constitution." Too little time has passed since the enactment of the legislation to evaluate the accuracy of his prediction. In the meantime, high school students wishing to meet with fellow students to pray or discuss the Bible can use classrooms equally available to their classmates who are meeting next door to discuss photography or soccer, so long as their participation is voluntary and initiated by the students themselves.[16]

22

THE SILENT PRAYER CASE

The Court holds only that Alabama has intentionally crossed the line between creating a quiet moment during which those so inclined may pray, and affirmatively endorsing the particular religious practice of prayer.
—Justice Sandra Day O'Connor

In 1978 the Alabama state legislature passed a statute that required a period of silence at the beginning of the school day; however, the original version of the statute was not the subject of the Supreme Court's scrutiny in the case of *Wallace v. Jaffree*.[1] Rather, the Supreme Court's attention was focused upon a subsequent version of the statute which added three words. The original statute had declared the purpose of the period of silence as being "for meditation," but three years later, in 1981, the Alabama legislature supplemented that declaration by adding another choice, stating that the silence was to be observed "for meditation or voluntary prayer."[2] The United States Supreme Court was asked to decide whether the addition of a stated alternate purpose of prayer violated the First Amendment.

At the time of the Court's decision, twenty-five states permitted or required public school teachers to direct their students in observing a moment of silence. Some of the state statutes declared the purpose as being for meditation only while others, like the Alabama statute, declared alternate purposes which included prayer. The trial courts that had heard constitutional challenges to some of these statutes were divided in their opinions, and there had been a great deal of speculation about the likely ruling by the Supreme Court during its consideration of the Alabama statute. During the Senate debates on the school prayer amendment most speakers had predicted that the Court would uphold the Alabama statute. Such predictions were wrong.

The Supreme Court held that the 1981 statute, by adding "or voluntary prayer" as an alternate purpose, violated the Establishment Clause of the First Amendment. The majority opinion, written by Justice

172

Stevens, was careful to distinguish the constitutionality of the original statute as opposed to the unconstitutionality of the supplemented version. "The legislative intent to return prayer to public schools is, of course, quite different from merely protecting every student's right to engage in voluntary prayer during an appropriate moment of silence during the school day. The 1978 statute already protected that right, containing nothing that prevented any student from engaging in voluntary prayer during a silent minute of meditation. . . . The addition of 'or voluntary prayer' indicates that the State intended to characterize prayer as a favored practice. Such an endorsement is not consistent with the established principle that Government must pursue a course of complete neutrality toward religion."

The legislative intent was ascertained from several sources, not the least of which was the testimony of the state senator who described himself as the "prime sponsor" of the bill to add "or voluntary prayer" to the language of the original statute. The bill he sponsored was enacted into law in 1981. He testified that the bill was an "effort to return voluntary prayer to our public schools . . . it is a beginning and a step in the right direction." When asked whether the bill had any other purpose, he testified unequivocally that he had no other purpose in mind. Clearly it was not enough for this senator, and the other legislators who joined in enacting the bill, that the 1978 statute already allowed an opportunity for school children to begin their day with a silent prayer during the meditation period. As the bill's sponsor, he felt something more was needed.

The Supreme Court found that the Alabama legislature had indeed provided the state's school children with something more than merely the opportunity to pray. The Court found that the 1981 statute was intended to convey a message of endorsement. Thus, the "step in the right direction" urged by the bill's sponsor was, according to the Court, an endorsement of prayer as the favored activity during the moment of silence and as such violated the Establishment Clause. The Court held that the Alabama legislators had gone a step too far.

In her concurring opinion Justice O'Connor emphasized that not all of the moment of silence laws of other states were unconstitutional. "By mandating a moment of silence, a State does not necessarily endorse any activity that might occur during the period. . . . The crucial question is whether the State has conveyed or attempted to convey the message that children should use the moment of silence for prayer. This question cannot be answered in the abstract, but instead requires courts to examine the history, language, and administration of a particular statute to determine whether it operates as an endorsement of religion."

Three justices dissented from the majority, and each of the three wrote a dissenting opinion. Among the dissenters was Chief Justice Burger who argued that "to suggest that a moment-of-silence statute that includes the word 'prayer' unconstitutionally endorses religion, while one that simply provides for a moment of silence does not, manifests not neutrality but hostility toward religion."

Justice White argued that the legislature had done no more than answer in advance the question that students were likely to ask their teachers if the moment of silence statute did not expressly mention prayer. Thus, he reasoned, "I would not invalidate a statute that at the outset provided the legislative answer to the question, 'May I pray?' "

The most vigorous dissent was written by Justice Rehnquist, much of which was devoted to a historical summary. Rehnquist concluded: "The Framers intended the Establishment Clause to prohibit the designation of any church as a 'national' one. The Clause was also designed to stop the Federal Government from asserting a preference for one religious denomination or sect over others. Given the 'incorporation' of the Establishment Clause as against the States via the Fourteenth Amendment in *Everson,* States are prohibited as well from establishing a religion or discriminating between sects. As its history abundantly shows, however, nothing in the Establishment Clause requires government to be strictly neutral between religion and irreligion, nor does that Clause prohibit Congress or the States from pursuing legitimate secular ends through nondiscriminatory sectarian means." Rehnquist quoted nineteenth-century constitutional authorities who interpreted the Constitution to allow a fostering of religious worship and religious institutions as a means of preserving public morals and public order. These constitutional scholars wrote that the Constitution was intended to exclude rivalry among Christian sects and prohibit a national religion, but, according to one former Supreme Court justice, "Probably at the time of the adoption of the Constitution, and of the Amendment to it now under consideration, the general if not the universal sentiment in America was, that Christianity ought to receive encouragement from the State so far as was not incompatible with the private rights of conscience and the freedom of religious worship." Thus, Rehnquist and the scholars he cited agreed with the Alabama legislature that it was appropriate to go further than merely providing an opportunity for prayer and affirmatively to endorse and encourage prayer by public school children.

Such a constitutional interpretation remains the minority view. The majority continued to employ the three-pronged test for evaluating a statute: (1) the statute must have a secular legislative purpose; (2) its primary effect must neither advance nor inhibit religion; and (3) it must not foster an excessive government entanglement with religion. Justice Powell wrote a concurring opinion expressly for the purpose of responding to criticism of the three-pronged *Lemon* test, so named because of its use in the case of *Lemon v. Kurtzman.*[3] Powell urged the importance of the test as being the only coherent test adopted by a majority of the Supreme Court, without which trial courts would be left to decide Establishment cases on an ad hoc basis. Rehnquist, in his dissent, however, pointed to the uneven results of cases in which the *Lemon* test had been applied. Nevertheless, the three-pronged test remains the Supreme Court-approved tool to assist lower courts in deciding Establishment Clause challenges to state statutes, and the tool that all Americans may employ to evaluate the constitutionality of laws proposed by their legislators.

Political reaction to the Court's decision was predictable. Senator Jeremiah Denton of Alabama, whose home state legislature had passed the law, said he was "extremely disappointed" and expressed his opinion that the ruling "represents a continuation of a distorted rationale that equates the opportunity to pray with the establishment of a state religion."[4] However, Senator Lowell Weicker, who had led the opposition to the school prayer amendment the previous year, said: "The Court's decision reaffirms that, uniquely in the United States, religion is a matter personal to each of us and not the business of government."[5] Many members of Congress expressed their intention to renew the push for an amendment.

The Reagan administration expressed regret that the Alabama statute was found unconstitutional, tempered only by relief that moment-of-silence laws of other states were left undisturbed. President Reagan continued thereafter to urge the need for a school prayer amendment in his annual State of the Union messages.

Other reactions were equally predictable. The legal director of the American Civil Liberties Union in Washington said, "The Court has made it fairly clear a moment of silence not dedicated to prayer is acceptable, and the ACLU doesn't disagree with that."[6] However, Jerry Falwell, president and founder of the Moral Majority, claimed that American school children "have no more rights than students in the Soviet Union, an officially atheistic state."[7]

Not all of the public criticism was directed toward the majority opinion, however. Justice Rehnquist's dissent came in for its own strong criticism. Although Rehnquist was alone in his dissent, he has, since writing the opinion, become chief justice, and therefore, the import of his position on the issue has increased. Justice Rehnquist based his opinion on his own analysis of history, saying, "It is impossible to build a sound constitutional doctrine upon a misunderstanding of constitutional history." According to one of his critics it is Rehnquist who "flunked history."[8] "Rehnquist quite literally does not know the facts relating to the constitutional history of the establishment clause, let alone understand them rightly. . . . [He] thinks that Madison, the sponsor of Jefferson's Statute of Religious Freedom, did not support neutrality between religion and irreligion and [he] thinks that an establishment of religion existed in Rhode Island from 1633 to 1842. Rhode Island, founded in 1636 by Roger Williams, a separatist, never had an establishment of religion. The man who makes such mistakes and passes fiction off as history makes historical judgments about the First Amendment that he would like to use as the anchor to a new establishment clause jurisprudence."[9]

Chief Justice Rehnquist has spoken specifically of his determination to guard against allowing personal moral principles to intrude in legal opinions. "The Supreme Court has on occasion been referred to as the conscience of the country, but I think this description has a considerable potential for mischief. If no more is meant by it than that the Supreme Court insofar as it upholds the principles of the Constitution is the conscience of the country, it is of course quite accurate. But the phrase is also subject to the more sweeping interpretation that the justices of the Supreme Court are to bring to bear on every constitutional question the moral principles found in each of their individual consciences. Yet to go beyond the language of the Constitution, and the meaning that may be fairly ascribed to the language, and into the consciences of individual judges, is to embark on a journey that is treacherous indeed."[10] Certainly, having such strong feelings against allowing his own moral values to color his judgment, Rehnquist intended to examine history for clues to the meaning of the words used in the establishment clause without allowing any bias resulting from his own personal beliefs.

Yet, a scholar analyzing Rehnquist's dissent concluded it represents distorted history. "Therefore, Rehnquist's attempt to use the intention of the Framers as an objective basis for constitutional law fails at its most fundamental and crucial point—its connection to history. The power of his argument rests on the claim that his position is derived from objectively determinable facts about the Framers' purposes. But his reconstruction of the Framers' intention not only fails to convince, it in fact seems susceptible to objective refutation. . . . By so misreading the Constitution's text and history, Rehnquist commits the precise emotivist error that he sets out to avoid: the erection of a judge's personal values and opinions into constitutional norms."[11]

Because the Court's opinion regarding the Alabama statute left open the question of constitutionality of other statutes, each state statute is left for review on a case by case basis. However, the pains taken by the Court in the Alabama case have provided lower courts making such determinations with guidelines to be applied, and the Court has reaffirmed the use of the three-pronged Lemon test.[12]

23
CONCLUSION

It has been said that the only thing we learn from history is that we do not learn. But surely we can learn if we have the will to do so.
                                    —Earl Warren, Eulogy to John F. Kennedy

If there are two things to be discovered from reading this book, they are, first, that devoutly religious people may differ on the issue of group school prayer, and second, that intelligent people have interpreted the lessons of history differently. One conlusion to be drawn from those two observations is the danger in simply accepting someone else's opinion on the issue of voluntary group prayer in public schools. Chief Justice Warren was correct in urging Americans to learn from history, but we cannot learn history's lessons if we lack the will to study America's history for ourselves.

There are a great many people on all sides of this issue—judges, politicians, authors, professors, and ministers among them—who are eager to share their opinions in hopes you will adopt theirs for your own. To do so is to adopt their knowledge of history—or lack of knowledge—and their unknown bias, along with their opinion. The American tradition of church-state separation requires not only your eternal vigilance for its preservation; it also requires your informed vigilance.

Each generation of Americans has played its role in developing the relationship between church and state that exists in this nation, and that responsibility must be faced anew by each generation that follows. History has taught that the goal to be sought is a matter of balance and not the supremacy of one over the other. In the opinion of John Adams, "Our constitution was made only for a moral and religious people. It is wholly inadequate for the government of any other."[1] Proponents of a constitutional amendment to allow spoken school prayer have expressed their concern that the effect of the *Engel v. Vitale* decision in 1962 has been the education of subsequent generations insufficiently moral and

177

religious to sustain America. As Senator Roth said during the debates, "I do not think it is coincidental that the decline in the moral climate in this nation and the breakdown of the family unit has come at a time when God was banned from our country's schools."[2]

Perhaps unexpectedly, others have pointed out the threat to religion from good-hearted people, including politicians, who have stolen the vigor from America's faithful, and replaced it with sentimentalism. "The chief danger in the situation is not conscious, creeping secularism or conscious creeping clericalism, but unconscious creeping sentimentalism. The underpinning of America's policy of church-state separation is being eroded by goodhearted people with exalted moral motives who are willing to make step-by-step concessions in order to maintain religious peace and good will."[3]

In the decade just prior to the *Engel v. Vitale* decision, there were several such good-hearted gestures by Washington. In 1954 the phrase "Under God" was added to the pledge of allegiance to the flag, and in 1956 "In God We Trust" was adopted as our national motto. The motto was placed on American currency the previous year, and a "Pray for Peace" cancellation stamp was used on American mail. The question is whether these gestures by government have enhanced the spiritual lives of American citizens in the years since or have trivialized religious concepts to the point that they go unnoticed by most Americans.

Although the appropriate degree of separation has varied among its advocates, both historical and contemporary writers have believed that separation of church and state affords the best protection of each. In 1808 Thomas Jefferson said: "I do not believe it is for the interest of religion to invite the civil magistrate to direct its exercises, its discipline, or its doctrines; nor of the religious societies, that the General Government should be invested with the power of effecting any uniformity of time or matter among them. Fasting and prayer are religious exercises; the enjoining them an act of discipline. Every religious society has a right to determine for itself the times for these exercises, and the objects proper for them, according to their own particular tenets, and this right can never be safer than in their own hands, where the Constitution has deposited it."[4]

In 1987 a contemporary religious writer said, "Tension between church and state is inherent and inevitable. . . . For from the constant tension—the chafing back and forth—a certain equilibrium is achieved. To maintain this balance the church and state must fulfill their respective roles. One cannot survive without the other; yet neither can do the work of the other. Both operate under God's rule, each in a different relationship to that rule."[5]

Several events in recent years illustrate the difficulties in maintaining that balance and the natural chafing back and forth between church and state that occurs in the process. Although these events do not relate directly or solely to the school prayer issue, they reflect the current status of the equilibrium and are included in this book because they, therefore, bear indirectly on the issue.

As one example, concerned by what they perceive to be a decline in the spiritual and moral values of their citizens, some states, acting through their elected legislators, have attempted to return religious instruction to their public school classrooms, and in order to avoid constitutional prohibitions they have ascribed secular purposes to the legislation. However, the courts have said that if the statement of secular purpose is merely a sham, it cannot protect legislation otherwise prohibited by the First Amendment.

In 1980 the Supreme Court reviewed a Kentucky law requiring the posting of the Ten Commandments in public schools.[6] The state law required that each public elementary and secondary classroom have posted in it a copy of the Ten Commandments, paid for with voluntary contributions to the state treasurer. In small print below the last commandment, the law required the printing of the following sentence. "The secular application of the Ten Commandments is clearly seen in its adoption as the fundamental legal code of Western Civilization and the Common Law of the United States." By stating a secular purpose, the Kentucky state legislators attempted to come within the first prong of the so-called Lemon test.[7] The majority of the United States Supreme Court found that, "[t]he pre-eminent purpose for posting the Ten Commandments on the schoolroom walls is plainly religious in nature. The Ten Commandments are undeniably a sacred text in the Jewish and Christian faiths, and no legislative recitation of a supposed secular purpose can blind us to that fact." The Court pointed out that while the Commandments do include secular prohibitions against such things as killing and stealing, that the first five concern religious duties. The Court went on to add, "This is not a case in which the Ten Commandments are integrated into the school curriculum, where the Bible may constitutionally be used in an appropriate study of history, civilization, ethics, comparative religion, or the like." Nor did the majority find that provision for the copies having been paid for by private contributions eliminated the obvious state support that arose from the very enactment of the law by the state legislature.

Two justices dissented from the majority without opinion, but Justice Rehnquist wrote a separate dissenting opinion, criticizing the cavalier manner in which the majority had treated the Kentucky law. His dissent emphasized that "[t]he fact that the asserted secular purpose may overlap with what some may see as a religious objective does not render it unconstitutional." As an example, he cited the Court's upholding of Sunday closing laws. He also stated his opinion that the rejection by the

Court of the stated secular purpose "articulated by the legislature and confirmed by the state court is without precedent."

Seven years later, the Court considered a Louisiana law which also attempted to avoid constitutional invalidation by stating a secular purpose. At issue was the Louisiana Balanced Treatment for Creation-Science and Evolution-Science in Public School Instruction Act.[8] The law forbade the teaching of the theory of evolution in Louisiana public schools unless accompanied by instruction in "creation science," and it stated as the secular purpose for its enactment the protection of academic freedom.

The Court found the act unconstitutional, stating, "While the Court is normally deferential to a State's articulation of a secular purpose, it is required that the statement of such purpose be sincere and not a sham." In this case the Court reviewed the legislative history of the act and found that the purpose of the legislation's sponsor was to narrow the science curriculum rather than to promote academic freedom. The Court said, "Such a ban on teaching does not promote—indeed, it undermines—the provision of a comprehensive scientific education. It is equally clear that requiring schools to teach creation science with evolution does not advance academic freedom. The Act does not grant teachers a flexibility that they did not already possess to supplant the present science curriculum with the presentation of theories, besides evolution, about the origin of life."

Only two members of the Court dissented; Justice Scalia wrote the dissenting opinion, joined by Chief Justice Rehnquist. Responding to the determination by the majority that the statement of secular purpose was a sham, Justice Scalia wrote: "Our task is not to judge the debate about teaching the origins of life, but to ascertain what the members of the Louisiana Legislature believed. The vast majority of them voted to approve a bill which explicitly stated a secular purpose; what is critical is not their *wisdom* in believing that purpose would be achieved by the bill, but their *sincerity* in believing it would be." Justice Scalia concluded, "We have, moreover, no adequate basis for disbelieving the secular purpose set forth in the Act itself, or for concluding that it is a sham enacted to conceal the legislators' violation of their oaths of office. I am astonished by the Court's unprecedented readiness to reach such a conclusion, which I can only attribute to an intellectual predisposition created by the facts and the legend of *Scopes v. State. . . .* "[9]

Just as Chief Justice Rehnquist had done in his dissent to the silent prayer case, Justice Scalia criticized the continued use by the Court of the three-pronged Lemon test, and just as he had done before, Justice Powell wrote a separate concurring opinion urging the propriety of reliance by the Court upon the Lemon test in sensitive cases involving the relationship between government and religion.

Because legal precedent is so important to any decision by the Supreme Court, and because lower courts are bound by the precedent of Supreme Court decisions, all of the church-state cases that have been reviewed in this book could be potentially relevant to the consideration of any case involving school prayer. It is difficult, however, to reconcile all of those holdings. Part of that difficulty is inevitable because of the formidable task judges face when they trace the line of separation between church and state; part of that difficulty is explainable because the personnel on the Supreme Court have changed over the years.

But one writer suggests that "[t]he Supreme court has been inexcusably inconsistent in its interpretation of the establishment clause. . . . The public which has little patience with legal distinction, is appalled by the contradictory results of the Court's various decisions on the establishment clause. New York's released time program of religious education for public school children does not violate the establishment clause, nor do compulsory Sunday closing laws, nativity scenes on public property, or free bus-rides and secular books for parochial school children. And taxpayers can write off the cost of tuition for private church schools, if a state provides the deductions. But a brief nondenominational prayer, even if voluntary, violates the establishment clause, as do remedial reading lessons for dyslectic children in parochial schools if their teachers or lessons are paid by our taxes. The gift by the government of a globe of the world or a videocassette of inaugural addresses by presidents of the United States would be unconstitutional if a religious school were the recipient. Nor can the government underwrite the costs of a field trip for the pupils of that school to watch our courts in action: that would advance the religious mission of the school unconstitutionally, even though sending the child to that school at public expense so that the child can receive a religious education is constitutionally permissible as a benefit to the child rather than to the school. No one can make much sense out of the Court's establishment clause opinions."[10]

The writer does not reserve his criticism for the Court, however. Of the Accommodationists (who believe in government accommodation of religion, even if incidental benefits to religion are the result), he writes, " . . . [they] seem insatiable and use every exception as precedents for still more exceptions. The Moral Majority does not compromise."[11] On the other hand, of the Separationists (who believe in strict separation), he writes, " . . . [they] see every exception as a disaster, tend to run around like Chicken Little screaming, 'The Wall is falling, the wall is falling.' " Although he concludes, "It really is not and will not, so long as it leaks just a little at the seams. If it did not leak a little, it might generate enough pressure to break it."[12]

In short, he accuses the Accommodationists of thinking the Supreme

Court has built the wall of separation too tall and too thick, and the Separatists of thinking the Court has bulldozed the wall, while through it all the Court rules inconsistently. His criticisms only emphasize the need for each reader to study the issues and reach his or her own conclusion.

Whether the Supreme Court has been inexcusably inconsistent or has only acted prudently in allowing the wall to leak a little, the personnel on the Court can make a difference in whether, in the future, the leaks are plugged or opened wider.

The Creation-Science case was decided on June 19, 1987, and one week later Justice Powell surprised most Court-observers by announcing his retirement. The effect on the Court will have to await the test of history, but it portends greater than normal significance. Justice Powell was generally regarded as occupying the ideological center of the Court, and only a short time before his resignation an American Civil Liberties Union lawyer had described Powell's position on the Court with these words: "This mild-mannered Virginia man has incredible power. His vote makes a bigger difference than maybe anybody else's in the whole country on a whole range of issues. . . . "[13] With Powell's resignation, President Reagan was given the opportunity to shift the Court away from center in a conservative direction.

Already President Reagan had enjoyed the opportunity to appoint more judges to the federal bench (which includes lower federal courts), than any other president in this century. On the Supreme Court itself, he had appointed two justices—Sandra Day O'Connor and Antonin Scalia—and when Chief Justice Burger unexpectedly resigned, Reagan had filled his position with William Rehnquist. All of these appointees were regarded as conservatives.

The legacy of a president's appointments to the federal bench can extend far beyond that president's term, depending upon the ages of his appointees. Reagan actively sought conservative candidates for his judicial appointments, and by selecting the relatively young Rehnquist he increased the likely longevity of a conservative chief justice. At the time of Powell's departure from the Court, the three conservatives— Rehnquist, O'Connor, and Scalia—were the three youngest members of the Court, and the two justices regarded as liberals were the two oldest members. Because of the split between conservatives and liberals on the Court, control of issues rested with the four justices in the ideological center, and often upon Powell himself. Therefore, in filling the vacancy left by Powell, Reagan was given the opportunity to replace a centrist with a conservative and thereby shift the balance of power.

President Reagan was forthright in declaring his intention to appoint a conservative; however, his first nominee, Robert H. Bork, was rejected by the Senate, and his second nominee, Douglas H. Ginsburg, withdrew after acknowledging marijuana use. Bork and Ginsburg joined twenty-five other nominees who, beginning with George Washington's candidate for chief justice, have failed to win confirmation.[14] President Reagan's third nominee, Anthony M. Kennedy, was more of a compromise candidate with little evidence in speeches and judicial opinions from which supporters or opponents could evaluate his ideological predisposition; however, indications are that he will prove to be more conservative than the man he replaced on the Court.[15]

Of the tendency by most presidents to strive to hand-pick jurists whose legal philosophies are consistent with the president's own goals, often referred to as "packing the court" (as opposed to considering the most qualified jurists without regard to philosophy), Chief Justice Rehnquist has stated his approval. "Thus a president who sets out to pack the Court does nothing more than seek to appoint people to the Court who are sympathetic to his political or philosophical principles. There is no reason in the world why a president should not do this."[16]

Presidents have not always correctly predicted the judicial temperament of their nominees. President Eisenhower, a conservative Republican, admitted his disappointment with the judicial activism of his chief justice appointee, Earl Warren. President Nixon, also a conservative Republican, appointed Justice Harry Blackmun, who authored the 1973 *Roe v. Wade* abortion ruling that conservatives continue to dispute. President Reagan himself may have been disappointed by Justice O'Connor's having aligned herself with the majority in the silent prayer and the creation-science decisions.[17]

During the confirmation hearings, Americans may learn certain things about the nominee's philosophy, or how the nominee has ruled in previous cases; however, once confirmed, a new justice is free to step away from the political fray and make his or her own decisions, which may or may not be consistent with what the president, Congress, or the public anticipated from the nomination and confirmation process. Americans can reasonably anticipate several new appointments to the Court within the next few years, because of the ages of five of the justices.[18] These appointments will play a controlling role in the direction of the Court, and active public comment during the confirmation hearings, just as occurred during the Bork hearings, provides citizens with an opportunity to influence the selection of justices.

The impact of Powell's resignation may be particularly significant in church-state cases because of the loss to the Court of Powell's strong support for the use of the Lemon test, especially in light of the strong opposition to its continued use that has been expressed by the chief justice. It remains to be seen whether the Lemon test has lost its only champion on the Court, but until the Supreme Court rules to the contrary, it remains the tool that will be employed by lower federal courts in deciding religious issues.

Because there are precedent Supreme Court decisions on the issue of school prayer, lower court cases dealing with school prayer have not generally been included in this book. However, two recent lower court cases that never reached the Supreme Court, both of which concern disputes over the content of textbooks, are important for what they reveal about the difficulty of compromising on issues of content when religious beliefs are involved. During the Senate debates on the school prayer amendment, one of the factors that the two sides could not reconcile was whether the content of a voluntary prayer could be worded so as not to offend any of the students. Although both of the following cases involve textbooks rather than prayer, they offer insight into the unique difficulties involved in the drafting of acceptable content for any voluntary prayer.

The first case involved a community in Tennessee called Church Hill. A group of parents and their children from different denominations but all considering themselves born-again Christians challenged the required use of the Holt, Rinehart & Winston reading series in the public schools of their community. They found the content of the texts offensive to their religious beliefs because, in their words, the texts contained stories concerning evolution, "secular humanism," "futuristic supernaturalism," pacifism, magic and false views of death. Although some of the specific stories to which they objected are generally regarded as children's literary classics, these plaintiffs found them offensive. As examples, they objected to *Cinderella* because it involves magic, to Shakespeare's *Macbeth* because it involves witchcraft, to *The Wizard of Oz* because it suggests that traits such as courage, intelligence, and compassion can be developed as opposed to being God-given, and to *The Diary of Anne Frank* because it suggests that all religions are equal. The basis for their complaint was that the use of the readers exposed their children to other forms of religion and to the feelings, attitudes, and values of other students that contradicted their own religious views, without including instruction that the other views were incorrect and that their own views were correct. The trial court found that the use of a prescribed set of reading textbooks violated their constitutional rights and entered an injunction requiring the schools to excuse the children from participating in reading class, and awarding damages.[19] However, on appeal, that finding was reversed.

The appellate court considered whether exposure to ideas that are objectionable on religious grounds constitutes a burden on the free exercise of a person's religion to an extent forbidden by the First Amendment and concluded that it did not. The court said, "It is abundantly clear that the exposure to materials in the Holt series did not compel the plaintiffs to 'declare a belief,' 'communicate by word and sign [their] acceptance' of the ideas presented, or make an 'affirmation of a belief and an attitude of mind.' " And, therefore, the court held that "the requirement that public school students study a basal reader series chosen by the school authorities does not create an unconstitutional burden under the Free Exercise Clause when the students are not required to affirm or deny a belief or engage or refrain from engaging in a practice prohibited or required by their religion."

Particularly noteworthy was the testimony of one of the parents that she objected to stories that develop "a religious tolerance that all religions are merely different roads to God." She testified that their religion would not allow acceptance of "other religious views on an equal basis with ours." This testimony should be remembered when evaluating the assumption by many senators during the debates on the constitutional amendment that children and their parents would be tolerant of the prayers of their classmates from different faiths.

The impact of the case upon the residents of the Church Hill community is also worthy of note in light of arguments during the Senate debates that passage of the amendment would be divisive. One of the plaintiffs observed that "[y]ou either love us, or you hate us. We've received great support from lots of people who believe as we do, and we've also received threatening phone calls." A resident who disagreed with the plaintiffs reported that the case had turned the community into "a battlefield" and that most of the citizens were embarrassed by the national publicity focused upon the case. He further objected to the participation of outsiders in the case, whom he claimed had come into the community to "tell us that we're ignorant, for letting them teach humanism to our children, or that we're godless because we don't agree with them."[20]

The second case involving a constitutional challenge to the content of public school textbooks also resulted in a judgment for the plaintiffs at the trial court level that was reversed on appeal. In this Alabama case, the plaintiffs objected that the offending textbooks advanced the religion of "secular humanism" and inhibited theistic faiths in such a way as to violate the First Amendment.[21] The trial court agreed and enjoined the use of the offending texts.

Upon appeal the court said, " . . . the message conveyed is not one of endorsement of secular humanism or any religion. Rather, the message conveyed is one of a governmental attempt to instill in Alabama public school children such values as independent thought, tolerance of diverse views, self-respect, maturity, self-reliance and logical decision-making. This is an entirely appropriate secular effect." With respect to the testimony that the textbooks created an inaccurate historical picture by their omission of religion in the relating of historical events and by the neglect of references to the influence of religion in American society, the court said, "There simply is nothing in this record to indicate that omission of certain facts regarding religion from these textbooks of itself constituted an advancement of secular humanism or an active hostility towards theistic religion prohibited by the establishment clause. While these textbooks may be inadequate from an educational standpoint, the wisdom of an educational policy or its efficiency from an educational point of view is not germane to the constitutional issue of whether that policy violates the establishment clause."

While these cases were being heard by the various trial and appellate courts, studies of textbooks were being conducted by researchers of differing ideological views. Yet, despite their differences, the researchers agreed that the textbooks used in America's public schools neglect or omit entirely the importance of religion in historical or social events. One professor, himself a textbook author, observed, "Publishers have shied away from anything that's perceived as controversial." But he admitted that authors and publishers are "in a tough position. They want to try to be as accurate and sensitive as possible to a variety of groups that influence the adoption of books."[22]

Responding to the criticism, one of America's top ten publishers of textbooks announced plans to revise its books. Its chief executive officer said, "Publishers have to take a different attitude. We have a moral obligation to present a realistic view of religion to the kids of our nation." For his company, the decision required some courage because of the possible economic consequences. The revenues from the sale of textbooks by that company during the previous year had approached thirty million dollars, and those profits may have resulted at least in part from the removal of controversial content in order to broaden marketability.[23]

A consideration of the separation of church and state cannot overlook the political process, for the ballot box may very well be the place most important to the reader in making his or her opinion on the school prayer issue known. Political campaigns and politicians have certainly played key roles in church-state, and specifically, school prayer issues recently. Politicians are in a particularly delicate position when it comes to preserving the separation of church and state, as we have seen from the Senate debates on school prayer.[24] "For them, church support is a constant political temptation; they are offered sweet rewards without unpleasant responsibilities. Since almost no one is against God, it is profitable to appear to be on God's side—which often means, in practice, on the side of some religious group. . . . "[25] The governor of at least one state has hired an advisor on church-state affairs to serve as an administrative assistant,[26] and candidates hire religious consultants to assist with campaigns.

During the 1988 presidential primaries, ordained ministers who had gained national reputations through their ministry, rather than as elected officials, were candidates of both the Republican and the Democratic parties. Their initial campaign workers were recruited largely from among their religious supporters rather than from the ranks of veteran party workers, and significant financial support for both candidates could be traced to religious constituents as well.[27]

Among the most outspoken politicians on church-state issues, and particularly on the issue of school prayer, during the decade of the 1980s was President Ronald Reagan. It was he who proposed the school prayer amendment debated by the Senate, and the return of group prayer to America's classrooms was a frequent subject of his campaign and presidential speeches, as well as his state of the union addresses. During the Senate debates "Mr. Reagan met with a group of Senators at the White House to tell them that as a child he had had no problems listening to a variety of prayers in school." The *New York Times* article of March 24, 1984 continued: "The years, of course, temper and sometimes alter memories. Court records show that on June 29, 1910, the Supreme Court of Illinois, in *People ex rel Ring et al. v. Board of Education of District 24,* issued a decision banning mandatory school prayer. The decision was handed down nearly eight months before Mr. Reagan was born February 6, 1911, in Tampico, Illinois. The decision said, in part, that 'religion is taught and should be taught in the churches' and imposing a prayer in which a student felt he could not take part 'subjects him to a religious stigma and places him at a disadvantage in the school which the law never contemplated.' " The deputy White House secretary later said that the president's recollection had been of public school group prayers on special occasions.[28] The words of the Illinois state supreme court prohibiting group school prayer in the classrooms of the president's youth sound very similar to the words of the United States Supreme Court that the president accused of having expelled God from America's classrooms.

Over three hundred years ago when Roger Williams established the colony of Rhode Island and prohibited the use of the "civil sword in religious matters," one Puritan predicted that such a policy would attract "Seducers to the Apostacy, Idolators, and Heretiks." Williams replied, "The Civil Sword may make a Nation of Hypocrites and Antichristians, but not one Christian." To which the Puritan responded, "If it did so, yet better to be hypocrites than prophane persons. Hypocrites give God part of his due, the outward man, but the prophane person giveth God neither outward nor inward man."[29] Much of the present debate over spoken group prayer relates, even today, to whether encouragement by civil government of prayer in public schools would make a more Christian, or only a more hypocritical, nation.

During the Constitution ratification debates in North Carolina, James Iredell, who had been a delegate to the convention and who later was among the first justices appointed to the United States Supreme Court, had this to say about the Constitution. "If any future Congress should pass an act concerning the religion of the country, it would be an act which they are not authorized to pass by the Constitution, and which the people would not obey."[30]

At the time of American independence, perhaps less than ten percent of the population were members of any church, and most of those were Protestant. Under the climate of religious liberty protected by the First Amendment, church membership rose to 15.5% in 1850, to 35.7% in 1900, to 43.5% in 1910,[31] to 58.7% today.[32] And, while Protestants still constitute approximately 56% of the population and Catholics another 29%, there are now 15% of America's citizens outside those two groups.[33] There are one thousand three hundred forty-seven different religious organizations in America, according to the Encyclopedia of American Religions,[34] and one-third of the population claims to attend church at least once a week.[35] Certainly any reasoned decision regarding possible changes to religious liberty in America must consider the growth and diversity of religions that have occurred under the present system. As one writer warned, "If we as a society choose to dismantle the system of using insulated and independent judges to define and enforce individual rights, no *deus ex machina* will descend from the text of the Constitution or in the form of John Marshall's ghost to protect us from ourselves. The political assaults . . . are not merely legitimate political gambits—they are assaults on the way Americans have learned to govern themselves as a free people."[36] A historian writing early in this century warned, "No man is fit to be entrusted with the control of the Present, who is ignorant of the Past, and no People, who are indifferent to their Past, need hope to make their future great."[37]

Americans have a simpler saying—"If it ain't broke, don't fix it." Former President Reagan, and his successor George Bush, a majority of the 1984 Senate, and a great many of the citizens of this nation passionately believe that something is broken within the Constitution, or the courts interpreting it, if school children are unable to join in group prayers in their classrooms, and that a constitutional amendment is needed to fix it. Former President Jimmy Carter, many religious leaders and constitutional scholars, and a great many citizens believe nothing is broken, since school children are already free to pray their own individual prayers and religion has prospered under the existing laws, all of which would be jeopardized by a constitutional amendment.

It is difficult to predict the outcome of the movement for voluntary spoken prayer in America's public schools. Ultimately the issue will be decided by the American people. Their expressions of opinion on the issue will be found in the votes they cast, the lawsuits they file,[38] the letters-to-the-editor they write, and the opinions they express over the dinner tables in their own homes. They may arrive at their opinions through an awareness of the religious, political, and legal history of the nation. Or they may feel as they do because of their own personal experiences. Unfortunately, they will probably have had little formal education on the history related to the issue, since America's public schools have avoided teaching religious history and the impact of religion upon political events from a fear of violating constitutional prohibitions. This book was written to make that history available so that the opinions of more Americans, regardless of what those opinions may ultimately be, will have benefitted from the lessons of history.

When the founding fathers drafted the First Amendment there were no public schools. Yet, in their amazing wisdom they created a law that has been employed by the citizens and the courts to protect the rights of American school children of all faiths. Has the price for extending that protection to all beliefs—majority, minority, and non-believers alike— caused a weakening of the morality and spirituality of the nation? Or is that protection, unique in all the world, the spiritual strength of America? Americans are being asked to decide, and the future character of this nation rests upon their answer.

APPENDIX A
James Madison's
MEMORIAL AND REMONSTRANCE
AGAINST RELIGIOUS ASSESSMENTS*

We, the subscribers, citizens of the said Commonwealth, having taken into serious consideration, a Bill printed by order of the last Session of General Assembly, entitled "A Bill establishing a provision for Teachers of the Christian Religion," and conceiving that the same, if finally armed with the sanctions of a law, will be a dangerous abuse of power, are bound as faithful members of a Free State, to remonstrate against it, and to declare the reasons by which we are determined. We remonstrate against the said Bill.

1. Because we hold it for a fundamental and undeniable truth, "that Religion or the duty which we owe to our Creator and the Manner of discharging it, can be directed only by reason and conviction, not by force or violence." The Religion then of every man must be left to the conviction and conscience of every man; and it is the right of every man to exercise it as these may dictate. This right is in its nature an unalienable right. It is unalienable; because the opinions of men, depending only on the evidence contemplated by their own minds, cannot follow the dictates of other men: It is unalienable also; because what is here a right towards men, is a duty towards the Creator. It is the duty of every man to render to the Creator such homage, and such only, as he believes to be acceptable to him. This duty is precedent both in order of time and degree of obligation, to the claims of Civil Society. Before any man can be considered as a member of Civil Society, he must be considered as a subject of the Governor of the Universe: And if a member of Civil Society, who enters into any subordinate Association, must always do it with a reservation of his duty to the general authority; much more must every man who becomes a member of any particular Civil Society, do it with a saving of his allegiance to the Universal Sovereign. We maintain therefore that in matters of Religion, no man's right is abridged by the institution of Civil Society, and that Religion is wholly exempt from its cognizance. True it is, that no other rule exists, by which any question which may divide a Society, can be ultimately determined, but the will of the majority; but it is also true, that the majority may trespass on the rights of the minority.

*Reprinted from Norman Cousins, ed., *"In God We Trust": The Religious Beliefs and Ideas of the American Founding Fathers.* New York: Harper and Brothers, 1958.

2. Because if religion be exempt from the authority of the Society at large, still less can it be subject to that of the Legislative Body. The latter are but the creatures and vicegerents [*sic*] of the former. Their jurisdiction is both derivative and limited: it is limited with regard to the coordinate departments, more necessarily is it limited with regard to the constituents. The preservation of a free government requires not merely, that the metes and bounds which separate each department of power may be invariably maintained; but more especially, that neither of them be suffered to over-leap the great Barrier which defends the rights of the people. The Rulers who are guilty of such an encroachment, exceed the commission from which they derive their authority, and are Tyrants. The People who submit to it are governed by laws made neither by themselves, nor by an authority derived from them, and are slaves.

3. Because, it is proper to take alarm at the first experiment on our liberties. We hold this prudent jealousy to be the first duty of citizens, and one of [the] noblest characteristics of the late Revolution. The freemen of America did not wait till usurped power had strengthened itself by exercise, and entangled the question in precedents. They saw all the consequences in the principle, and they avoided the consequences by denying the principle. We revere this lesson too much, soon to forget it. Who does not see that the same authority which can establish Christianity, in exclusion of all other Religions, may establish with the same ease any particular sect of Christians, in exclusion of all other Sects? That the same authority which can force a citizen to contribute three pence only of his property for the support of any one establishment, may force him to conform to any other establishment in all cases whatsoever?

4. Because, the bill violates that equality which ought to be the basis of every law, and which is more indispensible, in proportion as the validity or expediency of any law is more liable to be impeached. If "all men are by nature equally free and independent," all men are to be considered as entering into Society on equal conditions; as relinquishing no more, and therefore retaining no less, one than another, of their natural rights. Above all are they to be considered as retaining an "*equal* title to the free exercise of Religion according to the dictates of conscience". Whilst we assert for ourselves a freedom to embrace, to profess, and to observe the Religion which we believe to be of divine origin, we cannot deny an equal freedom to those whose minds have not yet yielded to the evidence which has convinced us. If this freedom be abused, it is an offense against God, not against man: To God, therefore, not to man, must an account of it be rendered. As the Bill violates equality by subjecting some to peculiar burdens; so it violates the same principle, by granting to others peculiar exemptions. Are the Quakers and Menonists the only sects who think a compulsive support of their religions unnecessary and unwarrantable? Can their piety alone be entrusted with the care of public worship? Ought their Religions to be endowed above all others, with extraordinary privileges, by which proselytes may be enticed from all others? We think too favorably of the justice and good sense of these denominations, to believe that they either covet preeminencies over their fellow citizens, or that they will be seduced by them, from the common opposition to the measure.

5. Because the bill implies either that the Civil Magistrate is a competent Judge of Religious truth; or that he may employ Religion as an engine of Civil

policy. The first is an arrogant pretension falsified by the contradictory opinions of Rulers in all ages, and throughout the world: The second an unhallowed perversion of the means of salvation.

6. Because the establishment proposed by the Bill is not requisite for the support of the Christian Religion. To say that it is, is a contradiction to the Christian Religion itself; for every page of it disavows a dependence on the powers of this world: it is a contradiction to fact; for it is known that this Religion both existed and flourished, not only without the support of human laws, but in spite of every opposition from them; and not only during the period of miraculous aid, but long after it had been left to its own evidence, and the ordinary care of Providence: Nay, it is a contradiction in terms; for a Religion not invented by human policy, must have pre-existed and been supported, before it was established by human policy. It is moreover to weaken in those who profess this Religion a pious confidence in its innate excellence, and the patronage of its Author; and to foster in those who still reject it, a suspicion that its friends are too conscious of its fallacies, to trust it to its own merits.

7. Because experience witnesseth that ecclesiastical establishments, instead of maintaining the purity and efficacy of Religion, have had a contrary operation. During almost fifteen centuries, has the legal establishment of Christianity been on trial. What have been its fruits? More or less in all places, pride and indolence in the Clergy; ignorance and servility in the laity; in both, superstition, bigotry and persecution. Enquire of the Teachers of Christianity for the ages in which it appeared in its greatest lustre; those of every sect, point to the ages prior to its incorporation with Civil policy. Propose a restoration of this primitive state in which its Teachers depended on the voluntary rewards of their flocks; many of them predict its downfall. On which side ought their testimony to have greatest weight, when for or when against their interests?

8. Because the establishment in question is not necessary for the support of Civil Government. If it be urged as necessary for the support of Civil Government only as it is a means of supporting Religion, and it be not necessary for the latter purpose, it cannot be necessary for the former. If Religion be not within [the] cognizance of Civil Government, how can its legal establishment be said to be necessary to civil Government? What influence in fact have ecclesiastical establishments had on Civil Society? In some instances they have been seen to erect a spiritual tyranny on the ruins of Civil authority; in many instances they have been seen upholding the thrones of political tyranny; in no instance have they been seen the guardians of the liberties of the people. Rulers who wished to subvert the public liberty, may have found an established clergy convenient auxiliaries. A just government, instituted to secure and perpetuate it, needs them not. Such a government will be best supported by protecting every citizen in the enjoyment of his Religion with the same equal hand which protects his person and his property; by neither invading the equal rights of any Sect, nor suffering any Sect to invade those of another.

9. Because the proposed establishment is a departure from that generous policy, which, offering an asylum to the persecuted and oppressed of every Nation and Religion, promised a lustre to our country, and an accession to the number of its citizens. What a melancholy mark is the Bill of sudden degeneracy? Instead of holding forth an asylum to the persecuted, it is itself a signal

of persecution. It degrades from the equal rank of Citizens all those whose opinions in Religion do not bend to those of the Legislative authority. Distant as it may be, in its present form, from the Inquisition it differs from it only in degree. The one is the first step, the other the last in the career of intolerance. The magnanimous sufferer under this cruel scourge in foreign Regions, must view the Bill as a Beacon on our Coast, warning him to seek some other haven, where liberty and philanthropy in their due extent may offer a more certain repose from his troubles.

10. Because, it will have a like tendency to banish our Citizens. The allurements presented by other situations are every day thinning their number. To superadd a fresh motive to emigration, by revoking the liberty which they now enjoy, would be the same species of folly which has dishonored and depopulated flourishing kingdoms.

11. Because, it will destroy that moderation and harmony which the forbearance of our laws to intermeddle with Religion, has produced amongst its several sects. Torrents of blood have been spilt in the old world, by vain attempts of the secular arm to extinguish Religious discord, by proscribing all difference in Religious opinions. Time has at length revealed the true remedy. Every relaxation of narrow and rigorous policy, wherever it has been tried, has been found to assuage the disease. The American Theatre has exhibited proofs, that equal and complete liberty, if it does not wholly eradicate it, sufficiently destroys its malignant influence on the health and prosperity of the State. If with the salutary effects of this system under our own eyes, we begin to contract the bonds of Religious freedom, we know no name that will too severely reproach our folly. At least let warning be taken at the first fruits of the threatened innovation. The very appearance of the Bill has transformed that "Christian forbearance, love and charity," which of late mutually prevailed, into animosities and jealousies, which may not soon be appeased. What mischiefs may not be dreaded should this enemy to the public quiet be armed with the force of a law?

12. Because, the policy of the Bill is adverse to the diffusion of the light of Christianity. The first wish of those who enjoy this precious gift, ought to be that it may be imparted to the whole race of mankind. Compare the number of those who have as yet received it with the number still remaining under the dominion of false Religions; and how small is the former! Does the policy of the Bill tend to lessen the disproportions? No; it at once discourages those who are strangers to the light of [revelation] from coming into the Region of it; and countenances, by example the nations who continue in darkness, in shutting out those who might convey it to them. Instead of leveling as far as possible, every obstacle to the victorious progress of truth, the Bill with an ignoble and unchristian timidity would circumscribe it, with a wall of defence, against the encroachments of error.

13. Because attempts to enforce by legal sanctions, acts obnoxious to so great a proportion of Citizens, tend to enervate the laws in general, and to slacken the bands of Society. If it be difficult to execute any law which is not generally deemed necessary or salutary, what must be the case where it is deemed invalid and dangerous? And what may be the effect of so striking an example of impotency in the Government, on its general authority.

14. Because a measure of such singular magnitude and delicacy ought not to be imposed, without the clearest evidence that it is called for by a majority of citizens: and no satisfactory method is yet proposed by which the voice of the majority in this case may be determined, or its influence secured. "The people of the respective counties are indeed requested to signify their opinion respecting the adoption of the Bill to the next Session of Assembly." But the representation must be made equal, be ore the voice either of the Representatives or of the Counties, will be that of the people. Our hope is that neither of the former will, after due consideration, espouse the dangerous principle of the Bill. Should the event disappoint us, it will still leave us in full confidence, that a fair appeal to the latter will reverse the sentence against our liberties.

15. Because, finally, "the equal right of every citizen to the free exercise of his Religion according to the dictates of conscience" is held by the same tenure with all our other rights. If we recur to its origin, it is equally the gift of nature; if we weigh its importance, it cannot be less dear to us; if we consult the Declaration of those rights which pertain to the good people of Virginia, as the "basis and foundation of Government," it is enumerated with equal solemnity, or rather studied emphasis. Either then, we must say, that the will of the Legislature is the only measure of their authority; and that in the plenitude of this authority, they may sweep away all our fundamental rights; or, that they are bound to leave this particular right untouched and sacred: Either we must say, that they may control the freedom of the press, may abolish the trial by jury, may swallow up the Executive and Judiciary Powers of the State; nay that they may despoil us of our very right of suffrage, and erect themselves into an independent and hereditary assembly: or we must say, that they have no authority to enact into law the Bill under consideration. We the subscribers say, that the General Assembly of this Commonwealth have no such authority: And that no effort may be omitted on our part against so dangerous an usurpation, we oppose to it, this remonstrance; earnestly praying, as we are in duty bound, that the Supreme Lawgiver of the Universe, by illuminating those to whom it is addressed, may on the one hand, turn their councils from every act which would affront his holy prerogative, or violate the trust committed to them: and on the other, guide them into every measure which may be worthy of his [blessing may re]dound to their own praise, and may establish more firmly the liberties, the prosperity, and the Happiness of the Commonwealth.

APPENDIX B
A BILL FOR ESTABLISHING RELIGIOUS FREEDOM

[Below is the complete text of Thomas Jefferson's Bill for Establishing Religious Freedom,* presented to the Virginia Assembly in 1779. The words that appear in italics were removed prior to passage of the bill in 1785.]

Well aware that the opinions and belief of men depend not on their own will, but follow involuntarily the evidence proposed to their minds; that Almighty God hath created the mind free, *and manifested His supreme will that free it shall remain by making it altogether insusceptible of restraint;* that all attempts to influence it by temporal punishments, or burthens, or by civil incapacitations, tend only to beget habits of hypocrisy and meanness, and are a departure from the plan of the holy author of our religion, who being lord both of body and mind, yet chose not to propagate it by coercions on either, as was in his Almighty power to do, *but to extend it by its influence on reason alone;* that the impious presumption of legislators and rulers, civil as well as ecclesiastical, who, being themselves but fallible and uninspired men, have assumed dominion over the faith of others, setting up their own opinions and modes of thinking as the only true and infallible, and as such endeavoring to impose them on others, hath established and maintained false religions over the greatest part of the world and through all time: That to compel a man to furnish contributions of money for the propagation of opinions which he disbelieves *and abhors,* is sinful and tyrannical; that even the forcing him to support this or that teacher of his own religious persuasion, is depriving him of the comfortable liberty of giving his contributions to the particular pastor whose morals he would make his pattern, and whose powers he feels most persuasive to righteousness; and is withdrawing from the ministry those temporary rewards, which proceeding from an approbation of their personal conduct, are an additional incitement to earnest and unremitting labours for the instruction of mankind; that our civil rights have no dependance on our religious opinions, and more than our opinions in physics or geometry; that therefore the proscribing any citizen as unworthy the public confidence by laying upon him an incapacity of being called to offices of trust and emolument, unless he profess or renounce this or that religious opinion, is depriving him injuriously of those privileges and advantages to which, in com-

---

*Thomas Jefferson, *A Biography in his Own Words.* Editors of Newsweek Books. New York: Newsweek, 1974.

mon with his fellow citizens, he has a natural right; that it tends also to corrupt the principles of that *very* religion it is meant to encourage, by bribing, with a monopoly of worldly honours and emoluments, those who will externally profess and conform to it; that though indeed these are criminal who do not withstand such temptation, yet neither are those innocent who lay the bait in their way; *that the opinions of men are not the object of civil government nor under its jurisdiction*; that to suffer the civil magistrate to intrude his powers into the field of opinion and to restrain the profession or propagation of principles on supposition of their ill tendency is a dangerous falacy, which at once destroys all religious liberty, because he being of course judge of that tendency will make his opinions the rule of judgment, and approve or condemn the sentiments of others only as they shall square with or differ from his own; that it is time enough for the rightful purposes of civil government for its officers to interfere when principles break out into overt acts against peace and good order; and finally, that truth is great and will prevail if left to herself; that she is the proper and sufficient antagonist to error, and has nothing to fear from the conflict unless by human interposition disarmed of her natural weapons, free argument and debate; errors ceasing to be dangerous when it is permitted freely to contradict them. *We the General Assembly of Virginia do enact* that no man shall be compelled to frequent or support any religious worship, place, or ministry whatsoever, nor shall be enforced, restrained, molested, or burthened in his body or goods, nor shall otherwise suffer, on account of his religious opinions or belief; but that all men shall be free to profess, and by argument to maintain, their opinions in matters of religion, and that the same shall in no wise diminish, enlarge, or affect their civil capacities.

And though we well know that this Assembly, elected by the people for the ordinary purposes of legislation only, have no power to restrain the acts of succeeding Assemblies, constituted with powers equal to our own, and that therefore to declare this act irrevocable would be of no effect in law; yet we are free to declare, and do declare, that the rights hereby asserted are of the natural rights of mankind, and that if any act shall be hereafter passed to repeal the present or to narrow its operation, such act will be an infringement of natural right.

APPENDIX C
HOUSE DEBATES OF AUGUST 15, 1789

[This report is from Volume One of The Debates and Proceedings in the Congress of the United States, commonly known as the Annals of Congress. The volume, despite its name, is not an official document but rather is an abstract composed from newspaper accounts written at the time of the debates. It should not be regarded as a verbatim transcript of the proceedings.]

Amendments to the Constitution

The House again went into a Committee of the Whole on the proposed amendments to the constitution, Mr. Boudinot in the chair.

The fourth proposition being under consideration, as follows:

Article I. Section 9. Between paragraphs two and three insert "no religion shall be established by law, nor shall the equal rights of conscience be infringed."

Mr. Sylvester had some doubts of the propriety of the mode of expression used in this paragraph. He apprehended that it was liable to a construction different from what had been made by the committee. He feared it might be thought to have a tendency to abolish religion altogether.

Mr. Vining suggested the propriety of transposing the two members of the sentence.

Mr. Gerry said it would read better if it was, that no religious doctrine shall be established by law.

Mr. Sherman thought the amendment altogether unnecessary, inasmuch as Congress had no authority whatever delegated to them by the constitution to make religious establishments; he would, therefore, move to have it struck out.

Mr. Carroll—As the rights of conscience are, in their nature, of peculiar delicacy, and will little bear the gentlest touch of governmental hand; and as many sects have concurred in opinion that they are not well secured under the present constitution, he said he was much in favor of adopting the words. He thought it would tend more towards conciliating the minds of the people to the Government than almost any other amendment he had heard proposed. He would not contend with gentlemen about the phraseology, his object was to secure the substance in such a manner as to satisfy the wishes of the honest part of the community.

Mr. Madison said, he apprehended the meaning of the words to be, that Congress should not establish a religion, and enforce the legal observation of it by law, nor compel men to worship God in any manner contrary to their conscience. Whether the words are necessary or not, he did not mean to say, but they had been required by some of the State Conventions, who seemed to entertain an opinion that under the clause of the constitution, which gave power to Congress to make all laws necessary and proper to carry into execution the constitution, and the laws made under it, enabled them to make laws of such a nature as might infringe the rights of conscience, and establish a national religion; to prevent these effects he presumed the amendment was intended, and he thought it as well expressed as the nature of the language would admit.

Mr. Huntington said that he feared, with the gentleman first up on this subject, that the words might be taken in such latitude as to be extremely harmful to the cause of religion. He understood the amendment to mean what had been expressed by the gentleman from Virginia; but others might find it convenient to put another construction upon it. The ministers of their congregations to the Eastward were maintained by the contributions of those who belonged to their society; the expense of building meeting-houses was contributed in the same manner. These things were regulated by by-laws. If an action was brought before a Federal Court on any of these cases, the person who had neglected to perform his engagements could not be compelled to do it; for a support of ministers, or building of places of worship might be construed into a religious establishment.

By the charter of Rhode Island, no religion could be established by law; he could give a history of the effects of such a regulation; indeed the people were now enjoying the blessed fruits of it. [Intended as irony.] He hoped, therefore, the amendment would be made in such a way as to secure the rights of conscience, and a free exercise of the rights of religion, but not to patronize those who professed no religion at all.

Mr. Madison thought, if the word national was inserted before religion, it would satisfy the minds of honorable gentlemen. He believed that the people feared one sect might obtain a pre-eminence, or two combine together, and establish a religion to which they would compel others to conform. He thought if the word national was introduced, it would point the amendment directly to the object it was intended to prevent.

Mr. Livermore was not satisfied with that amendment; but he did not wish them to dwell long on the subject. He thought it would be better if it was altered, and made to read in this manner, that Congress shall make no laws touching religion, or infringing the rights of conscience.

Mr. Gerry did not like the term national, proposed by the gentleman from Virginia, and he hoped it would not be adopted by the House. It brought to his mind some observations that had taken place in the conventions at the time they were considering the present constitution. It had been insisted upon by those who were called antifederalists, that this form of Government consolidated the Union; the honorable gentleman's motion shows that he considers it in the same light. Those who were called antifederalists at that time complained that they had injustice done them by the title, because they were in favor of a Federal Government, and the others were in favor of a national one; the federalists were for ratifying the constitution as it stood, and the others not until amendments were made. Their names then ought not to have been distinguished by federalists and antifederalists, but rats and antirats.

Mr. Madison withdrew his motion, but observed that the words "no national religion shall be established by law," did not imply that the Government was a national one; the question was then taken on Mr. Livermore's motion, and passed in the affirmative, thirty-one for, and twenty against it.

APPENDIX D
THOMAS JEFFERSON'S LETTER TO THE
DANBURY BAPTIST ASSOCIATION*

To Nehemiah Dodge, Ephraim Robbins, and Stephen S. Nelson: A Committee of the Danbury Baptist Association, Connecticut, January 1, 1802

The affectionate sentiments of esteem and approbation which you are so good as to express towards me, on behalf of the Danbury Baptist Association, give me the highest satisfaction.

My duties dictate a faithful and zealous pursuit of the interests of my constituents, and in proportion as they are persuaded of my fidelity to those duties, the discharge of them becomes more and more pleasing.

Believing with you that religion is a matter which lies solely between man and his God, that he owes account to none other for his faith or his worship, that the legislative powers of government reach actions only, and not opinions, I contemplate with sovereign reverence that act of the whole American people which declared that their legislature should "make no law respecting an establishment of religion, or prohibiting the free exercise thereof," thus building a wall of separation between Church and State. Adhering to this expression of the supreme will of the nation in behalf of the rights of conscience, I shall see with sincere satisfaction the progress of those sentiments which tend to restore to man all his natural rights, convinced he has no natural right in opposition to his social duties.

I reciprocate your kind prayers for the protection and blessing of the common Father and Creator of man, and tender you for yourselves and your religious association, assurances of my high respect and esteem.

---

*Reprinted from Norman Cousins, ed., *"In God We Trust": The Religious Beliefs and Ideas of the American Founding Fathers.* New York: Harper and Brothers, 1958.

APPENDIX E
OPINIONS IN *ENGEL V. VITALE*

STEVEN I. ENGEL et al., Petitioners,

v

WILLIAM J. VITALE, Jr., et al.

Argued April 3, 1962. Decided June 25, 1962.

Mr. Justice Black delivered the opinion of the Court.

The respondent Board of Education of Union Free School District No. 9, New Hyde Park, New York, acting in its official capacity under state law, directed the School District's principal to cause the following prayer to be said aloud by each class in the presence of a teacher at the beginning of each school day:

"Almighty God, we acknowledge our dependence upon Thee, and we beg Thy blessings upon us, our parents, our teachers and our Country."

This daily procedure was adopted on the recommendation of the State Board of Regents, a governmental agency created by the State Constitution to which the New York Legislature has granted broad supervisory, executive, and legislative powers over the State's public school system.[1] These state officials composed the prayer which they recommended and published as a part of their "Statement on Moral and Spiritual Training in the Schools," saying: "We believe that this Statement will be subscribed to by all men and women of good will, and we call upon all of them to aid in giving life to our program."

Shortly after the practice of reciting the Regents' prayer was adopted by the School District, the parents of ten pupils brought this action in a New York State Court insisting that use of this official prayer in the public schools was contrary to the beliefs, religions, or religious practices of both themselves and their children. Among other things, these parents challenged the constitutionality of both the state law authorizing the School District to direct the use of prayer in public schools and the School District's regulation ordering the recitation of this particular prayer on the ground that these actions of official governmental agencies violate that part of the First Amendment of the Federal Constitution which commands that "Congress shall make no law respecting an establishment of religion"—a command which was "made applicable to the State of New York by the Fourteenth Amendment of the said Constitution." The New York Court of Appeals, over the dissents of Judges Dye and Fuld,

---

1. See New York Constitution, Art 5, § 4; New York Education Law, §§ 101, 120 et seq, 202, 214–219, 224, 245 et seq, 704, and 801 et seq.

sustained an order of the lower state courts which had upheld the power of New York to use the Regents' prayer as a part of the daily procedures of its public schools so long as the schools did not compel any pupil to join in the prayer over his or his parents' objection.[2] We granted certiorari to review this important decision involving rights protected by the First and Fourteenth Amendments.[3]

We think that by using its public school system to encourage recitation of the Regents' prayer, the State of New York has adopted a practice wholly inconsistent with the Establishment Clause. There can, of course, be no doubt that New York's program of daily classroom invocation of God's blessings as prescribed in the Regents' prayer is a religious activity. It is a solemn avowal of divine faith and supplication for the blessings of the Almighty. The nature of such a prayer has always been religious, none of the respondents has denied this and the trial court expressly so found:

"The religious nature of prayer was recognized by Jefferson and has been concurred in by theological writers, the United States Supreme Court and State courts and administrative officials, including New York's Commissioner of Education. A committee of the New York Legislature has agreed.

"The Board of Regents as amicus curiae, the respondents and intervenors all concede the religious nature of prayer, but seek to distinguish this prayer because it is based on our spiritual heritage. . . . "[4]

The petitioners contend among other things that the state laws requiring or permitting use of the Regents' prayer must be struck down as a violation of the Establishment Clause because that prayer was composed by governmental officials as a part of a governmental program to further religious beliefs. For this

2. 10 NY2d 174, 218 NYS2d 659, 176 NE2d, 579. The trial court's opinion, which is reported at 18 Misc 2d 659, 191 NYS2d 453, had made it clear that the Board of Education must set up some sort of procedures to protect those who objected to reciting the prayer: "This is not to say that the rights accorded petitioners and their children under the 'free exercise' clause do not mandate safeguards against such embarrassments and pressures. It is enough on this score, however, that regulations, such as were adopted by New York City's Board of Education in connection with its released time program, be adopted, making clear that neither teachers nor any other school authority may comment on participation or nonparticipation in the exercise nor suggest or require that any posture or language be used or dress be worn or be not used or not worn. Nonparticipation may take the form either of remaining silent during the exercise, or if the parent or child so desires, of being excused entirely from the exercise. Such regulations must also make provision for those nonparticipants who are to be excused from the prayer exercise. The exact provision to be made is a matter for decision by the board, rather than the court, within the framework of constitutional requirements. Within that framework would fall a provision that prayer participants proceed to a common assembly while nonparticipants attend other rooms, or that nonparticipants be permitted to arrive at school a few minutes late or to attend separate opening exercises, or any other method which treats with equality both participants and nonparticipants." 18 Misc 2d, at 696, 191 NYS2d, at 492, 493. See also the opinion of the Appellate Division affirming that of the trial court, reported at 11 App Div 2d 340, 206 NYS2d 183.

3. 368 US 924, 7 L ed 2d 189, 82 S Ct 367.

4. 18 Misc 2d, at 671, 672, 191 NYS 2d, at 468, 469.

reason, petitioners argue, the State's use of the Regents' prayer in its public school system breaches the constitutional wall of separation between Church and State. We agree with that contention since we think that the constitutional prohibition against laws respecting an establishment of religion must at least mean that in this country it is no part of the business of government to compose official prayers for any group of the American people to recite as a part of a religious program carried on by government.

It is a matter of history that this very practice of establishing governmentally composed prayers for religious services was one of the reasons which caused many of our early colonists to leave England and seek religious freedom in America. The Book of Common Prayer, which was created under governmental direction and which was approved by Acts of Parliament in 1548 and 1549,[5] set out in minute detail the accepted form and content of prayer and other religious ceremonies to be used in the established, tax-supported Church of England.[6] The controversies over the Book and what should be its content repeatedly threatened to disrupt the peace of that country as the accepted forms of prayer in the established church changed with the views of the particular ruler that happened to be in control at the time.[7] Powerful groups representing some of the varying religious views of the people struggled among themselves to impress their particular views upon the Government and obtain amendments of the Book more suitable to their respective notions of how religious services should be conducted in order that the official religious establishment would advance their particular religious beliefs.[8] Other groups, lacking the necessary

---

5. 2 & 3 Edward VI, c 1, entitled "An Act for Uniformity of Service and Administration of the Sacraments throughout the Realm"; 3 & 4 Edward VI, c 10, entitled "An Act for the abolishing and putting away of divers Books and Images."

6. The provisions of the various versions of the Book of Common Prayer are set out in broad outline in the Encyclopedia Britannica, Vol 18 (1957 ed), pp 420–423. For a more complete description, see Pullan, The History of the Book of Common Prayer (1900).

7. The first major revision of the Book of Common Prayer was made in 1552 during the reign of Edward VI. 5 & 6 Edward VI, c 1. In 1553, Edward VI died and was succeeded by Mary who abolished the Book of Common Prayer entirely. 1 Mary, c 2. But upon the accession of Elizabeth in 1558, the Book was restored with important alterations from the form it had been given by Edward VI. 1 Elizabeth, c 2. The resentment to this amended form of the Book was kept firmly under control during the reign of Elizabeth but, upon her death in 1603, a petition signed by more than 1,000 Puritan ministers was presented to King James I asking for further alterations in the Book. Some alterations were made and the Book retained substantially this form until it was completely suppressed again in 1645 as a result of the successful Puritan Revolution. Shortly after the restoration in 1660 of Charles II, the Book was again reintroduced, 13 & 14 Charles II, c 4, and again with alterations. Rather than accept this form of the Book some 2,000 Puritan ministers vacated their benefices. See generally Pullan, The History of the Book of Common Prayer (1900), pp vii–xvi; Encyclopedia Britannica (1957 ed), Vol 18, pp 421–422.

8. For example, the Puritans twice attempted to modify the Book of Common Prayer and once attempted to destroy it. The story of their struggle to modify the Book in the reign of Charles I is vividly summarized in Pullan, History of the Book of Common

political power to influence the Government on the matter, decided to leave England and its established church and seek freedom in America from England's governmentally ordained and supported religion.

It is an unfortunate fact of history that when some of the very groups which had most strenuously opposed the established Church of England found themselves sufficiently in control of colonial governments in this country to write their own prayers into law, they passed laws making their own religion the official religion of their respective colonies.[9] Indeed, as late as the time of the Revolutionary War, there were established churches in at least eight of the thirteen former colonies and established religions in at least four of the other five.[10] But the successful Revolution against English political domination was shortly followed by intense opposition to the practice of establishing religion by law. This opposition crystallized rapidly into an effective political force in Virginia where the minority religious groups such as Presbyterians, Lutherans, Quakers and Baptists had gained such strength that the adherents to the established Episcopal Church were actually a minority themselves. In 1785–1786, those opposed to the established Church, led by James Madison and Thomas Jefferson, who, though themselves not members of any of those dissenting religious groups, opposed all religious establishments by law on grounds of principle, obtained the enactment of the famous "Virginia Bill for Religious Liberty" by which all religious groups were placed on an equal footing so far as the State

---

Prayer, at p xiii: "The King actively supported those members of the Church of England who were anxious to vindicate its Catholic character and maintain the ceremonial which Elizabeth had approved. Laud, Archbishop of Canterbury, was the leader of this school. Equally resolute in his opposition to the distinctive tenets of Rome and of Geneva, he enjoyed the hatred of both Jesuit and Calvinist. He helped the Scottish bishops, who had made large concessions to the uncouth habits of Presbyterian worship, to draw up a Book of Common Prayer for Scotland. It contained a Communion Office resembling that of the book of 1549. It came into use in 1637, and met with a bitter and barbarous opposition. The vigour of the Scottish Protestants strengthened the hands of their English sympathisers. Laud and Charles were executed, Episcopacy was abolished, the use of the Book of Common Prayer was prohibited."

9. For a description of some of the laws enacted by early theocratic governments in New England, see Parrington, Main Currents in American Thought (1930), Vol 1, pp 5–50; Whipple, Our Ancient Liberties (1927), pp 63–78; Wertenbaker, The Puritan Oligarchy (1947).

10. The Church of England was the established church of at least five colonies: Maryland, Virginia, North Carolina, South Carolina and Georgia. There seems to be some controversy as to whether that church was officially established in New York and New Jersey but there is no doubt that it received substantial support from those States. See Cobb, The Rise of Religious Liberty in America (1902), pp 338, 408. In Massachusetts, New Hampshire and Connecticut, the Congregationalist Church was officially established. In Pennsylvania and Delaware, all Christian sects were treated equally in most situations but Catholics were discriminated against in some respects. See generally Cobb, The Rise of Religious Liberty in America (1902). In Rhode Island all Protestants enjoyed equal privileges but it is not clear whether Catholics were allowed to vote. Compare Fiske, The Critical Period in American History (1899), p 76 with Cobb, The Rise of Religious Liberty in America (1902), pp 437–438.

was concerned.[11] Similar though less far-reaching legislation was being considered and passed in other States.[12]

By the time of the adoption of the Constitution, our history shows that there was a widespread awareness among many Americans of the dangers of a union of Church and State. These people knew, some of them from bitter personal experience, that one of the greatest dangers to the freedom of the individual to worship in his own way lay in the Government's placing its official stamp of approval upon one particular kind of prayer or one particular form of religious services. They knew the anguish, hardship and bitter strife that could come when zealous religious groups struggled with one another to obtain the Government's stamp of approval from each King, Queen, or Protector that came to temporary power. The Constitution was intended to avert a part of this danger by leaving the government of this country in the hands of the people rather than in the hands of any monarch. But this safeguard was not enough. Our Founders were no more willing to let the content of their prayers and their privilege of praying whenever they pleased be influenced by the ballot box than they were to let these vital matters of personal conscience depend upon the succession of monarchs. The First Amendment was added to the Constitution to stand as a guarantee that neither the power nor the prestige of the Federal Government would be used to control, support or influence the kinds of prayer the American people can say—that the people's religions must not be subjected to the pressures of government for change each time a new political administration is elected to office. Under the Amendment's prohibition against governmental establishment of religion, as reinforced by the provisions of the Fourteenth Amendment, government in this country, be it state or federal, is without power to prescribe by law any particular form of prayer which is to be used as an official prayer in carrying on any program of governmentally sponsored religious activity.

There can be no doubt that New York's state prayer program officially establishes the religious beliefs embodied in the Regents' prayer. The respondents' argument to the contrary, which is largely based upon the contention that the Regents' prayer is "non-denominational" and the fact that the program, as modified and approved by state courts, does not require all pupils to recite the prayer but permits those who wish to do so to remain silent or be excused from the room, ignores the essential nature of the program's constitutional defects. Neither the fact that the prayer may be denominationally neutral nor the fact that its observance on the part of the students is voluntary can serve to free it from the limitations of the Establishment Clause, as it might from the Free Exercise Clause, of the First Amendment, both of which are operative against

11. 12 Hening, Statutes of Virginia (1823), 84, entitled "An act for establishing religious freedom." The story of the events surrounding the enactment of this law was reviewed in Everson v Board of Education, 330 US 1, 91 L ed 711, 67 S Ct 504, 168 ALR 1392, both by the Court, 330 US at pp 11–13, and in the dissenting opinion of Mr. Justice Rutledge, at 330 US pp 33–42. See also Fiske, The Critical Period in American History (1899), pp 78–82; James, The Struggle for Religious Liberty in Virginia (1900); Thom, The Struggle for Religious Freedom in Virginia: The Baptists (1900); Cobb, The Rise of Religious Liberty in America (1902), pp 74–115, 482–499.

12. See Cobb, The Rise of Religious Liberty in America (1902), pp 482–509.

the States by virtue of the Fourteenth Amendment. Although these two clauses may in certain instances overlap, they forbid two quite different kinds of governmental encroachment upon religious freedom. The Establishment Clause, unlike the Free Exercise Clause, does not depend upon any showing of direct governmental compulsion and is violated by the enactment of laws which establish an official religion whether those laws operate directly to coerce nonobserving individuals or not. This is not to say, of course, that laws officially prescribing a particular form of religious worship do not involve coercion of such individuals. When the power, prestige and financial support of government is placed behind a particular religious belief, the indirect coercive pressure upon religious minorities to conform to the prevailing officially approved religion is plain. But the purposes underlying the Establishment Clause go much further than that. Its first and most immediate purpose rested on the belief that a union of government and religion tends to destroy government and to degrade religion. The history of governmentally established religion, both in England and in this country, showed that whenever government had allied itself with one particular form of religion, the inevitable result had been that it had incurred the hatred, disrespect and even contempt of those who held contrary beliefs.[13] That same history showed that many people had lost their respect for any religion that had relied upon the support of government to spread its faith.[14] The Establishment Clause thus stands as an expression of principle on the part of the Founders of our Constitution that religion is too personal, too sacred, too holy, to permit its "unhallowed perversion" by a civil magistrate.[15] Another purpose of the Establishment Clause rested upon an awareness of the historical fact that governmentally established religions and religious persecutions go hand in hand.[16] The Founders knew that only a few years after the

---

13. "[A]ttempts to enforce by legal sanctions, acts obnoxious to so great a proportion of Citizens, tend to enervate the laws in general, and to slacken the bands of Society. If it be difficult to execute any law which is not generally deemed necessary or salutary, what must be the case where it is deemed invalid and dangerous? and what may be the effect of so striking an example of impotency in the Government, on its general authority." Memorial and Remonstrance against Religious Assessments, II Writings of Madison 183, 190.

14. "It is moreover to weaken in those who profess this Religion a pious confidence in its innate excellence, and the patronage of its Author; and to foster in those who still reject it, a suspicion that its friends are too conscious of its fallacies, to trust it to its own merits . . . [E]xperience witnesseth that ecclesiastical establishments, instead of maintaining the purity and efficacy of Religion, have had a contrary operation. During almost fifteen centuries, has the legal establishment of Christianity been on trial. What have been its fruits? More or less in all places, pride and indolence in the Clergy; ignorance and servility in the laity; in both, superstition, bigotry and persecution. Enquire of the Teachers of Christianity for the ages in which it appeared in its greatest lustre; those of every sect, point to the ages prior to its incorporation with Civil policy." Id., at 187.

15. Memorial and Remonstrance against Religious Assessments, II Writings of Madison, at 187.

16. "[T]he proposed establishment is a departure from that generous policy, which, offering an asylum to the persecuted and oppressed of every Nation and Religion, promised a lustre to our country, and an accession to the number of its citizens. What a

Book of Common Prayer became the only accepted form of religious services in the established Church of England, an Act of uniformity was passed to compel all Englishmen to attend those services and to make it a criminal offense to conduct or attend religious gatherings of any other kind[17]—a law which was consistently flouted by dissenting religious groups in England and which contributed to widespread persecutions of people like John Bunyan who persisted in holding "unlawful [religious] meetings . . . to the great disturbance and distraction of the good subjects of this kingdom. . . . "[18] And they knew that similar persecutions had received the sanction of law in several of the colonies in this country soon after the establishment of official religions in those colonies.[19] It was in large part to get completely away from this sort of systematic religious persecution that the Founders brought into being our Nation, our Constitution, and our Bill of Rights with its prohibition against any governmental establishment of religion. The New York laws officially prescribing the Regents' prayer are inconsistent both with the purposes of the Establishment Clause and with the Establishment Clause itself.

It has been argued that to apply the Constitution in such a way as to prohibit state laws respecting an establishment of religious services in public schools is to indicate a hostility toward religion or toward prayer. Nothing, of course, could be more wrong. The history of man is inseparable from the history of religion.

---

melancholy mark is the Bill of sudden degeneracy? Instead of holding forth an asylum to the persecuted, it is itself a signal of persecution. . . . Distant as it may be, in its present form, from the Inquisition it differs from it only in degree. The one is the first step, the other the last in the career of intolerance. The magnanimous sufferer under this cruel scourge in foreign Regions, must view the Bill as a Beacon on our Coast, warning him to seek some other haven, where liberty and philanthropy in their due extent may offer a more certain repose from his troubles." Id., at 188.

17. 5 & 6 Edward VI, c1, entitled "An Act for the Uniformity of Service and Administration of Sacraments throughout the Realm." This Act was repealed during the reign of Mary but revived upon the accession of Elizabeth. See note 7, supra. The reasons which led to the enactment of this statute were set out in its preamble: "Where there hath been a very godly Order set forth by the Authority of Parliament, for Common Prayer and Administration of the Sacraments to be used in the Mother Tongue within the Church of *England,* agreeable to the Word of God and the Primitive Church, very comfortable to all good People desiring to live in Christian Conversation, and most profitable to the Estate of this Realm, upon the which the Mercy, Favour and Blessing of Almighty God is in no wise so readily and plenteously poured as by Common Prayers, due using of the Sacraments, and often preaching of the Gospel, with the Devotion of the Hearers: (1) And yet this notwithstanding, a great Number of People in divers Parts of this Realm, following their own Sensuality, and living either without Knowledge or due Fear of God, do wilfully and damnably before Almighty God abstain and refuse to come to their Parish Churches and other Places where Common Prayer, Administration of the Sacraments, and Preaching of the Word of God, is used upon *Sundays* and other Days ordained to be Holydays."

18. Bunyan's own account of his trial is set forth in A Relation of the Imprisonment of Mr. John Bunyan, reprinted in Grace Abounding and The Pilgrim's Progress (Brown ed 1907), at 103–132.

19. For a vivid account of some of these persecutions, see Wertenbaker, The Puritan Oligarchy (1947).

And perhaps it is not too much to say that since the beginning of that history many people have devoutly believed that "More things are wrought by prayer than this world dreams of." It was doubtless largely due to men who believed this that there grew up a sentiment that caused men to leave the cross-currents of officially established state religions and religious persecution in Europe and come to this country filled with the hope that they could find a place in which they could pray when they pleased to the God of their faith in the language they chose.[20] And there were men of this same faith in the power of prayer who led the fight for adoption of our Constitution and also for our Bill of Rights with the very guarantees of religious freedom that forbid the sort of governmental activity which New York has attempted here. These men knew that the First Amendment, which tried to put an end to governmental control of religion and of prayer, was not written to destroy either. They knew rather that it was written to quiet well-justified fears which nearly all of them felt arising out of an awareness that governments of the past had shackled men's tongues to make them speak only the religious thoughts that government wanted them to speak and to pray only to the God that government wanted them to pray to. It is neither sacrilegious nor antireligious to say that each separate government in this country should stay out of the business of writing or sanctioning official prayers and leave that purely religious function to the people themselves and to those the people choose to look to for religious guidance.[21]

---

20. Perhaps the best example of the sort of men who came to this country for precisely that reason is Roger Williams, the founder of Rhode Island, who has been described as "the truest Christian amongst many who sincerely desired to be Christian." Parrington, Main Currents in American Thought (1930), Vol 1, at p 74. Williams, who was one of the earliest exponents of the doctrine of separation of church and state, believed that separation was necessary in order to protect the church from the danger of destruction which he thought inevitably flowed from control by even the best-intentioned civil authorities: "The unknowing zeale of *Constantine* and other Emperours, did more hurt to *Christ Jesus* his Crowne and Kingdome, then the raging fury of the most bloody *Neroes*. In the *persecutions* of the later, *Christians* were sweet and fragrant, like spice pounded and beaten in morters: But those *good* Emperours, persecuting some erroneous persons, *Arrius, &c.* and advancing the professours of some Truths of Christ (for there was no small number of *Truths* lost in those times) and maintaining their *Religion* by the materiall Sword, I say by this meanes *Christianity* was *eclipsed,* and the Professors of it fell asleep. . . . " Williams, The Bloudy Tenent, of Persecution, for cause of Conscience, discussed in A Conference betweene Truth and Peace (London, 1644), reprinted in Narragansett Club Publications, Vol III, p 184. To Williams, it was no part of the business or competence of a civil magistrate to interfere in religious matters. "[W]hat imprudence and *indiscretion* is it in the most common affaires of Life, to conceive that *Emperours, Kings* and *Rulers* of the earth must not only be qualified with *politicall* and *state abilities* to *make* and *execute* such *Civill Lawes* which may concerne the common *rights, peace* and *safety* (which is worke and businesse, load and burthen enough for the ablest shoulders in the Commonweal) but also furnished with such *Spirituall* and heavenly *abilities* to governe the *Spirituall* and *Christian Commonweal. . . .* " Id., at 366. See also id., at 136–137.

21. There is of course nothing in the decision reached here that is inconsistent with the fact that school children and others are officially encouraged to express love for our country by reciting historical documents such as the Declaration of Independence which

It is true that New York's establishment of its Regents' prayer as an officially approved religious doctrine of that State does not amount to a total establishment of one particular religious sect to the exclusion of all others—that, indeed, the governmental endorsement of that prayer seems relatively insignificant when compared to the governmental encroachments upon religion which were commonplace 200 years ago. To those who may subscribe to the view that because the Regents' official prayer is so brief and general there can be no danger to religious freedom in its governmental establishment, however, it may be appropriate to say in the words of James Madison, the author of the First Amendment: "[I]t is proper to take alarm at the first experiment on our liberties. . . . Who does not see that the same authority which can establish Christianity, in exclusion of all other Religions, may establish with the same ease any particular sect of Christians, in exclusion of all other Sects? That the same authority which can force a citizen to contribute three pence only of his property for the support of any one establishment, may force him to conform to any other establishment in all cases whatsoever?"[22]

The judgment of the Court of Appeals of New York is reversed and the cause remanded for further proceedings not inconsistent with this opinion.

Reversed and remanded.

Mr. Justice Frankfurter took no part in the decision of this case.

Mr. Justice White took no part in the consideration or decision of this case.

Separate Opinions

Mr. Justice Douglas, concurring.

It is customary in deciding a constitutional question to treat it in its narrowest form. Yet at times the setting of the question gives it a form and content which no abstract treatment could give. The point for decision is whether the Government can constitutionally finance a religious exercise. Our system at the federal and state levels is presently honeycombed with such financing.[1] Nevertheless, I think it is an unconstitutional undertaking whatever form it takes.

---

contain references to the Deity or by singing officially espoused anthems which include the composer's professions of faith in a Supreme Being, or with the fact that there are many manifestations in our public life of belief in God. Such patriotic or ceremonial occasions bear no true resemblance to the unquestioned religious exercise that the State of New York has sponsored in this instance.

22. Memorial and Remonstrance against Religious Assessments, II Writings of Madison 183, at 185–186.

1. There are many 'aids' to religion in this country at all levels of government. To mention but a few at the federal level, one might begin by observing that the very First Congress which wrote the First Amendment provided for chaplains in both Houses and in the armed services. There is compulsory chapel at the service academies, and religious services are held in federal hospitals and prisons. The President issues religious proclamations. The Bible is used for the administration of oaths. N.Y.A. and W.P.A. funds were available to parochial schools during the depression. Veterans receiving money under the 'G.I.' Bill of 1944 could attend denominational schools, to which payments were made directly by the government. During World War II, federal money was contributed to denominational schools for the training of nurses. The benefits of the National School Lunch Act are available to students in private as well as public schools. The Hospital

First, a word as to what this case does not involve.

Plainly, our Bill of Rights would not permit a State or the Federal Government to adopt on official prayer and penalize anyone who would not utter it. This, however, is not that case, for there is no element of compulsion or coercion in New York's regulation requiring that public schools be opened each day with the following prayer:

"Almighty God, we acknowledge our dependence upon Thee, and we beg Thy blessings upon us, our parents, our teachers and our Country."

The prayer is said upon the commencement of the school day, immediately following the pledge of allegiance to the flag. The prayer is said aloud in the presence of a teacher, who either leads the recitation or selects a student to do so. No student, however, is compelled to take part. The respondents have adopted a regulation which provides that "Neither teachers nor any school authority shall comment on participation or non-participation . . . nor suggest or request that any posture or language be used or dress be worn or be not used or not worn." Provision is also made for excusing children, upon written request of a parent or guardian, from the saying of the prayer or from the room in which the prayer is said. A letter implementing and explaining this regulation has been sent to each taxpayer and parent in the school district. As I read this regulation, a child is free to stand or not stand, to recite or not recite, without fear of reprisal or even comment by the teacher or any other school official.

In short, the only one who need utter the prayer is the teacher; and no teacher is complaining of it. Students can stand mute or even leave the classroom, if they desire.[2]

Illinois ex rel. McCollum v Board of Education, 333 US 203, 92 L ed 649, 68 S Ct 461, 2 ALR2d 1338, does not decide this case. It involved the use of public school facilities for religious education of students. Students either had to attend religious instruction or "go to some other place in the school building for pursuit of their secular studies. . . . Reports of their presence or absence were to be made to their secular teachers." Id. 333 US at 209. The influence of the teaching staff was therefore brought to bear on the student body, to support

Survey and Construction Act of 1946 specifically made money available to non-public hospitals. The slogan 'In God We Trust' is used by the Treasury Department, and Congress recently added God to the pledge of allegiance. There is Bible-reading in the schools of the District of Columbia, and religious instruction is given in the District's National Training School for Boys. Religious organizations are exempt from the federal income tax and are granted postal privileges. Up to defined limits—15 per cent of the adjusted gross income of individuals and 5 per cent of the net income of corporations—contributions to religious organizations are deductible for federal income tax purposes. There are no limits to the deductibility of gifts and bequests to religious institutions made under the federal gift and estate tax laws. This list of federal 'aids' could easily be expanded, and of course there is a long list in each state." Fellman, the Limits of Freedom (1959), pp 40–41.

2. West Point Cadets are required to attend chapel each Sunday. Reg, c. 21, § 2101. The same requirement obtains at the Naval Academy (Reg, c. 9, § 0901, (1) (a)), and at the Air Force Academy except First Classmen. Catalogue, 1962–1963, p 110. And see Honeywell, Chaplains of the United States Army (1958); Jorgensen, The Service of Chaplains to Army Air Units, 1917–1946, Vol I (1961).

the instilling of religious principles. In the present case, school facilities are used to say the prayer and the teaching staff is employed to lead the pupils in it. There is, however, no effort at indoctrination and no attempt at exposition. Prayers of course may be so long and of such a character as to amount to an attempt at the religious instruction that was denied the public schools by the McCollum Case. But New York's prayer is of a character that does not involve any element of proselytizing as in the McCollum Case.

The question presented by this case is therefore an extremely narrow one. It is whether New York oversteps the bounds when it finances a religious exercise.

What New York does on the opening of its public schools is what we do when we open court. Our Crier has from the beginning announced the convening of the Court and then added "God save the United States and this Honorable Court." That utterance is a supplication, a prayer in which we, the judges, are free to join, but which we need not recite any more than the students need recite the New York prayer.

What New York does on the opening of its public schools is what each House of Congress[3] does at the opening of each day's business.[4] Reverend Frederick B. Harris is Chaplain of the Senate; Reverend Bernard Braskamp is Chaplain of the House. Guest chaplains of various denominations also officiate.[5]

In New York the teacher who leads in prayer is on the public payroll; and the time she takes seems minuscule as compared with the salaries appropriated by

3. The New York Legislature follows the same procedure. See e.g., Vol 1, NY Assembly Jour, 184th Sess, 1961, p 8; Vol 1, NY Senate Jour, 184th Sess, 1961, p 5.

4. Rules of the Senate provide that each calendar day's session shall open with prayer. See Rule III, Senate Manual, S Doc No. 2, 87th Cong, 1st Sess. The same is true of the Rules of the House. See Rule VII, Rules of the House of Representatives, HR Doc No. 459, 86th Cong, 2d Sess. The Chaplains of the Senate and of the House receive $8,810 annually. See 75 Stat 320, 324.

5. It would, I assume, make no difference in the present case if a different prayer were said every day or if the ministers of the community rotated, each giving his own prayer. For some of the petitioners in the present case profess no religion.

The Pledge of Allegiance, like the prayer, recognizes the existence of a Supreme Being. Since 1954 it has contained the words "one Nation *under God,* indivisible, with liberty and justice for all." 36 USC § 172. The House Report recommending the addition of the words "under God" stated that those words in no way run contrary to the First Amendment but recognize "only the guidance of God in our national affairs." HR Rep No. 1693, 83d Cong, 2d Sess, p 3. And see S Rep No. 1287, 83d Cong, 2d Sess. Senator Ferguson, who sponsored the measure in the Senate, pointed out that the words "In God We Trust" are over the entrance to the Senate Chamber. 100 Cong Rec 6348. He added:

"I have felt that the Pledge of Allegiance to the Flag which stands for the United States of America should recognize the Creator who we really believe is in control of the destinies of this great Republic.

"It is true that under the Constitution no power is lodged anywhere to establish a religion. This is not an attempt to establish a religion; it has nothing to do with anything of that kind. It relates to belief in God, in whom we sincerely repose our trust. We know that America cannot be defended by guns, planes, and ships alone. Appropriations and expenditures for defense will be of value only if the God under whom we live

state legislatures and Congress for chaplains to conduct prayers in the legislative halls. Only a bare fraction of the teacher's time is given to reciting this short 22-word prayer, about the same amount of time that our Crier spends announcing the opening of our sessions and offering a prayer for this Court. Yet for me the principle is the same, no matter how briefly the prayer is said, for in each of the instances given the person praying is a public official on the public payroll, performing a religious exercise in a governmental institution.[6] It is said that the element of coercion is inherent in the giving of this prayer. If that is true here, it is also true of the prayer with which this Court is convened, and of those that open the Congress. Few adults, let alone children, would leave our courtroom or the Senate or the House while those prayers are being given. Every such audience is in a sense a "captive" audience.

At the same time I cannot say that to authorize this prayer is to establish a religion in the strictly historic meaning of those words.[7] A religion is not es-

---

believes that we are in the right. We should at all times recognize God's province over the lives of our people and over this great Nation." Ibid. And see 100 Cong Rec 7757 et seq. for the debates in the House.

The Act of March 3, 1865, 13 Stat 517, 518, authorized the phrase "In God We Trust" to be placed on coins. And see 17 Stat 427. The first mandatory requirement for the use of that motto on coins was made by the Act of May 18, 1908, 35 Stat 164. See HR Rep No. 1106, 60th Cong, 1st Sess; 42 Cong Rec 3384 et seq. The use of the motto on all currency and coins were directed by the Act of July 11, 1955, 69 Stat 290. See HR Rep No. 662, 84th Cong, 1st Sess; S Rep No. 637, 84th Cong, 1st Sess. Moreover by the Joint Resolution of July 30, 1956, our national motto was declared to be "In God We Trust." 70 Stat 732. In reporting the Joint Resolution, the Senate Judiciary Committee stated:

"Further official recognition of this motto was given by the adoption of the Star-Spangled Banner as our national anthem. One stanza of our national anthem is as follows:

" 'O, thus be it ever when freemen shall stand
Between their lov'd home and the war's desolation!
Blest with vict'ry and peace may the heav'n rescued land
Praise the power that hath made and preserved us a nation!
Then conquer we must when our cause it is just,
And this be our motto—"In God is our trust."
And the Star-Spangled Banner in triumph shall wave
O'er the land of the free and the home of the brave.'

"In view of these words in our national anthem, it is clear that 'In God we trust' has a strong claim as our national motto." S Rep No. 2703, 84th Cong, 2d Sess, p. 2.

6. The fact that taxpayers do not have standing in the federal courts to raise the issue (Frothingham v Mellon, 262 US 447, 67 L ed 1078, 43 S Ct 597) is of course no justification for drawing a line between what is done in New York on the one hand and on the other what we do and what Congress does in this matter of prayer.

7. The Court analogizes the present case to those involving the traditional Established Church. We once had an Established Church, the Anglican. All baptisms and marriages had to take place there. That church was supported by taxation. In these and other ways the Anglican Church was favored over the others. The First Amendment put an end to placing any one church in a preferred position. It ended support of any church or all

tablished in the usual sense merely by letting those who choose to do so say the prayer that the public school teacher leads. Yet once government finances a religious exercise it inserts a divisive influence into our communities.[8] The New York Court said that the prayer given does not conform to all of the tenets of the Jewish, Unitarian, and Ethical Culture groups. One of the petitioners is an agnostic.

"We are a religious people whose institutions presuppose a Supreme Being." Zorach v Clauson, 343 US 306, 313, 96 L ed 954, 962, 72 S Ct 679. Under our Bill of Rights free play is given for making religion an active force in our lives.[9] But "if a religious leaven is to be worked into the affairs of our people, it is to be done by individuals and groups, not by the Government." McGowan v Maryland, 366 US 420, 563, 6 L ed 2d 393, 525, 81 S Ct 1101 (dissenting opinion). By reason of the First Amendment government is commanded "to have no interest in theology or ritual" (id. 366 US at 564), for on those matters, "government must be neutral." Ibid. The First Amendment leaves the Government in a position not of hostility to religion but of neutrality. The philosophy is that the atheist or agnostic—the nonbeliever—is entitled to go his own way. The philosophy is that if government interferes in matters spiritual, it will be a divisive force. The First Amendment teaches that a government neutral in the field of religion better serves all religious interests.

My problem today would be uncomplicated but for Everson v Board of Education, 330 US 1, 17, 91 L ed 711, 724, 67 S Ct 504, 168, ALR 1392, which allowed taxpayers' money to be used to pay "the bus fares of parochial school pupils as a part of a general program under which" the fares of pupils attending public and other schools were also paid. The Everson Case seems in retrospect to be out of line with the First Amendment. Its result is appealing, as it allows aid to be given to needy children. Yet by the same token, public funds could be used to satisfy other needs of children in parochial schools—lunches, books, and tuition being obvious examples. Mr. Justice Rutledge stated in dissent what I think is durable First Amendment philosophy:

"The reasons underlying the Amendment's policy have not vanished with time or diminished in force. Now as when it was adopted the price of religious freedom is double. It is that the church and religion shall live both within and upon that freedom. There cannot be freedom of religion, safeguarded by the state, and intervention by the church or its agencies in the state's domain or

---

churches by taxation. It went further and prevented secular sanction to any religious ceremony, dogma, or rite. Thus, it prevents civil penalties from being applied against recalcitrants or nonconformists.

8. Some communities have a Christmas tree purchased with the taxpayers' money. The tree is sometimes decorated with the words "Peace on earth, goodwill to men." At other times the authorities draw from a different version of the Bible which says "Peace on earth to men of goodwill." Christmas, I suppose, is still a religious celebration, not merely a day put on the calendar for the benefit of merchants.

9. Religion was once deemed to be a function of the public school system. The Northwest Ordinance, which antedated the First Amendment, provided in Article III that "Religion, morality, and knowledge being necessary to good government and the happiness of mankind, schools and the means of education shall forever be encouraged."

dependency on its largesse. Madison's Remonstrance, Par. 6, 8. The great condition of religious liberty is that it be maintained free from sustenance, as also from other interferences, by the state. For when it comes to rest upon that secular foundation it vanishes with the resting. Id., Par. 7, 8. Public money devoted to payment of religious costs, educational or other, brings the quest for more. It brings too the struggle of sect against sect for the larger share or for any. Here one by numbers alone will benefit most, there another. That is precisely the history of societies which have had an established religion and dissident groups. Id., Par. 8, 11. It is the very thing Jefferson and Madison experienced and sought to guard against, whether in its blunt or in its more screened forms. Ibid. The end of such strife cannot be other than to destroy the cherished liberty. The dominating group will achieve the dominant benefit; or all will embroil the state in their dissensions. Id., Par. 11." Id. 330 US pp. 53, 54.

What New York does with this prayer is a break with that tradition. I therefore join the Court in reversing the judgment below.

Mr. Justice Stewart, dissenting.

A local school board in New York has provided that those pupils who wish to do so may join in a brief prayer at the beginning of each school day, acknowledging their dependence upon God and asking His blessing upon them and upon their parents, their teachers, and their country. The court today decides that in permitting this brief non-denominational prayer the school board has violated the Constitution of the United States. I think this decision is wrong.

The Court does not hold, nor could it, that New York has interfered with the free exercise of anybody's religion. For the state courts have made clear that those who object to reciting the prayer must be entirely free of any compulsion to do so, including any "embarrassments and pressures." Cf. West Virginia State Board of Education v Barnette, 319 US 624, 87 L ed 1628, 63 S Ct 1178, 147 ALR 674. But the Court says that in permitting school children to say this simple prayer, the New York authorities have established "an official religion."

With all respect, I think the Court has misapplied a great constitutional principle. I cannot see how an "official religion" is established by letting those who want to say a prayer say it. On the contrary, I think that to deny the wish of these school children to join in reciting this prayer is to deny them the opportunity of sharing in the spiritual heritage of our Nation.

The Court's historical review of the quarrels over the Book of Common Prayer in England throws no light for me on the issue before us in this case. England had then and has now an established church. Equally unenlightening, I think, is the history of the early establishment and later rejection of an official church in our own States. For we deal here not with the establishment of a state church, which would, of course, be constitutionally impermissible, but with whether school children who want to begin their day by joining in prayer must be prohibited from doing so. Moreover, I think that the Court's task, in this as in all areas of constitutional adjudication, is not responsibly aided by the uncritical invocation of metaphors like the "wall of separation," a phrase nowhere to be found in the Constitution. What is relevant to the issue here is not the history of an established church in sixteenth century England or in eighteenth century America, but the history of the religious traditions of our people, reflected in countless practices of the institutions and officials of our government.

At the opening of each day's Session of this Court we stand, while one of our officials invokes the protection of God. Since the days of John Marshall our Crier has said, "God save the United States and this Honorable Court."[1] Both the Senate and the House of Representatives open their daily Sessions with prayer.[2] Each of our Presidents, from George Washington to John F. Kennedy, has upon assuming his office asked the protection and help of God.[3]

---

1. See Warren, The Supreme Court in United States History, Vol I, p 469.

2. See Rule III, Senate Manual, S Doc No. 2, 87th Cong, 1st Sess. See Rule VII, Rules of the House of Representatives, HR Doc No. 459, 86th Cong, 2d Sess.

3. For example:

On April 30, 1789, President George Washington said:

" . . . it would be peculiarly improper to omit in this first official act my fervent supplications to that Almighty Being who rules over the universe, who presides in the councils of nations, and whose providential aids can supply every human defect, that His benediction may consecrate to the liberties and happiness of the people of the United States a Government instituted by themselves for these essential purposes, and may enable every instrument employed in its administration to execute with success the functions allotted to his charge. In tendering this homage to the Great Author of every public and private good, I assure myself that it expresses your sentiments not less than my own, nor those of my fellow-citizens at large less than either. No people can be bound to acknowledge and adore the Invisible Hand which conducts the affairs of men more than those of the United States. . . .

.   .   .   .   .

"Having thus imparted to you my sentiments as they have been awakened by the occasion which brings us together, I shall take my present leave; but not without resorting once more to the benign Parent of the Human Race in humble supplication that, since He has been pleased to favor the American people with opportunities for deliberating in perfect tranquillity, and dispositions for deciding with unparalleled unanimity on a form of government for the security of their union and the advancement of their happiness, so His divine blessing may be equally *conspicuous* in the enlarged views, the temperate consultations, and the wise measures on which the success of this Government must depend."

On March 4, 1797, President John Adams said:

"And may that Being who is supreme over all, the Patron of Order, the Fountain of Justice, and the Protector in all ages of the world of virtuous liberty, continue His blessing upon this nation and its Government and give it all possible success and duration consistent with the ends of His providence."

On March 4, 1805, President Thomas Jefferson said:

" . . . I shall need, too, the favor of that Being in whose hands we are, who led our fathers, as Israel of old, from their native land and planted them in a country flowing with all the necessaries and comforts of life; who has covered our infancy with His providence and our riper years with His wisdom and power, and to whose goodness I ask you to join in supplications with me that He will so enlighten the minds of your servants, guide their councils, and prosper their measures that whatsoever they do shall result in your good, and shall secure to you the peace, friendship, and approbation of all nations."

On March 4, 1809, President James Madison said:

The Court today says that the state and federal governments are without constitutional power to prescribe any particular form of words to be recited by any group of the American people on any subject touching religion.[4] One of the

---

"But the source to which I look . . . is in . . . my fellow-citizens, and in the counsels of those representing them in the other departments associated in the care of the national interests. In these my confidence will under every difficulty be best placed, next to that which we have all been encouraged to feel in the guardianship and guidance of that Almighty Being whose power regulates the destiny of nations, whose blessings have been so conspicuously dispensed to this rising Republic, and to whom we are bound to address our devout gratitude for the past, as well as our fervent supplications and best hopes for the future."

On March 4, 1865, President Abraham Lincoln said:

" . . . Fondly do we hope, fervently do we pray, that this mighty scourge of war may speedily pass away. Yet, if God wills that it continue until all the wealth piled by the bondsman's two hundred and fifty years of unrequited toil shall be sunk, and until every drop of blood drawn with the lash shall be paid by another drawn with the sword, as was said three thousand years ago, so still it must be said 'the judgments of the Lord are true and righteous altogether.'

"With malice toward none, with charity for all, with firmness in the right as God gives us to see the right, let us strive on to finish the work we are in, to bind up the nation's wounds, to care for him who shall have borne the battle and for his widow and his orphan, to do all which may achieve and cherish a just and lasting peace among ourselves and with all nations."

On March 4, 1885, President Grover Cleveland said:

" . . . And let us not trust to human effort alone, but humbly acknowledging the power and goodness of Almighty God, who presides over the destiny of nations, and who has at all times been revealed in our country's history, let us invoke His aid and His blessing upon our labors."

On March 5, 1917, President Woodrow Wilson said:

" . . . I pray God I may be given the wisdom and the prudence to do my duty in the true spirit of this great people."

On March 4, 1933, President Franklin D. Roosevelt said:

"In this dedication of a Nation we humbly ask the blessing of God. May He protect each and every one of us. May He guide me in the days to come."

On January 21, 1957, President Dwight D. Eisenhower said:

"Before all else, we seek, upon our common labor as a nation, the blessings of Almighty God. And the hopes in our hearts fashion the deepest prayers of our whole people."

On January 20, 1961, President John F. Kennedy said:

"The world is very different now. . . . And yet the same revolutionary beliefs for which our forebears fought are still at issue around the globe—the belief that the rights of man come not from the generosity of the state but from the hand of God.

"With a good conscience our only sure reward, with history the final judge of our deeds, let us go forth to lead the land we love, asking His blessing and His help, but knowing that here on earth God's work must truly be our own."

4. My brother Douglas says that the only question before us is whether government "can constitutionally finance a religious exercise." The official chaplains of Congress are paid with public money. So are military chaplains. So are state and federal prison chaplains.

stanzas of "The Star-Spangled Banner," made our National Anthem by Act of Congress in 1931,[5] contains these verses:

"Blest with victory and peace, may the heav'n rescued land
Praise the Pow'r that hath made and preserved us a nation!
Then conquer we must, when our cause it is just,
And this be our motto 'In God is our Trust.' "

In 1954 Congress added a phrase to the Pledge of Allegiance to the Flag so that it now contains the words "one Nation *under God* indivisible, with liberty and justice for all."[6] In 1952 Congress enacted legislation calling upon the President each year to proclaim a National Day of Prayer.[7] Since 1865 the words "IN GOD WE TRUST" have been impressed on our coins.[8]

Countless similar examples could be listed, but there is no need to belabor the obvious.[9] It was all summed up by this Court just ten years ago in a single sentence: "We are a religious people whose institutions presuppose a Supreme Being." Zorach v Clauson, 343 US 306, 313, 96 L ed 954, 962, 72 S Ct 679.

I do not believe that this Court, or the Congress, or the President has by the actions and practices I have mentioned established an "official religion" in violation of the Constitution. And I do not believe the State of New York has done so in this case. What each has done has been to recognize and to follow the deeply entrenched and highly cherished spiritual traditions of our Nation— traditions which come down to us from those who almost two hundred years ago avowed their "firm Reliance on the Protection of divine Providence" when they proclaimed the freedom and independence of this brave new world.[10]

I dissent.

---

5. 36 USC § 170.

6. 36 USC § 172.

7. 36 USC § 185.

8. 13 Stat 517, 518; 17 Stat 427; 35 Stat 164; 69 Stat 290. The current provisions are embodied in 31 USC §§ 324, 324a.

9. I am at a loss to understand the Court's unsupported ipse dixit that these official expressions of religious faith in and reliance upon a Supreme Being "bear no true resemblance to the unquestioned religious exercise that the State of New York has sponsored in this instance." See p 610, supra note 21. I can hardly think that the Court means to say that the First Amendment imposes a lesser restriction upon the Federal Government than does the Fourteenth Amendment upon the States. Or is the Court suggesting that the Constitution permits judges and Congressmen and Presidents to join in prayer, but prohibits school children from doing so?

10. The Declaration of Independence ends with this sentence: "And for the support of this Declaration, with a firm reliance on the protection of divine Providence, we mutually pledge to each other our Lives, our Fortunes and our sacred Honor."

APPENDIX F
EQUAL ACCESS ACT
20 United States Code, Section 4071

§ 4071. Denial of equal access prohibited

(a) **Restriction of limited open forum on basis of religious, political, philosophical, or other speech content prohibited**

It shall be unlawful for any public secondary school which receives Federal financial assistance and which has a limited open forum to deny equal access or a fair opportunity to, or discriminate against, any students who wish to conduct a meeting within that limited open forum on the basis of the religious, political, philosophical, or other content of the speech at such meetings.

(b) **"Limited open forum" defined**

A public secondary school has a limited open forum whenever such school grants an offering to or opportunity for one or more noncurriculum related student groups to meet on school premises during noninstructional time.

(c) **Fair opportunity criteria**

Schools shall be deemed to offer a fair opportunity to students who wish to conduct a meeting within its limited open forum if such school uniformly provides that—

(1) the meeting is voluntary and student-initiated;

(2) there is no sponsorship of the meeting by the school, the government, or its agents or employees;

(3) employees or agents of the school or government are present at religious meetings only in a nonparticipatory capacity;

(4) the meeting does not materially and substantially interfere with the orderly conduct of educational activities within the school; and

(5) nonschool persons may not direct, conduct, control, or regularly attend activities of student groups.

(d) **Federal or State authority nonexistent with respect to certain rights**

Nothing in this subchapter shall be construed to authorize the United States or any State or political subdivision thereof—

(1) to influence the form or content of any prayer or other religious activity;

219

(2) to require any person to participate in prayer or other religious activity;

(3) to expend public funds beyond the incidental cost of providing the space for student-initiated meetings;

(4) to compel any school agent or employee to attend a school meeting if the content of the speech at the meeting is contrary to the beliefs of the agent or employee;

(5) to sanction meetings that are otherwise unlawful;

(6) to limit the rights of groups of students which are not of a specified numerical size; or

(7) to abridge the constitutional rights of any person.

(e) Unaffected Federal financial assistance to schools

Notwithstanding the availability of any other remedy under the Constitution or the laws of the United States, nothing in this subchapter shall be construed to authorize the United States to deny or withhold Federal financial assistance to any school.

(f) Authority of schools with respect to order-and-discipline, well-being, and voluntary-presence concerns

Nothing in this subchapter shall be construed to limit the authority of the school, its agents or employees, to maintain order and discipline on school premises, to protect the well-being of students and faculty, and to assure that attendance of students at meetings is voluntary.

§ 4072. Definitions

As used in this subchapter—

(1) The term "secondary school" means a public school which provides secondary education as determined by State law.

(2) The term "sponsorship" includes the act of promoting, leading, or participating in a meeting. The assignment of a teacher, administrator, or other school employee to a meeting for custodial purposes does not constitute sponsorship of the meeting.

(3) The term "meeting" includes those activities of student groups which are permitted under a school's limited open forum and are not directly related to the school curriculum.

(4) The term "noninstructional time" means time set aside by the school before actual classroom instruction begins or after actual classroom instruction ends.

§ 4073. Severability

If any provision of this subchapter or the application thereof to any person or circumstances is judicially determined to be invalid, the provisions of the remainder of the subchapter and the application to other persons or circumstances shall not be affected thereby.

§ 4074. Construction

The provisions of this subchapter shall supersede all other provisions of Federal law that are inconsistent with the provisions of this subchapter.

Notes

Notes to Introduction

1. *Engel v. Vitale*, 370 U.S. 421, 435 (1962).
2. *George C. Wallace, Governor of the State of Alabama, et al. v. Ishmael Jaffree et al.; Douglas T. Smith et al. v. Ishmael Jaffree et al.*, 472 U.S. 38 (1985).
3. Colson, *Kingdoms in Conflict*, 113.
4. Noll et al., *Handbook to Christianity*, unnumbered flyleaf.

Notes to Chapter 1

1. Olmstead, *Religion in the U.S.*, 16; Kennedy, *Dictionary of Religion*, 16.

Notes to Chapter 2

1. Hudson, *American Protestantism*, 4; Sweet, *Religion in America*, 7.
2. Folsom, *Give Me Liberty*, 7.
3. Judge, *"Forgotten Century,"* 346.
4. Cate, *Todays & Yesterdays*, 22–23.
5. Gaustad, *Religion in America*, 31.
6. Hennesey, *American Catholics*, 23.
7. Rossiter, *Seedtime of the Republic*, 153.
8. Gaustad, *Religion in America*. Because of the tabular nature of this work, specific page references are not appropriate; material cited is obtained from a comparison of information presented in numerous places.
9. Ibid.
10. Goodwin, *Dutch and English*, 18.
11. Augustus H. Van Buren, Proceedings of the New York Historical Society, XI:133, quoted in Goodwin, *Dutch and English*, 23.
12. Rev. Johannes Megapolensis to the Classis of Amsterdam, March 18, 1655, in Jameson, *New Netherland*, 392–393.
13. Sweet, *Religion in America*, 130.
14. Levy, *Establishment Clause*, 10.
15. Ibid., 11.
16. Rossiter, *Seedtime of the Republic*, 42.
17. Levy, *Establishment Clause*, 13.

18. Olmstead, *Religion in the U.S.*, 18.
19. Marty, *Pilgrims in their Own Land*, 56.
20. Judge, "Forgotten Century," 360.
21. Gaustad, *Religion in America*, 41.
22. In 1965 the new Immigration Act repudiated the national origins quotas that had basically maintained the ethnic balance during this century. Under the 1965 law all nationalities were able to compete equally, and the traditional European patterns of immigration have changed radically, until today about 84% of the immigrants are from Asia, Latin America, and the Caribbean. *Fortune*, May 9, 1988, p. 94.

Notes to Chapter 3

1. Blair, Hornberger, and Stewart, *Literature of the U.S.*, 24.
2. Ibid., 22.
3. Ibid., 32.
4. Ibid.
5. Commager, *Documents of American History*, 16.
6. Noll et al., *Handbook to Christianity*, 78.
7. Jernegan, *American Colonies*, 182.
8. Hennesey, *American Catholics*, 37.
9. Gaustad, *Religion in America*, 35.
10. Olmstead, *Religion in the U.S.*, 110.
11. Folsom, *Give Me Liberty*, 31.
12. Hudson, *American Protestantism*, 14.
13. Commager, *Documents of American History*, 26.

Notes to Chapter 4

1. Armstrong and Armstrong, *Indomitable Baptists*, 46.
2. Ibid., 47.
3. Miller, *New England Mind*, 93.
4. Folsom, *Give Me Liberty*, 16.
5. Miller, *New England Mind*, 51.
6. Armstrong and Armstrong, *Indomitable Baptists*, 51.
7. Rossiter, *Seedtime of the Republic*, 191.
8. Ibid.
9. Armstrong and Armstrong, *Indomitable Baptists*, 55.
10. In a 1744 revision to the Rhode Island Code, Catholics were disenfranchised, based upon a restriction purportedly enacted in 1663. Research revealed that the provision had been interpolated, probably in 1705, without legislative action, by some official or committee, and it was officially expunged in 1783. Beth, *Church and State*, 54–55.
11. Miller, *New England Mind*, 173.
12. Beth, *Church and State*, 54.
13. Rossiter, *Seedtime of the Republic*, 199.
14. Gaustad, *Religion in America*, 1.
15. Rossiter, *Seedtime of the Republic*, 192.

Notes to Chapter 5

1. Sweet, *Religion in America*, 147.
2. Folsom, *Give Me Liberty*, 49.
3. Sweet, *Religion in America*, 145.
4. Gabriel Thomas to William Penn, in Myers, *Early Pennsylvania*, 315–316.
5. Ver Steeg, *Formative Years*, 167.
6. Gabriel Thomas to William Penn, in Myers, *Early Pennsylvania*, 317, 319, 325, 329.
7. Commager, *Documents of American History*, 40.
8. Ibid.
9. Cohen et al., *Bill of Rights*, 252.
10. Folsom, *Give Me Liberty*, 53.

Notes to Chapter 6

1. Commager, *Documents of American History*, 21.
2. Hennesey, *American Catholics*, 39.
3. Sweet, *Religion in America*, 117.
4. Hennesey, *American Catholics*, 39.
5. Bridenbaugh, *Jamestown*, 66.
6. Commager, *Documents of American History*, 31–32.
7. Ibid.
8. Hennesey, *American Catholics*, 42.

Notes to Chapter 7

1. Bridenbaugh, *Jamestown*, 120.
2. Ibid.
3. Rouse, *Planters and Pioneers*, 20.
4. Gaustad, *Religion in America*, 6.
5. Eckenrode, *Separation of Church and State*, 13.
6. Jernegan, *American Colonies*, 101.
7. Rouse, *Planters and Pioneers*, 102.
8. Sweet, *Religion in America*, 56.
9. Hudson, *American Protestantism*, 7.
10. Sweet, *Religion in America*, 57.
11. Commager, *Documents of American History*, 9.
12. Rouse, *Planters and Pioneers*, 104.
13. Commager, *Documents of American History*, 12.
14. Rossiter, *Seedtime of the Republic*, 152.
15. Gewehr, *Great Awakening*, 155.

Notes to Chapter 8

1. Saye, *Georgia's Charter*, 33.
2. McPherson, *Journal*, xiii.

3. McCain, *Proprietary Province,* 39; McCain studied the trust records to determine who among the trustees actually attended meetings and shaped ideas for the colony. He determined that of the 1,162 reports for committee duty, half of these were made by seven men, whom he identified as Vernon, Egmont, L'Apostre, Smith, T. Towers, Laroche, Hucks, Hales, Oglethorpe, and Shaftesbury.

4. *The Most Delightful Country,* 118.
5. Saye, *Georgia's Charter,* 49.
6. McCain, *Proprietary Province,* 150.
7. Ibid., 303–305.
8. Saye, *Georgia's Charter,* 35.
9. Strickland, *Religion in Georgia,* 18.
10. *The Most Delightful Country,* 207–208.
11. White, *Historical Collections,* 178.
12. Coleman, *Colonial Georgia,* 20, crediting the work of Saye.
13. *The Most Delightful Country,* 130–131.
14. Ibid., 183.
15. Ibid., 176.
16. McPherson, *Journal,* 7.
17. Ver Steeg, *Southern Mosaic,* 79.
18. Lane, *General Oglethorpe's Georgia,* xviii.
19. Ibid.
20. Vaughan, *Colony of Georgia,* 28.
21. Lane, *General Oglethorpe's Georgia,* xxii; Davis, *Fledgling Province,* 10; Coleman, *Colonial Georgia,* 51.
22. McPherson, *Journal,* 4.
23. Davis, *Fledgling Province,* 17.
24. McPherson, *Journal,* 12.
25. Coleman, *Colonial Georgia,* 33–34.
26. Lane, *General Oglethorpe's Georgia,* 20–21.
27. McPherson, *Journal,* 12.
28. Ver Steeg, *Tailfer's Narrative,* 48.
29. Lane, *General Oglethorpe's Georgia,* 29.
30. Coleman, *Colonial Georgia,* 27.
31. Lane, *General Oglethorpe's Georgia,* 7, 15.
32. Ibid., xxxii.
33. Ibid.
34. Ibid., 540.
35. Ibid., 436.
36. White, *Historical Collections,* 17.
37. Lane, *General Oglethorpe's Georgia,* 488.
38. Ibid., 437–441.
39. Coleman, *Colonial Georgia,* 167.
40. Strickland, *Religion in Georgia,* 96.
41. McCain, *Proprietary Province,* 337.
42. Ibid., 337, 269.
43. Ver Steeg, *Southern Mosaic,* 77.
44. Lane, *General Oglethorpe's Georgia,* 397.
45. *The Most Delightful Country,* 208.

46. Lane, *General Oglethorpe's Georgia*, 389.
47. Strickland, *Religion in Georgia*, 97.
48. Ibid., 131.
49. Knollenberg, *American Revolution*, 5.
50. Strickland, *Religion in Georgia*, 102.
51. Davis, *Fledgling Province*, 207.
52. Ibid., 225–226.
53. Ibid., 226.

Notes to Chapter 9

1. Sweet, *Religion in America*, 187.
2. Noll et al., *Handbook to Christianity*, 72.
3. Gaustad, *Religion in America*, 3, 4.
4. Sweet, *Religion in America*, 189.
5. Gewehr, *Great Awakening*, 4–5, 12.
6. Marty, *Pilgrims in their Own Land*, 127.
7. Gross, *American Methodism*, 37–38; Noll et al., *Handbook to Christianity*, 111.
8. Rouse, *Planters and Pioneers*, 110.
9. Noll et al., *Handbook to Christianity*, unnumbered flyleaf.
10. Ibid., 128.
11. Marty, *Pilgrims in their Own Land*, 120.
12. Jernegan, *American Colonies*, 410.
13. Gross, *American Methodism*, 71, quoting Bernard Weisberger, *They Gathered at the River* (Boston: Little, Brown, 1958), 45.

Notes to Chapter 10

1. Noll et al., *Handbook to Christianity*, 133.
2. Rossiter, *Seedtime of the Republic*, 329.
3. Noll et al., *Handbook to Christianity*, 138.
4. Ibid., 137.
5. Ibid., 143.
6. Sweet, *Religion in America*, 266.
7. Noll et al., *Handbook to Christianity*, 144.
8. White, *Historical Collections*, 62.
9. Strickland, *Religion in Georgia*, 156.
10. Eckenrode, *Separation of Church and State*, 84.

Notes to Chapter 11

1. Levy, *Establishment Clause*, xvi.
2. Noll et al., *Handbook to Christianity*, 79–80.
3. Jameson, *Social Movement*, 86.
4. Jefferson, *Writings*, 34.
5. Gewehr, *Great Awakening*, 201.
6. Jefferson, *Cyclopedia*, No. 7263.
7. Jefferson, *Writings*, 34.
8. Ibid.

9. Eckenrode, *Separation of Church and State,* 48.
10. Commager, *Documents of American History,* 124–125.
11. Cousins, *In God We Trust,* 300–301.
12. Jefferson, *Writings,* 34.
13. Eckenrode, *Separation of Church and State,* 66.
14. Ibid., 67.
15. Cousins, *In God We Trust,* 299.
16. Ibid., 322.
17. Ibid., 308–313.
18. Ibid, 306–307.
19. Eckenrode, *Separation of Church and State,* 89.
20. Cousins, *In God We Trust,* 308–309.
21. Eckenrode, *Separation of Church and State,* 84.
22. Ibid., 99.
23. Ibid., 105–106.
24. Ibid., 102.
25. Ibid., 95.
26. Ibid., 97.
27. Ibid., 109.
28. Madison, *Writings,* 175.
29. Eckenrode, *Separation of Church and State,* 110.
30. Ibid., 114.
31. Cousins, *In God We Trust,* 121.
32. Jefferson, *Own Words,* 87.
33. Ibid., 86.
34. Cousins, *In God We Trust,* 121.

Notes to Chapter 12

1. Rutland, *Ordeal of the Constitution,* 50.
2. Ibid., 33.
3. Ibid.
4. Beard, *Supreme Court,* 118.
5. Cousins, *In God We Trust,* 315–316.
6. Commager, *Documents of American History,* 107–108.
7. Rutland, *Ordeal of the Constitution,* 216.
8. Ibid., 218.
9. Ibid., 223.
10. See Levy, *Establishment Clause,* 66–73, for a state by state review of the ratification records as they relate to religion and the need for a bill of rights.
11. Hunt, *Writings of Madison,* 5:372–374.
12. Levy, *Establishment Clause,* 77–79, 187–189.
13. *Everson v. Board of Education,* 330 U.S. 1 (1947).

Notes for Chapter 13

1. Cousins, *In God We Trust,* 314–315.
2. Ibid.

3. Commager, *Documents of American History*, 211.
4. Ibid.
5. de Tocqueville, *Democracy in America*, 308.
6. Ibid.
7. Ibid., 303.
8. Rossiter, *Seedtime of the Republic*, 197.
9. Commager, *Documents of American History*, 125.
10. Jefferson, *Notes on Virginia*, 160.
11. Jefferson, *Own Words*, 83.
12. de Tocqueville, *Democracy in America*, 310.

Notes to Chapter 14

1. Cousins, *In God We Trust*, 66.
2. Eckenrode, *Separation of Church and State*, 105–106.
3. Cousins, *In God We Trust*, 63.
4. Ibid., 56.
5. Ibid., 60.
6. Ibid., 59.
7. Ibid., 71–72.
8. Meyers, *Mind of the Founder*, 432.
9. Jefferson, *Cyclopedia*, No. 1269, n.
10. Cousins, *In God We Trust*, 135.
11. Ibid., 325.
12. Meyers, *Mind of the Founder*, 432.
13. de Tocqueville, *Democracy in America*, 305–306.
14. Cousins, *In God We Trust*, 320.
15. Ibid., 265.

Notes to Chapter 15

1. Freund, *Supreme Court*, 25, quoting philosopher Alexander Meiklejohn.
2. Freund, *Supreme Court*, 89.
3. Hand, *Bill of Rights*, 69.
4. Ibid., 71.
5. Frankfurter, *Mr. Justice Holmes*, 45.
6. *Missouri v. Holland*, 252 U.S. 416, 433 (1920).
7. *Marbury v. Madison*, 1 Cranch 137, 2 L.Ed 60 (1803).
8. *Passenger Cases*, 7 How 282, 470; 48 U.S. 122, 200 (1849).
9. *Minersville School Dist. v. Gobitis*, 310 U.S. 586 (1940), and *West Virginia State Board of Education v. Barnette*, 319 U.S. 624 (1943).
10. Warren, *Memoirs*, 333.
11. Ibid.
12. *Home Bldg & Loan Ass'n v. Blaisdell*, 290 U.S. 398, 442–3 (1943).
13. *Missouri v. Holland*, 252 U.S. 416, 433 (1920).
14. *Gompers v. U.S.*, 233 U.S. 604, 610 (1914).
15. Rehnquist, *Supreme Court*, 317.
16. Burger, "Judiciary," 33.

17. Constitutional amendments have been successfully used to overturn a Supreme Court decision only four times: *Chisholm v. Georgia,* 2 U.S. 419, decided in 1793, was overturned by the 11th Amendment; *Dred Scott v. Sandford,* 60 U.S. 393, decided in 1857, was overturned by the 14th Amendment; *Pollock v. Farmers' Loan & Trust Co.,* 157 U.S. 429, 158 U.S. 601, decided in 1895, was overturned at least in part by the 16th Amendment; and *Oregon v. Mitchell,* 400 U.S. 112, decided in 1970, was overturned by the 26th Amendment.

18. Senate Committee on the Judiciary, 75th Cong., 1st Sess., 1937, S. Rept. 711, 13–14.

19. *Dodge v. Woolsey,* 59 U.S. (18 How.) 331, 350 (1855).

20. *Martin v. Hunter's Lease,* 14 U.S. (1 Wheat) 304, 347–348 (1816).

21. *Congressional Record,* 98th Cong., 2nd sess., March 20, 1984, S. 2901.

22. *Congressional Record,* 97th Cong., 1st sess., February 16, 1981, S. 1284.

23. *Ex parte McCardle,* 74 U.S. 506 (1869).

24. Perry, "Human Rights Cases," 343.

25. Sager, "Constitutional Limitations," 89.

26. McCloskey, *American Supreme Court,* Boorstin's Preface.

27. Pollack, *Earl Warren,* 210.

Notes to Chapter 16

1. *Reynolds v. U.S.,* 98 U.S. 145 (1878).

2. *Watson v. Jones,* 80 U.S. 679 (1872).

3. *Meyer v. Nebraska,* 262 U.S. 390 (1923).

4. *Pierce v. Society of the Sisters of the Holy Names,* 268 U.S. 510 (1925).

5. *U.S. v. Schwimmer,* 279 U.S. 644 (1929).

6. *U.S. v. Carolene Products Co.,* 304 U.S. 144 (1938).

7. *Cantwell v. Connecticut,* 310 U.S. 296 (1940).

8. *Minersville School Dist. v. Gobitis,* 310 U.S. 586 (1940), and *West Virginia State Board of Education v. Barnette,* 319 U.S. 624 (1943).

9. Habenstreit, *Changing America,* 136.

10. *Everson v. Board of Education,* 330 U.S. 1 (1947); rehearing denied, 330 U.S. 855.

11. *McCollum v. Board of Education,* 333 U.S. 203 (1948).

12. *Zorach v. Clauson,* 343 U.S. 306 (1952).

13. *McGowan v. Maryland,* 366 U.S. 420 (1961).

14. The Sunday closing decisions have been criticized because of the unfairness toward Americans whose sabbath does not fall on Sunday. "The Court should have ruled that forced Sunday laws have the effect of advancing religion. In two of the four Sunday closing cases, forced closure penalized those for whom the Sabbath comes on Saturday. The failure of the Statutes before the Court to give observant Jews and Seventh-Day Adventists, among others, an alternate day of rest should have been held unconstitutional on ground of preference of one set of religious beliefs over another. The state may have a legitimate stake in forcing all citizens to take a day off from work, but no argument can show that one's health or welfare is improved by resting on Sunday rather than Saturday." Levy, *Establishment Clause,* 154.

15. *Torcaso v. Watkins,* 367 U.S. 488 (1961).

16. Madison's Memorial & Remonstrance, Point 4; see Appendix A for complete text.

17. *U.S. v. Seeger,* 85 U.S. 850 (1965).

Notes to Chapter 17

1. *Engel v. Vitale,* 370 U.S. 421 (1962).

2. *Time,* July 6, 1962, 8.

3. Liston, *Tides of Justice,* 2.

4. Ibid. The author of the bill was Rep. Robert T. Ashmore of South Carolina.

5. *Newsweek,* July 9, 1962, 43.

6. Warren, *Memoirs,* 315–316.

7. *New York Times,* July 1, 1962, Sec. 4.

8. Ibid.

9. Liston, *Tides of Justice,* 3.

10. *Newsweek,* July 9, 1962, 45.

11. Pollack, *Earl Warren,* 212.

12. *Time,* July 6, 1962, 7.

13. Warren, *Memoirs,* 316.

14. *New York Times,* July 1, 1962, Sec. 4.

15. Ibid.

16. Ibid.

17. Resolution of the Annual Governors' Conference, July 3, 1962, quoted in the *New York Times,* July 4, 1962, 8.

18. *Time,* August 24, 1962, 8.

19. *Time,* July 6, 1962, 8.

20. Ibid.

21. *New York Times,* July 1, 1962, Sec. 4. The congressman was Rep. Emanuel Celler.

22. *Newsweek,* July 9, 1962, 45.

23. Ibid.

24. Dierenfield, "Religious Influence," 173–179.

25. *Carden v. Bland,* 288 S.W.2d 718.

26. *Newsweek,* July 9, 1962, 45.

27. Sheldon, *Supreme Court,* 83–87, taken from an article about the Clairton School System, Cornwall-Lebanon Joint School District in central Pennsylvania, by Ben A. Franklin, *New York Times,* March 26, 1969.

28. *DeSpain v. DeKalb County Community School Dist.,* 384 F2d 836 (1967, CA 7 Ill); certiorari denied 390 U.S. 906.

29. Sorauf, *Wall of Separation,* 297; taken from charts contained in R. B. Dierenfield, "The Impact of the Decisions on Religion in Public Schools," *Religious Education* 62, Sept-Oct 1967, 444–451.

30. *Public Papers of the Presidents of the United States: John F. Kennedy, 1960–1963.* 1962, President Kennedy's news conference, Washington: Government Printing Office, 1963.

Notes to Chapter 18

1. *Abington School District v. Schempp; Murray v. Curlett,* 374 U.S. 203 (1963).

2. *Minor v. Board of Education of Cincinnati,* Superior Court of Cincinnati, February 1870. The opinion is not reported but is published under the title, The Bible in the Common Schools (Cincinnati: Robert Clarke & Co., 1870).

3. At the time of the *Abington* decision, twelve states and the District of Columbia required bible reading in their public schools, seventeen states permitted Bible reading, and nine states expressly prohibited it. Table prepared by Congressional Research Service, June 6, 1983. *Congressional Record,* 98th Cong., 2nd sess., March 5, 1984, S. 2293.

4. *West Virginia State Board of Education v. Barnette,* 319 U.S. 624 (1943).

5. Warren, *Memoirs,* 316.

6. In 1842 a Roman Catholic bishop had asked that Catholic children in the Philadelphia public schools be allowed to use the Catholic Bible and that they be excused from other religious instruction. His request resulted in "two years of bitterness and mob violence, the burning of two Catholic churches and a seminary, and finally three days of rioting in which thirteen people were killed and fifty wounded." Levy, *Establishment Clause,* 170, quoting from James O'Neill, *Religion & Education Under the Constitution* (New York: Harper and Bros., 1949), 26–27.

7. *Time,* August 16, 1963, 48, quoting the Very Reverend Howard S. Kennedy, Dean of the Episcopal Cathedral of St. James in Chicago.

8. *U.S. News & World Report,* May 11, 1964, 72. The Reverend Dr. Edwin H. Tuller of Valley Forge, Pennsylvania testified on April 29, 1964, before the House Judiciary Committee, introducing himself as a representative of the National Council of Churches and as general secretary of the American Baptist Convention.

9. *Time,* June 19, 1964, quoting Dr. Eugene Carson Blake.

10. *U.S. News & World Report,* May 18, 1964, 63–64.

11. Sorauf, *Wall of Separation,* 297; statistics from R. B. Dierenfield, "The Impact of the Decisions on Religion in Public Schools," *Religious Education* 62, Sept–Oct 1967, 444–451.

12. House Joint Resolution 9, introduced January 9, 1963. It never got out of committee.

13. *U.S. News & World Report,* May 11, 1964, 72–74.

Notes to Chapter 19

1. The full senate debates lasted for two weeks and may be found in the *Congressional Record,* 98th Cong., 2nd sess., March 5–20, 1984, S. 2290–2904. The footnotes that follow refer to the particular page on which the quoted remarks may be found.

2. S. 2705.

3. S. 2290.

4. S. 2772.

5. S. 2314.

6. S. 2888.

7. S. 2689.

8. Although there were two women serving in the Senate during this time, neither one spoke on the issue. On the final vote, one woman voted yea and the other nay.

9. S. 2895.

10. S. 2557.

11. S. 2555.

12. S. 2732.

13. S. 2687–8.

14. S. 2688.

15. S. 2345.

16. S. 2846.

17. S. 2732.

18. S. 2432.

19. S. 2391.

20. S. 2892.

21. S. 2518.

22. S. 2290.

23. S. 2435.

24. S. 2394.

25. S. 2392.

26. S. 2896.

27. S. 2891.

28. S. 2347.

29. S. 2778.

30. S. 2345.

31. S. 2401.

32. S. 2401.

33. S. 2356.

34. S. 2883.

35. S. 2703.

36. S. 2692.

37. S. 2886.

38. S. 2701.

39. S. 2846.

40. S. 2705.

41. S. 2847.

42. S. 2352.

43. S. 2494.

44. S. 2892.

45. S. 2849.

46. S. 2704.

47. S. 2701.

48. S. 2698.

49. S. 2352.

50. S. 2887.

51. S. 2887.

52. S. 2557.
53. S. 2394.
54. S. 2702.
55. S. 2299.
56. S. 2304.
57. S. 2759.
58. S. 2702.

Notes for Chapter 20

1. S. 2702.
2. S. 2891.
3. S. 2760.
4. S. 2884.
5. S. 2396.
6. S. 2849.
7. S. 2898.
8. S. 2885.
9. S. 2899.
10. S. 2686.
11. S. 2880.
12. S. 2895.
13. S. 2896.
14. S. 2889.
15. S. 2898.
16. S. 2554.
17. S. 2701.
18. S. 2847.
19. S. 2556.
20. S. 2696.
21. S. 2697.
22. S. 2302.
23. S. 2887.
24. S. 2430.
25. S. 2304.
26. S. 2777.
27. S. 2351.
28. S. 2392.
29. S. 2428.
30. S. 2885.
31. S. 2888.
32. S. 2692.
33. S. 2892.
34. S. 2704.
35. S. 2350.
36. S. 2302.
37. S. 2304.

38. S. 2393.
39. S. 2892.
40. S. 2557.
41. S. 2701.
42. S. 2558.
43. S. 2780.
44. S. 2490.
45. S. 2347.
46. S. 2703.
47. S. 2393.
48. S. 2891.
49. S. 2885.
50. S. 2699.
51. S. 2848.
52. S. 2690.
53. S. 2431.
54. S. 2883.
55. S. 2900.
56. S. 2900.
57. As previously mentioned, the final vote was not cast along party lines. Those in favor of the amendment included 37 Republicans and 19 Democrats; those opposed included 18 Republicans and 26 Democrats.

Notes to Chapter 21

1. S. 2901.
2. S. 2903.
3. S. 2904.
4. S. 2394.
5. S. 2432.
6. S. 2315.
7. S. 2315; see also S. 2690.
8. 20 United States Code, Sec. 4071(a).
9. [1984] U.S. Code Cong. & Adm. News, 2383.
10. [1984] U.S. Code Cong. & Adm. News, 2380.
11. *Tinker v. Des Moines Independent School District*, 393 U.S. 503 (1969).
12. *Widmar v. Vincent*, 454 U.S. 263 (1981).
13. *Stone v. Graham*, 449 U.S. 39 (1980).
14. *Engel v. Vitale*, 370 U.S. 421 (1962) and *Abington School District v. Schempp*, 374 U.S. 203 (1963).
15. [1984] U.S. Code Cong. & Adm. News, 2360.
16. The key issue in many of the cases involving the Equal Access Act will be the determination of whether the school has established a limited open forum. For two examples of how courts considered this issue and arrived at opposite holdings, see *Mergens v. Board of Education of Westside Com. Schools*, 867 F.2d 1076 (8th Cir. 1989), and *Garnett by Smith v. Renton School District*, 865 F.2d 1121 (9th Cir. 1989).

Notes to Chapter 22

1. *Wallace v. Jaffree,* 105 S. Ct 2479 (1985).
2. Alabama Code Section 16–1–20.1: "At the commencement of the first class of each day in all grades in all public schools the teacher in charge of the room in which each class is held may announce that a period of silence not to exceed one minute in duration shall be observed for meditation or voluntary prayer, and during any such period no other activities shall be engaged in."
3. *Lemon v. Kurtzman,* 403 US 602 (1972).
4. Choyke, "Justices Reject Silent Time," 10A.
5. Ibid.
6. Ibid.
7. Ibid.
8. Levy, *Establishment Clause,* xii.
9. Levy, *Original Intent,* 379, 380.
10. Rehnquist, *Supreme Court,* 317.
11. Powell, "The Compleat Jeffersonian," 1369–70.
12. On October 6, 1987 the case of May v. Cooperman was argued before the United States Supreme Court. It involved a New Jersey statute which permitted a one-minute period of silence "to be used solely at the discretion of the individual student." The district court, at 572 F.Supp. 1561, declared the statute unconstitutional, and the Court of Appeals for the Third Circuit, at 780 F.2d 240, affirmed that finding.

Notes to Chapter 23

1. Reichley, *Religion in Public Life,* 105.
2. S. 2887.
3. Blanshard, *God and Man,* 213.
4. Thomas Jefferson to the Reverend Samuel Miller, January 23, 1808; quoted in Cousins, *In God We Trust,* 136–137.
5. Colson, *Kingdoms in Conflict,* 121.
6. *Stone v. Graham,* 449 US 39 (1980).
7. *Lemon v. Kurtzman,* 403 US 602, 612–613 (1971).
8. *Edwards v. Aguillard,* 482 US ____ , 96 L. Ed 2d 510, 107 S. Ct. 2573 (1987).
9. Justice Scalia referred to the famous *Scopes v. State* trial, 154 Tenn 105, 289 SW 363 (1927), in which John T. Scopes, defended by Clarence Darrow, was prosecuted for teaching Darwinian theory contrary to Tennessee law. The prosecuting attorney was William Bryan, and the case served as the basis for subsequent theatrical and motion picture productions.
10. Levy, *Establishment Clause,* 162–163.
11. Ibid., 176.
12. Ibid.
13. Taylor, "Justice Powell," 13, quoting Janet Benshoof.
14. *Dallas Morning News,* November 8, 1987, H-2.
15. Taylor, "Rehnquist's Court," 39, 94.
16. Rehnquist, *Supreme Court,* 235.

17. Taylor, "Rehnquist's Court," 39, 40, 95.

18. Brennan, appointed by Eisenhower in 1956, is 83; Marshall, appointed by Johnson in 1967, is 81; Blackmun, appointed by Nixon in 1970, is 80; White, appointed by Kennedy in 1962, is 72; and Stevens, appointed by Ford in 1975, is 69. Even the relatively young Chief Justice Rehnquist is 65.

19. *Mozert v. Hawkins County Board of Education,* 827 F.2d 1058 (6th Cir. 1987); reversing and remanding 647 F.Supp. 1194.

20. Frank Trejo, "Textbooks feelings run deep," *Dallas Morning News,* October 26, 1986; quoting Plaintiff Bob Mozert, a part-time principal at a Christian school, and Michael Grubbs, whose wife was president of a group called People Recommending Improvement and Development of Education (Pride), which was formed shortly after the lawsuit was filed.

21. *Smith v. Board of School Commissioners of Mobile County,* 827 F.2d 684 (11th Cir. 1987); reversing and remanding 655 F.Supp. 939. This case had originally begun as a part of the case referred to in this book as the Silent Prayer case, *Jaffree v. Wallace,* 472 US 924, prior to the bifurcation of the claims and realignment of the parties.

22. Taft, "Religion's beacon fails to shine in textbooks," *Dallas Morning News,* November 29, 1986, 3C, quoting Robert P. Green, professor of social studies education at Clemson University.

23. Connell, "Publisher to increase religion references in school texts," *Dallas Morning News,* March 14, 1987, 43A, quoting Herbert P. Adams, chief executive officer for Laidlaw Educational Publishers, the textbook division of Doubleday.

24. According to an advertisement that was run in newspapers during the 1988 political campaigns, a *Times Mirror* survey of 2,109 Americans nationwide, conducted by the Gallup Organization, showed that 70% of all Americans who had an opinion said they would be less likely to vote for a candidate who opposes a constitutional amendment permitting prayer in public schools. *New York Times,* June 12, 1988, E-27.

25. Blanshard, *God and Man,* 210.

26. Governor William Clements of Texas asked Richard Land to take a leave of absence from his position as vice president of Criswell College in Dallas in order to advise the governor on such church-state issues as pornography, abortion, and drug abuse.

27. The Reverend Jesse Jackson was a candidate on the Democratic ticket and Reverend Pat Robertson was the Republican candidate.

28. Pfeffer, *Religion,* 99.

29. Covey, *Gentle Radical,* 140.

30. Levy, *Establishment Clause,* 72.

31. Altholz, *Churches in 19th Century,* 200.

32. *1989 World Almanac,* 591; Sources: 1988 Yearbook of American and Canadian Churches, for the year 1986.

33. 1983 Gallup Poll.

34. *Encyclopedia of American Religions* (second edition), 1987.

35. General Social Survey of the National Opinion Research Center, 1984, University of Chicago. (Margin of error is plus or minus three percentage points.) Specifically, people were asked: "How often do you attend religious

services?" and their responses were as follows: Less than once a year, 20%; a few times a year, 26%; one to four times a month, 21%; and at least once a week, 33%.

36. Burt Neuborne, "The Supreme Court and the Judicial Process," in Dorsen, ed., *ACLU Report*, 40; Mr. Neuborne's warning referred specifically to the dismantling of judicial review, which is more vulnerable to political attack because the ability to alter judicial review lacks the safeguards which protect against casual constitutional amendment. However, regardless of the political means employed to change the existing system, any such efforts must be regarded cautiously because they threaten the system which has protected religious liberty for over two centuries.

37. Jernegan, *American Colonies*, v., unreferenced epigraph.

38. Among the ongoing legal challenges concerning public school prayer, a high school student in Georgia objected to pre-game prayers at the football games of his school. As a band member, he was criticized by other students for standing silently, rather than joining in the prayers, and in September of 1986, he and his father filed a federal lawsuit. On January 3, 1989, the 11th Circuit Court of Appeals ruled that the invocations at Douglas County High School football games were unconstitutional, and on May 30, 1989, the United States Supreme Court allowed the circuit court ruling to stand without comment. *Jager v. Douglas County School District*, 862 F.2d 824.

REFERENCES

Altholz, Josef L. *The Churches in the Nineteenth Century*. Indianapolis, IN: Bobbs-Merrill, 1967.

Armstrong, O. K. and Marjorie Moore Armstrong. *The Indomitable Baptists: A Narrative of Their Role in Shaping American History*. Garden City, NY: Doubleday, 1967.

Baum, Lawrence. *The Supreme Court*. Washington: Congressional Quarterly Press, 1981.

Beard, Charles A. *The Supreme Court and the Constitution*. Englewood Cliffs, NJ: Prentice Hall, 1962.

Berns, Walter. "Do We Have a Living Constitution?" *National Forum* (Fall 1984): 29–32.

Beth, Loren P. *The American Theory of Church and State*. Gainesville: University of Florida Press, 1958.

Blair, Walter, Theodore Hornberger, and Randall Stewart. *The Literature of the United States*. Chicago: Scott, Foresman and Co., 1957.

Blanshard, Paul. *God and Man in Washington*. Boston: Beacon Press, 1960.

Bridenbaugh, Carl. *Jamestown, 1544–1699.* New York: Oxford University Press, 1980.

Bradford, William. *The History of Plymouth Plantation*. Edited by W. T. Davis. New York: 1908.

Burger, Warren E. "The Judiciary: The Origins of Judicial Review." *National Forum* (Fall 1984): 26–28, 33.

Cate, Margaret Davis. *Our Todays and Yesterdays, A Story of Brunswick and the Coastal Islands*. Spartanburg, SC: The Reprint Company, 1972.

Catton, Bruce and William B. Catton. *The Bold and Magnificent Dream: America's Founding Years, 1492–1815*. Garden City, NY: Doubleday, 1978.

Choyke, William J. "Justices Reject Silent Time." *Dallas Morning News*, June 5, 1985, 10A.

Cohen, William, Murray Schwartz, and DeAnne Sobul. *The Bill of Rights: A Source Book*. New York: Benziger Books, 1968.

Collier, James Lincoln and Christopher Collier. *Decisions in Philadelphia: The Constitutional Convention of 1787*. New York: Random House, 1986.

Coleman, Kenneth. *Colonial Georgia*. New York: Charles Scribner's Sons, 1976.

Colson, Charles W. *Kingdoms in Conflict*. Rapid City: Zondervan, 1987.

Corwin, Edward Samuel. *John Marshall and the Constitution*. New Haven: Yale University Press, 1919.

Commager, Henry Steele, ed. *Documents of American History.* New York: Appleton-Century-Crofts, 1968.

Connell, Joan. "Publisher to Increase Religion References in School Texts." *Dallas Morning News,* March 4, 1987, 43A.

Cousins, Norman, ed. *"In God We Trust": The Religious Beliefs and Ideas of the American Founding Fathers.* New York: Harper & Brothers, 1958.

Covey, Cyclone. *The Gentle Radical: A Biography of Roger Williams.* New York: Macmillian, 1966.

Cushman, Robert F. *Leading Constitutional Cases* (15th ed.). Englewood Cliffs, NJ: Prentice Hall, 1977.

Dallas Morning News, November 8, 1987, H-2.

Davis, Harold R. *The Fledgling Province: Social and Cultural Life in Colonial Georgia, 1733–1776.* Chapel Hill: University of North Carolina Press, 1976.

Dierenfield, R. B. "The Extent of Religious Influence in American Public Schools." *Religious Education* 56 (1961): 173–179.

Dierenfield, R. B. "The Impact of the Decisions on Religion in Public Schools." *Religious Education* 62 (1967): 444–451.

Dorsen, Norman W., ed. *Our Endangered Rights: The ACLU Report on Civil Rights Today.* New York: Pantheon Books, 1984.

Eckenrode, H. J. *Separation of Church and State in Virginia: A Study in the Development of the Revolution.* New York: Da Capo Press, 1971.

Edwards, Jonathan. *A Divine and Supernatural Light* (1st ed.). Boston, 1734.

Encyclopedia of American Religions (2nd edition). Edited by J. Gordon Melton. Detroit: Gale Research Co., 1987.

de Tocqueville, Alexis. *Democracy in America.* New York: Alfred A. Knopf, 1960.

Farrand, Max. *The Framing of the Constitution of the United States.* New Haven: Yale University Press, 1972.

Folsom, Franklin. *Give Me Liberty: America's Colonial Heritage.* Chicago: Rand McNally, 1974.

Friendly, Fred W. and Martha J. Elliott. *The Constitution: That Delicate Balance.* New York: Random House, 1984.

Frankfurter, Felix. *Mr. Justice Holmes and the Supreme Court.* Cambridge, MA: Harvard University Press, 1961.

Freund, Paul A. *The Supreme Court of the United States: Its Business, Purposes, and Performance.* Cleveland, OH: Meridian Books, 1961.

Gaustad, Edwin Scott. *Historical Atlas of Religion in America.* New York: Harper and Row, 1962.

Gewehr, Wesley M. *The Great Awakening in Virginia, 1740–1790.* Durham, NC: Duke University Press, 1965.

Goodwin, Maud Wilder. *Dutch and English on the Hudson.* New Haven: Yale University Press, 1919.

Gross, John O. *The Beginnings of American Methodism.* New York: Abingdon Press, 1961.

Habenstreit, Barbara. *Changing America and the Supreme Court.* New York: Julian Messner, 1970.

Hamilton, Alexander, James Madison and John Jay. *The Federalists.* Edited by Benjamin Fletcher Wright. Cambridge, MA: Harvard University Press, 1966.

Hand, Learned. *The Bill of Rights*. Cambridge, MA: Harvard University Press, 1958.

Handy, Robert T. *A Christian America: Protestant Hopes and Historical Realities*. New York: Oxford University Press, 1971.

Handy, Robert T. *A History of the Churches in the United States and Canada*. New York: Oxford University Press, 1977.

Hennesey, James J. *American Catholics: A History of the Roman Catholic Community in the United States*. New York: Oxford University Press, 1981.

Hudson, Winthrop S. *American Protestantism*. Chicago: University of Chicago Press, 1951.

Hunt, Gaillard, ed. *The Writings of James Madison, Comprising his Public Papers and his Private Correspondence*, vol. 5: *1787–1790*. New York: G. P. Putnam's Sons, 1904.

Jameson, J. Franklin, ed. *Narratives of New Netherland, 1609–1664*. New York: Charles Scribner's Sons, 1909.

Jameson, J. Franklin. *The American Revolution Considered as a Social Movement*. Princeton, NJ: Princeton University Press, 1926.

Jefferson, Thomas. *A Biography in His Own Words*. Edited by Newsweek Books, with an introduction by Joseph L. Gardner. New York: Newsweek, 1974.

Jefferson, Thomas. *The Jeffersonian Cyclopedia*. Edited by John P. Foley. New York: Funk and Wagnalls, 1900.

Jefferson, Thomas. *Notes on the State of Virginia*. Edited by William Peden. Chapel Hill: University of North Carolina Press, 1954.

Jefferson, Thomas. *Writings, Notes, and Selected Texts*. Edited by Merrill D. Peterson. New York: Library of America, 1984.

Jernegan, Marcus Wilson. *The American Colonies, 1492–1750*. New York: Longmans, Green and Co., 1929.

Judge, Joseph. "Exploring Our Forgotten Century." *National Geographic* 173 (March 1988): 330–363.

Katz, Wilbur G. *Religion and American Constitutions*. Evanston, IL: Northwestern University Press, 1964.

Kennedy, John F. *Public Papers of the Presidents of the United States: John F. Kennedy 1960–1963*. Washington: Government Printing Office, 1963.

Kennedy, Richard. *The International Dictionary of Religion*. New York: Crossroads, 1984.

Killion, Ronald G. and Charles T. Waller. *Georgia and the Revolution*. Atlanta: Cherokee Publishing Co., 1975.

Knollenberg, Bernhard. *Growth of the American Revolution, 1766–1775*. New York: The Free Press, 1975.

Lane, Mills, ed. *General Oglethorpe's Georgia, Colonial Letters, 1733–1743*, Vols. I and II. Savannah, GA: Beehive Press, 1975.

Levy, Leonard W. *The Establishment Clause: Religion and the First Amendment*. New York: Macmillan, 1986.

Levy, Leonard W. *Original Intent and the Framers of the Constitution*. New York: Macmillan, 1988.

Liston, Robert A. *Tides of Justice: The Supreme Court and the Constitution in Our Time*. New York: Delacorte Press, 1966.

Lundin, Roger and Mark A. Noll, eds. *Voices from the Heart: Four Centuries of American Piety.* Grand Rapids, MI: Eerdmans, 1987.

Madison, James. *Writings of James Madison,* Vol. I, *1769–1793.* Philadelphia: J. B. Lippincott and Co., 1865.

Marty, Martin E. *Pilgrims in Their Own Land: Five Hundred Years of Religion in America.* Boston: Little, Brown and Co., 1984.

McCain, James Ross. *Georgia as a Proprietary Province: The Execution of a Trust.* Spartanburg, SC: The Reprint Co., 1972, reprint of 1917 edition.

McCloskey, Robert G. *The American Supreme Court.* Chicago: University of Chicago Press, 1960.

McPherson, Robert G., ed. *The Journal of The Earl of Egmont, Abstract of the Trustees Proceedings for Establishing the Colony of Georgia, 1732–1738.* Athens: University of Georgia Press, 1962.

Meyers, Marvin, ed. *The Mind of the Founder: Sources of the Political Thought of James Madison.* Indianapolis, IN: Bobbs-Merrill, 1973.

Miller, John. *Origins of the American Revolution.* Stanford, CA: Stanford University Press, 1959.

Miller, Perry. *The New England Mind: The Seventeenth Century.* Boston: Beacon Press, 1968.

Miller, Robert T. and Ronald B. Flowers. *Toward Benevolent Neutrality: Church, State, and the Supreme Court.* Waco, TX: Markham Press Fund of Baylor University Press, 1987.

Morgan, Richard E. *The Supreme Court and Religion.* New York: The Free Press, 1972.

Morris, Richard B. "Creating and Ratifying the Constitution." *National Forum* 64 (Fall 1984): 9–13.

The Most Delightful Country of the Universe, Promotional Literature of the Colony of Georgia, 1717–1734. Introduction by Trevor R. Reese. Savannah, GA: Beehive Press, 1972.

Muir, William K., Jr. *Prayer in the Public School: Law and Attitude Change.* Chicago: University of Chicago Press, 1967.

Myers, Albert Cook, ed. *Narratives of Early Pennsylvania, West New Jersey, and Delaware, 1630–1707.* New York: Barnes and Noble, 1912, reprinted 1959.

Noll, Mark A., Nathan O. Hatch, George M. Marsden, David F. Wells, and John D. Woodbridge, eds. *Eerdmans Handbook to Christianity in America.* Grand Rapids, MI: Eerdmans, 1983.

Olmstead, Clifton E. *History of Religion in the United States.* Englewood Cliffs, NJ: Prentice Hall, 1960.

Perry, Michael J. "Noninterpretive Review in Human Rights Cases: A Functional Justification." *New York University Law Review* 56 (1981): 259, 278.

Pfeffer, Leo. *God, Caesar, and the Constitution.* Boston: Beacon Press, 1975.

Pfeffer, Leo. *Religion, State and the Burger Court.* Buffalo, NY: Prometheus Books, 1985.

Pollack, Jack Harrison. *Earl Warren, The Judge Who Changed America.* Englewood Cliffs, NJ: Prentice Hall, 1979.

Powell, H. Jefferson. "The Compleat Jeffersonian: Justice Rehnquist and Federalism." *Yale Law Journal* 91 (1982): 1317–70.

Rehnquist, William H. *The Supreme Court: The Way It Was—The Way It Is.* New York: Morrow, 1987.

Reichley, A. James. *Religion in American Public Life.* Washington: Brookings Institution, 1985.

Rossiter, Clinton. *Seedtime of the Republic.* New York: Harcourt, Brace, Jovanovich, 1953.

Rosten, Leo, ed. *Religion in America.* New York: Simon and Schuster, 1963.

Rouse, Parke, Jr. *Planters and Pioneers: Life in Colonial Virginia.* New York: Hastings House, 1968.

Rutland, Robert Allen. *The Ordeal of the Constitution: The Anti-Federalists and the Ratification Struggle of 1787–1788.* Norman: University of Oklahoma Press, 1965.

Sager, Lawrence Gene. "Constitutional Limitations on Congress' Authority to Regulate the Jurisdiction of the Federal Courts." *Harvard Law Review* 95 (1981): 17.

Saye, Albert B., ed. *Georgia's Charter of 1732.* Athens: University of Georgia Press, 1942.

Schachner, Nathan. *Thomas Jefferson, A Biography.* New York: Appleton-Century-Crofts, 1951.

Sheldon, Charles H. *The Supreme Court: Politicians in Robes.* Beverly Hills: Glencoe Press, 1970.

Sorauf, Frank J. *The Wall of Separation: The Constitutional Politics of Church and State.* Princeton: Princeton University Press, 1976.

Strickland, Reba Carolyn. *Religion and the State in Georgia in the Eighteenth Century.* New York: AMS Press, 1967.

Swancara, Frank. *Thomas Jefferson versus Religious Oppression.* New York: University Books, 1969.

Swindler, William F. *Court and Constitution in the 20th Century: The Modern Interpretation.* Indianapolis, IN: Bobbs-Merrill, 1974.

Sweet, William Warren. *The Story of Religion in America.* New York: Harper & Bros., 1930.

Taft, Adon. "Religion's Beacon Fails to Shine in Textbooks." *Dallas Morning News,* November 29, 1986, 3C.

Taylor, Stuart, Jr. "Justice Powell Shaping Law as Swing Man on High Court." *New York Times,* April 26, 1987, 13.

Taylor, Stuart, Jr. "Rehnquist's Court, Tuning Out the White House." *New York Times Magazine,* September 11, 1988.

Trejo, Frank. "Textbooks, Feelings Run Deep," *Dallas Morning News,* October 26, 1986.

Tyler, Lyon Gardiner. *England in America, 1580–1652.* New York: Cooper Square Publishers, 1968, reprint of 1904 edition.

Tyler, Lyon Gardiner, ed. *Narratives of Early Virginia, 1606–1625.* New York: Barnes and Noble, 1966, reprint of 1907 edition.

Van Doren, Carl C. *The Great Rehearsal.* New York: Viking Press, 1948.

Vaughan, Harold Cecil. *The Colony of Georgia.* New York: Franklin Watts, 1975.

Ver Steeg, Clarence L. *The Formative Years, 1607–1763.* New York: Hill and Wang, 1964.

Ver Steeg, Clarence L. *Origins of a Southern Mosaic: Studies of Early Carolina and Georgia*. Athens: University of Georgia Press, 1975.

Ver Steeg, Clarence L. *A True and Historical Narrative of the Colony of Georgia by Par. Tailfer and Others With Comments by the Earl of Egmont*. Athens: University of Georgia Press, 1960.

Warren, Earl. *The Memoirs of Earl Warren*. Garden City, NY: Doubleday, 1977.

Wertenbaker, Thomas J. *The Planters of Colonial Virginia*. New York: Russell and Russell, 1958, reprint of 1922 edition.

Wertenbaker, Thomas J. *The First Americans, 1607–1690*. Chicago: Quadrangle Books, 1955.

White, Rev. George M. A. *Historical Collections of Georgia*. Danielsville, GA: Heritage Papers, 1968.

Williams, Roger. *The Bloudy Tenent*. Edited by Samuel Caldwell, III. Naragansett Club Publications, 1867.

Winslow, Ola Elizabeth. *Jonathan Edwards 1703–1758*. New York: Macmillan, 1940.

Index

243